# Styles
# of Acting

Prentice-Hall International (UK) Limited, *London*
Prentice-Hall of Australia Pty. Limited, *Sydney*
Prentice-Hall Canada Inc., *Toronto*
Prentice-Hall Hispanoamericana, S.A., *Mexico*
Prentice-Hall of India Private Limited, *New Delhi*
Prentice-Hall of Japan, Inc., *Tokyo*
Prentice-Hall of Southeast Asia Pte. Ltd., *Singapore*
Whitehall Books Limited, *Wellington, New Zealand*
Editora Prentice-Hall do Brasil Ltda., *Rio de Janeiro*

# STYLES
# OF ACTING

## A SCENEBOOK
## FOR ASPIRING ACTORS

### ELAINE ADAMS NOVAK

A SPECTRUM BOOK

Prentice-Hall, Inc.,
Englewood Cliffs, New Jersey 07632

Library of Congress Cataloging in Publication Data

Novak, Elaine Adams.
    Styles of acting.

    "A Spectrum Book."
    Bibliography: p.
    Includes index.
    1. Acting.    2. Drama—Collections.    I. Title.
PN2080.N6   1985        792'.028        85-6407
ISBN 0-13-858804-X
ISBN 0-13-858796-5 (pbk.)

A SPECTRUM BOOK

Printed in the United States of America

1   2   3   4   5   6   7   8   9   10

ISBN 0-13-858804-X

ISBN 0-13-858796-5 {PBK.}

Cover design © 1985 by Jeannette Jacobs
Manufacturing buyer: Anne P. Armeny

# Contents

# Preface

This book is for aspiring actors who want to study the major theatrical styles and act in scenes from representative plays. Such authors as Sophocles, Euripides, Shakespeare, Jonson, Molière, Sheridan, Ibsen, Chekhov, Brecht, O'Neill, Beckett, and others created some of the greatest dramas of all time, and this book was written to help you discover methods for acting them. In this text you will find the historical information you need to understand the plays and original productions plus suggestions for acting and presenting them today.

This book, however, is not for beginning actors. It is assumed that you have worked on your voice and stage movement, have experimented with different theories and methods of acting, have some experience with improvisation and scenework, and are ready now to explore major styles and difficult scenes.

Chapter 1 gives an overview of the subject of theatrical styles, a ten-point plan for preparing scenes, a list of reference books, and some warm-up exercises. The rest of the chapters are designed to explain the major styles, starting with the classicism of ancient Greece and proceeding to the contemporary theatre. These chapters include:

1. A brief description of important plays.
2. Information about how they were first produced.
3. Suggestions on how they may be performed today.

4. A list of books for further reading.
5. Exercises to help you get ready for scenework.
6. Scenes for two or three actors from well-known plays for you to study and rehearse.

Now it's up to you. How well you succeed in interpreting the styles depends on your dedication, and willingness to work. Other artists, such as musicians, know that long hours of practice are vital to attaining and maintaining mastery of their instrument. Actors, too, need the self-discipline to work diligently at their craft. As many have pointed out, no book can teach you how to act. You must teach yourself.

Grateful acknowledgment is made to my daughter Deborah Novak, and to Milton Brooks of Empire States for their assistance and to the following for permission to reprint passages from their publications:

From *The Antigone of Sophocles:* An English version by Dudley Fitts and Robert Fitzgerald, copyright 1939 by Harcourt Brace Jovanovich, Inc.; renewed 1967 by Dudley Fitts and Robert Fitzgerald. Reprinted by permission of the publisher. CAUTION: All rights, including professional, amateur, motion picture, recitation, lecturing, performance, public reading, radio broadcasting, and television, are strictly reserved. Inquiries on all rights should be addressed to Harcourt Brace Jovanovich, Inc., 111 Fifth Avenue, New York, New York 10003.

From *Cawdor and Medea* by Robinson Jeffers, copyright 1956 by Robinson Jeffers. Reprinted by permission of New Directions Publishing Corporation.

From *The Oedipus Rex of Sophocles:* An English Version by Dudley Fitts and Robert Fitzgerald, copyright 1949 by Harcourt Brace Jovanovich, Inc.; renewed 1977 by Cornelia Fitts and Robert Fitzgerald. Reprinted by permission of Harcourt Brace Jovanovich, Inc., and Faber and Faber Ltd. Performing rights controlled by Margaret Ramsay Ltd., 14a Goodwin's Court, London WC2N 4LL. CAUTION: All rights, including professional, amateur, motion picture, recitation, lecturing, performance, public reading, radio broadcasting, and television, are strictly reserved. Inquiries on all rights should be addressed to Harcourt Brace Jovanovich, Inc., 111 Fifth Avenue, New York, New York 10003.

From *Lysistrata* by Aristophanes. From *The Complete Greek Drama,* edited by Whitney J. Oates and Eugene O'Neill, Jr. Copyright 1938 and renewed 1966 by Random House, Inc. Reprinted by permission of the publisher.

From *The Menaechmi* by Plautus, translated by Richard W. Hyde and Edward C. Weist, published by Harvard University Press. Copyright © 1930 by the President and Fellows of Harvard College, renewed 1958 by Richard W. Hyde and Edward C. Weist. Reprinted by permission.

From Seneca's *Medea,* translated by Frank Justus Miller. From *The Complete Roman Drama,* edited by George E. Duckworth. Copyright 1942 and renewed 1970 by Random House, Inc. Reprinted by permission of the publisher.

From *The Twin Captains* by Flaminio Scala. Reprinted from *Scenarios of the Commeida dell'Arte: Flaminio Scala's Il Teatro delle favole rappresentative,* translated by Henry F. Salerno, by permission of New York University Press.

From Molière's *The School for Wives,* translated by Richard Wilbur, copyright © 1971 by Richard Wilbur. Reprinted by permission of Harcourt Brace Jovanovich, Inc. CAUTION:

# Styles
# of Acting

# Chapter One

# Introduction

## WHAT IS STYLE?

The term *style* is difficult to define, and definitions range from simple to complex. A simple definition, which is sufficient for our purposes, is that style is the quality that results from a distinctive manner of expression.

We may speak about a style that is characteristic of many artists who lived in a particular country or time period, such as the classicism of ancient Greece in the fifth century B.C. We may discuss the style of an artistic school or movement, like German expressionism, or the style of an individual artist, such as Samuel Beckett's style of writing or Laurence Olivier's style of acting. This book, however, is limited to discussing the *major* playwriting and acting styles.

Today, we use certain labels to describe plays, others for acting, and still others for the production elements of scenery, properties, costumes, makeup, lighting, and sound. Some people do not like to categorize theatrical elements, but labels often help you to see similarities in the work of artists—or the differences, because plays and productions can vary greatly within the same category.

The major playwriting styles are: classical, neoclassical, romantic, realistic, naturalistic, symbolistic, expressionistic, epic theatre, and theatre of the absurd.

Acting styles may be termed: classical or heroic, romantic, realistic, high comedy, low comedy, epic, or nonrealistic.

Some of the names of production styles used today are: formalistic, romantic, realistic, naturalistic, selective realistic, impressionistic, symbolistic, constructivistic, expressionistic, theatrical, epic theatre, and multimedia. If these labels are unfamiliar to you, you will find a brief description of each in the appendix.

There are four general points to know about style:

1. All plays have style, whether they fit neatly into one of our major categories or not.

2. Everything onstage is illusion, but some styles are more illusory than others. (*Illusion* may be defined as the attempt to deceive an audience into believing that the events of a play are actually occurring.)

3. All theatrical styles can be classified as either presentational or representational. From the classicism of the fifth century B.C. to the growth of realism in the nineteenth century, plays, acting, and productions were mainly presentational; that is, the plays were primarily presented directly to the audience. Actors spoke to the spectators much of the time; unrealistic poetry, soliloquies, and asides were frequent; scenery merely suggested a locale; and there was little attempt at illusion. (See Chapters 2 through 8.) The representational style came into vogue in the nineteenth century with realism and naturalism. Actors then spoke mainly to the other actors onstage, ignoring the spectators who were allowed to watch the events through the "fourth wall" of the room. The dialogue sounded like real conversations, and the scenery appeared to be the actual locale. (See Chapter 9.) Productions were highly illusory until there was a swing back in the late nineteenth and twentieth centuries to more presentational styles with symbolism, expressionism, epic theatre, and theatre of the absurd. (See Chapter 10.)

4. While presentational styles may not show much illusion on the stage, illusion can be achieved in the minds of the spectators if they are willing to accept the theatrical conventions used; so it is possible for an audience to empathize with a classical play as much as a naturalistic one so long as the conventions are believed.

Today, in the contemporary theatre of the United States, various styles are used. Although realism is still our dominant style, it is a realism that has been influenced and modified by other styles. And because our theatre is not limited to one style, as it has been in some countries and time periods, there is experimentation with new modes of expression. (See Chapter 11.)

## WHICH STYLES TO USE?

The acting and production styles should stem from the style of the play. The author has carefully selected the characters, plot, themes, dialogue, sounds, and spectacle to present a vision of life; and the director, actors, and designers must study and analyze the playwright's choices. To find the best acting and production styles to interpret that play—and each play must be approached differently—we should also investigate the criticism and history of the work, the life and other compositions of the dramatist, and the artistic, social, and political developments of the period in which the piece was written.

The major styles of playwriting often have the same organizational structure as other arts of the same era; for example, romantic plays and romantic art may both express freedom from restraint, as opposed to the restrictions of classical plays and classical art. For this reason, a play written in a particular style is usually acted and produced in a related style. As an illustration, a realistic drama such as Ibsen's *A Doll's House* is likely to be produced with realistic scenery and acting because this seems to be the best way to achieve the purpose of the dramatist. Some plays seem to call for one and only one style of acting and production; but other shows, especially those that express universal ideas, can sometimes gain excitement by changing to another style or time period for the acting and/or production. For example, Shakespeare's *Julius Caesar* has been presented effectively in this century with modern dress and scenery.

Today, a production cannot reproduce an old play exactly as it was first done. Even if it were possible, it is doubtful that such authenticity would be aesthetically pleasing to modern audiences. We should view the past with contemporary eyes and attitudes—with knowledge and appreciation for the style—and then interpret it so it is theatrically effective for our audiences as we work with twentieth-century fabrics, construction materials, lighting equipment, and stage facilities that were not available to former generations.

Today, we usually do not want to act plays as they were performed originally. If an actor now were to walk down center and declaim the lines of a Restoration tragedy with large, formal gestures, as they did in England in the seventeenth century, he would be laughed off the stage. Because of the popularity of realism and "the Method," all styles of acting are more realistic today than they were before the twentieth century.

A modern production of an old show, however, can and should capture the spirit, mood, and atmosphere of the original. This may mean adapting the play for modern audiences and stages by heightening some aspects of the script and ignoring others or changing the time or production and acting styles from what the period of the show would suggest.

In any event, the director must be the arbiter of style, and his or her selection should guide the work of the actors, designers, and crews, who must approach each play differently.

## TEN-POINT PLAN FOR PREPARING SCENES

To help you prepare your characterizations for acting the scenes in this book, here is a ten-point plan for approaching all styles from the Greek to the contemporary:

1. *Research and analyze the play.* After reading the scene and the chapter in this book on the style of the play, go to your school or public library to study the entire script. If you do not understand the plot, the characters and their relationships, the themes, and the words of the dialogue, look for more information in the library. The plays in this text are famous, and many books have been written about them.

2. *Analyze your character.* What does your character look and sound like? How would you describe your character's personality? What has your character's life been like from birth to the time of the play? What motivates your character? In the scene you are preparing, what is your character's main objective? Do you know what your character is thinking and feeling at every moment to accomplish that objective?

3. *Personalize the character by examining your own life.* What similarities are there between you and your character? What sensory and emotional experiences have you had that are the same or close to your character's? If you have had similar experiences, recreate what happened to you. What did you think? How did you feel? Do these experiences give you an insight into what your character should be thinking and feeling?

4. *Observe other people who are similar to your character.*

5. *Use your imagination to build the character.* Try Stanislavski's "magic if," and say to yourself, "What would I do IF I were the character in this situation?"

6. *Prepare internally for your character.* All of the points above will help you with this. Your goal is to try to think the thoughts and feel the emotions that your character should have in the scene.

7. *Prepare externally for your character.* External involves work on your voice, dialect or accent, posture, movements, blocking, and stage business. Are your movements and speech appropriate for your character? Can you be heard and understood? Are you warming up your body and voice by exercising daily before rehearsals and performances? (See the exercises at the end of this chapter.) If you have difficult actions to do, such as fighting, falling, dancing, kissing, or dying, have they been well rehearsed? Try to find clothes, including shoes, that are close to what your character might wear. Many professional actors believe that shoes are a key to the character and use them from the first day of rehearsal. Styling your hair like the character's may also help. And here is a note for those who wear glasses: if your character would not wear them, rehearse without them as soon as possible.

8. *Learn your lines accurately.* Never paraphrase. Remember that the playwright has spent months or years to get the words exactly as he or she wants them. Your job is to interpret them.

9. *Experiment in rehearsal.* Improvise what has happened immediately before the scene begins so that you have the right mood, thoughts,

and feelings for the scene. See what develops intuitively when you absorb yourself in your part and concentrate completely on communicating the ideas and emotions of your character to the other actor(s). Discuss your options with your director, if you have one or, if not, with your partner(s).

10. *Examine the style of the play.* Read the chapter in this book again on the style of the scene. Are the choices you have made appropriate for the style of the play?

You may find it useful to complete the character analysis form in the appendix. Writing down your ideas may help you determine whether you do understand the play, your character, and your scene. Many professional actors keep a notebook on each character they play. During rehearsals, they write down their ideas and refer to those notes often throughout rehearsals and performances.

For scenework, it is not necessary to have a director, scenery, stage lighting, sound, makeup, or actors to play the parts with no lines or a few lines (those playing the principal roles can imagine their presence); however, you should know what your stage environment should be like so that you can visualize it and react to it. Some chairs and a table are all that need be available for your use; however, it is helpful to have hand props (that is, a glass, a fan, a cane, sewing, and so forth) if they are easy to obtain. If any unavailable props are called for in the scene, you can pantomime handling them or use substitute props.

## SUGGESTED READING

The following are general reference books that offer information about all or most of the styles described in this book. Also, within each of the following chapters is a list of books with more detailed information on that particular style.

### General

Albright, Hardie, and Arnita Albright. *Acting: The Creative Process.* 3d ed. Belmont, Calif.: Wadsworth Publishing Company, 1980.

Brockett, Oscar G. *History of the Theatre.* 4th ed. Boston: Allyn and Bacon, Inc., 1982.

———. *The Theatre: An Introduction.* 4th ed. New York: Holt, Rinehar t and Winston, Inc., 1979.

Crawford, Jerry L. *Acting in Person and in Style.* 3d ed. Dubuque, Iowa: Wm. C. Brown Publishing Company, 1983.

Duerr, Edwin. *The Length and Depth of Acting.* New York: Holt, Rinehart and Winston, Inc., 1962.

Gassner, John, and Ralph Allen (eds.). *Theatre and Drama in the Making.* 2 vols. Boston: Houghton Mifflin Company, 1964.

Gassner, John, and Edward Quinn (eds.). *The Reader's Encyclopedia of World Drama.* New York: Thomas Y. Crowell Company, 1969.

Grose, B. Donald, and O. Franklin Kenworthy. *A Mirror to Life: A History of Western Theatre.* New York: Holt, Rinehart, and Winston, Inc., 1985.

Harrop, John, and Sabin R. Epstein. *Acting with Style.* Englewood Cliffs, N.J.: Prentice-Hall, Inc., 1982.

Matlaw, Myron. *Modern World Drama: An Encyclopedia.* New York: E.P. Dutton & Co., Inc., 1972.

*McGraw-Hill Encyclopedia of World Drama.* 4 vols. New York: McGraw-Hill Book Co., 1972.

Roberts, Vera M. *On Stage: A History of the Theatre.* 2d ed. New York: Harper & Row, Publishers, 1974.

Russell, Douglas A. *Period Style for the Theatre.* Boston: Allyn and Bacon, Inc., 1980.

Saint-Denis, Michel. *Theatre: The Rediscovery of Style.* New York: Theatre Arts Books, 1969.

Schreck, Everett M. *Principles and Styles of Acting.* Reading, Mass.: Addison-Wesley Publishing Company, 1970.


## Scene Design

Bay, Howard. *Stage Design.* New York: Drama Book Specialists, 1974.

Bellman, Willard F. *Scene Design, Stage Lighting, Sound, Costume & Makeup.* New York: Harper & Row, Publishers, 1983.

Oenslager, Donald. *Stage Design: Four Centuries of Scenic Invention.* New York: The Viking Press, Inc., 1975.

Parker, W. Oren, and Harvey K. Smith. *Scene Design and Stage Lighting.* 4th ed. New York: Holt, Rinehart and Winston, Inc., 1979.


## Costumes

Barton, Lucy. *Historic Costume for the Stage.* Rev. ed. Boston: Walter H. Baker Co., 1963.

Boucher, François León Louis. *20,000 Years of Fashion.* New York: Harry N. Abrams, Inc., 1967.

Brooke, Iris. *Western European Costume and Its Relation to the Theatre.* 2d ed. New York: Theatre Arts Books, 1964.

Lister, Margot. *Costume: An Illustrated Survey from Ancient Times to the Twentieth Century.* Boston: Plays, Inc., 1968.

Payne, Blanche. *History of Costume from the Ancient Egyptians to the Twentieth Century.* New York: Harper & Row, Publishers, 1965.

Russell, Douglas A. *Stage Costume Design: Theory, Technique, and Style.* 2d ed. Englewood Cliffs, N.J.: Prentice-Hall, Inc., 1985.

## Makeup and Masks

Corson, Richard. *Stage Makeup.* 6th ed. Englewood Cliffs, N.J.: Prentice-Hall, Inc., 1981.

Smith, C. Ray (ed.). *The Theatre Crafts Book of Make-up, Masks and Wigs.* Emmaus, Pa.: Rodale Press, 1974.

Terry, Ellen, and Lynne Anderson. *Make-up and Masks.* New York: Richards Rosen Press, Inc., 1971.

## Manners and Movements

Boehn, Max von. *Modes and Manners.* Tr. by Joan Joshua. 4 vols. Philadelphia: J. B. Lippincott Company, 1932–1936.

Chisman, Isobel, and H. E. Raven-Hart. *Manners and Movements in Costume Plays.* London: H.F.W. Deane and Sons, 1934.

Oxenford, Lyn. *Playing Period Plays.* London: J. Garnet Miller Ltd., 1958.

## Period Dances

Guthrie, John. *Historical Dances for the Theatre.* Worthing, Sussex: Aldridge Bros., Ltd., 1950.

Wood, Melusine. *Advanced Historical Dances.* London: Imperial Society of Teachers of Dancing, 1960.

———. *More Historical Dances.* London: Imperial Society of Teachers of Dancing, 1956.

———. *Some Historical Dances 12th to 19th Century.* London: Imperial Society of Teachers of Dancing, 1952.

The following are exercises for warming up before rehearsals and performances:

1. Stretch. Bend over and grab your ankles; pull your head between your legs for eight counts. Rise to a good posture and reach up over your head as far as you can; go up on your toes and stretch for four counts. With arms above your head, lunge forward on your right leg, gently stretching for four counts. Repeat on your left leg.

2. Dance vigorously for several minutes—do your favorite aerobic exercises.

3. Relax. Lie on your back on the floor; close your eyes, and try to remove all tension from the body. Put one hand on your upper abdomen to be aware of the movement in the midsection of your body as you breathe.

4. Stand in an upright but relaxed position. Yawn as you inhale and hum, until you run out of air. On the next exhalations, sing "ah," "oh," "ee," "ay," "oo."

5. Sing "mee" up the scale for one octave using one syllable for each tone. Breathe at the top, and then sing down the scale. Repeat using "mah," "moh," "may," "moo," "nee," "nah," "noh," "nay," "noo."

6. Glide up and down the octave singing one "mee" for all tones. Repeat using the other syllables in Exercise 5.

7. Repeat Exercise 5 going from a soft tone at the bottom of the scale and swelling to a loud sound at the top and then returning to a soft tone at the bottom. Reverse starting softly at the top of the scale; reach your loudest tone at the bottom, and diminish the loudness as you return to the top.

8. Tense all of the muscles of the face for four counts; then relax by moving the jaw around, sticking out the tougue and moving it around, moving the lips from pucker to smile, and shaking the head.

9. Repeat the following words rapidly eight times each: "bee," "fee," "gee," "he," "key," "lee," "me," "knee," "pea," "see," "tee," "we," "ye."

10. Recite any poem that you know from memory (nursery rhyme? limerick? a passage from Shakespeare?) as though you were standing on a stage addressing an audience of thousands. Project!

# Chapter Two

# Classicism
# of Ancient Greece

The first record of drama in Greece dates from 534 B.C., when the actor-playwright Thespis won the first contest for tragedy at a religious festival in honor of the god Dionysus. His play needed one actor, who took all of the parts by changing masks, and a chorus. We know little about the sixth-century B.C. Greek theatre, but we know that in the fifth and fourth centuries B.C. the Greeks presented some of the finest plays ever created. This style of playwriting is now called classicism.

## PLAYS

Although the ancient Greeks wrote many plays, only forty-five (plus some fragments of others) have come down to us by Aeschylus, Sophocles, Euripides, Aristophanes, and Menander. Thirty-two are serious plays, twelve are comedies, and one is a satyr play (a comedy, usually burlesquing a myth, which has a chorus of satyrs).

Seven of the existing tragedies are by Aeschylus (525–456 B.C.), who was concerned primarily with man's relationship to the gods and the universe. Seven tragedies are by Sophocles (c. 496–406 B.C.), who was more interested in human relationships than religious themes. Eighteen

9

serious plays, some of which are tragedies and some melodramas or tragi-comedies, and the one complete satyr play, *The Cyclops*, were written by Euripides (c. 480–406 B.C.). More realistic than his predecessors, he was concerned mainly with man's psychological motivations and reactions and is credited with writing the first domestic dramas.

The usual plot of a tragedy has a prologue (primarily exposition), the *parodos* (entry of the chorus), three to five episodes separated by choral passages, and the *exodos* (the departure). Control, order, and compression of events are evident throughout the tragedies. The unity of action is adhered to; but the Greek dramatists did not always observe the unities of time and place as Renaissance neoclassicists, who insisted upon one action in one locale within a twenty-four hour period, believed. Life in Greek tragedies is idealized and intensified: the writers were not trying to present realistic life but a story, sometimes on a religious theme, which was already well known to their audiences. The language is poetic, dignified, and formal to tell a single plot that usually has a late point of attack (that is, the play begins in the middle or near the climax of the story and then moves forward to its conclusion). Outside of the processions and choral movements, there is little action in the tragedies, because violence takes place offstage and is merely reported onstage.

The eleven comedies of Aristophanes (c. 448–380 B.C.) are concerned primarily with making fun of gods, contemporary problems, politics, playwrights, and other important people. The usual structure is to have a *prologue* in which a fantastic idea is conceived, the *parodos*, the *agon* (debate of the idea), the *parabasis* (choral passage that has advice for the audience), a series of episodes showing the results of the idea, and the *exodos*. Aristophanes' plays, which are termed Old Comedy, are filled with boisterous action, satire, farcical parodies, fantasy, exaggeration, and some serious comments and poetry.

Later, Menander (c. 343–291 B.C.), often called the father of modern comedy, wrote about the human foibles of the ordinary people of Athens. Called New Comedy, this kind deals with young lovers, clever slaves, braggart soldiers, parasites, courtesans, angry fathers, long-lost relatives, and other types that appear later in Roman comedies, in the *commedia dell'arte*, and in plays by Shakespeare, Molière, and many others. Only one complete comedy by Menander exists, *Dyskolos*, although parts of several other plays are extant.

Some of the most famous classical plays are the following: Aeschylus' *The Persians, Seven Against Thebes, The Suppliants, Prometheus Bound*, and his trilogy called the *Oresteia*; Sophocles' *Antigone, Oedipus Rex, Electra*, and *Oedipus at Colonus*; Euripides' *Alcestis, Medea, Hippolytus, Electra, The Trojan Women, The Bacchae*, and *Iphigenia at Aulis*; and Aristophanes' *The Knights, The Clouds, The Wasps, The Birds, Lysistrata*, and *The Frogs*.

# PRODUCTIONS THEN

**Amphitheatres.**   In the fifth and fourth centuries B.C., plays were presented at religious festivals in large outdoor amphitheatres that seated thousands of people. Not all amphitheatres were alike, but probably in most instances the audience at first sat on the slopes of hills to watch two or three male actors, who played all of the characters, and the male chorus and its leader (*choregus*) perform in the daylight in a large circular playing area (the *orkestra*), which contained a statue of the god Dionysus. Gradually wooden and then stone seats were installed for the spectators, and a scene house (*skene*) was built at the edge of the *orkestra* so that the actors might have a place to dress and change masks. What the *skene* looked like is not known, but it may have had a low platform stage backed by a facade that had three doors and niches for statues of gods.

**Scenery.**   The stage settings were nonillusionistic for the most part, yet there were some attempts at illusion: horses and chariots were occasionally used; there were movable platforms (*eccyclema*), trap doors, cranes for lowering gods to earth from the roof of the scene building (*deus ex machina*), thunder machines, and perhaps revolving painted prisms (*periaktoi*) at the sides of the stage, painted scenery (*pinakes*) between the columns of the *skene,* and other scenic devices.

**Costumes.**   The actors wore masks, which they changed to indicate different characters or various moods for the same character. By the fifth century B.C., the tragic actor probably wore a long, decorated tunic with sleeves, belted below the breast, with perhaps a cloak or mantle, in different colors that may have had symbolic meanings.

In the later days of this period, actors used boots with thickened soles (*cothurni*), a high headdress (the *onkos*), and padding to make the tragedians appear larger than ordinary humans. Heavily encumbered, actors must have moved slowly and their gestures must have been broad, which may explain why little physical action is called for by the plots. The comedians, however, were free to move actively in low, soft boots (*socci*) and short, grotesquely padded tunics over tights, with male characters often wearing a phallus of red leather.

**Acting.**   Sophocles is credited with adding the third actor in tragedies, and some comedies apparently used four or five male actors. These were professionals who enjoyed a high reputation in the community because they were revered as leaders as well as artists. The chorus was composed usually of twelve to fifty men in the tragedies and twenty-four in the comedies. Women were not permitted to perform, but they were allowed to be in the audience.

There is little evidence to tell us what the acting was like, but by studying the plays and amphitheatres we can assume that it was presentational, with the actors and chorus speaking, chanting, and singing directly to the spectators much of the time. Accompanied by flute music and occasionally by other instruments, the performers must have had excellent projection and articulation to be understood in these large amphitheatres. Voices and gestures could not be small; they, of necessity, had to be enlarged to be heard and seen.

## PRODUCTIONS NOW

Productions today of these ancient Greek plays are frequent and notable for their great variety of form. At one extreme are those done in a realistic style; at the other end are those filled with highly unrealistic conventions. One reason for the popularity of these plays is that there is no one way to perform them: directors and designers, therefore, can feel free to see what their imaginations and creative abilities can produce.

**Acting.**   When doing classical tragedies today, directors usually wish to emulate the presentational acting of the original with its beauty, simplicity, passion, and grandeur. Accordingly, those actors playing principal roles should realize that they are portraying heroes and heroines and act accordingly in a majestic manner. A conversational, realistic style of speaking is usually not suitable; the powerful poetry of the lines demands a smooth-flowing delivery with appropriate resonance and clear enunciation.

Remember that when you are using a poetic translation, you must not pause at the end of each line just because it is the end of the line. You must continue until the end of the thought. For example, in the opening speech of *Antigone,* as translated by Dudley Fitts and Robert Fitzgerald, you would probably pause at the end of lines 1, 3, 5, and 6, but you should not pause at the end of lines 2 and 4 because the thoughts continue into the following lines:

ANTIGONÊ:
Ismenê, dear sister,
You would think that we had already suffered enough
For the curse on Oedipus:
I cannot imagine any grief
That you and I have not gone through. And now—
Have they told you the new decree of our King Creon?

Punctuation marks may be a guide for when to pause. Ordinarily, you will pause at periods, question marks, exclamation points, semicolons,

colons, and dashes. When you see a comma, though, look at the sentence carefully; it may or may not indicate the end of a thought.

While pausing, you can use that moment to inhale: you should never break into the middle of a thought-group because you need air. Remember, too, to control your exhalations so that the final words may be said as strongly as those at the beginning. Often actors are accused of dropping the ends of sentences to the point where they cannot be heard. Good breath control is the answer to this problem.

Another problem faced by classical players is to sustain audience interest during long speeches. To do this, actors need skillful vocal variation of loudness, rate, pitch, and quality to project the meaning and the dramatic intensity of the lines. For classical acting, you need a routine of daily exercises in relaxation, breath control, projection, variety, resonance, and articulation.

In classical plays, movements for principal actors are mainly deliberate, graceful, and rhythmical with an upright posture. For the most part, actors stand and talk with each other. Touching other characters and sitting down were seldom done in the original productions and are not common today. Gestures may be flowing, enlarged, and powerful with hands above the waist much of the time.

The acting in classical comedies is presentational for the most part and similar to playing boisterous, low-comedy farces of all periods. The satire in the play must be emphasized with exaggerated characterizations. There should be much action, horseplay, and slapstick, often at a fast pace. Unlike tragedies, comedies involve a lot of physical contact. Gestures may be drawn from actual life but should be enlarged to be funny. To get laughs, the actor must play with gusto, skillfully time and point key lines, and devise funny business, vocal tricks, and peculiar costuming. Some scenic devices, such as crude cranes for descending gods and the appearance of an *eccyclema*, may also be funny.

Chorus. The chorus may be, as it was originally, a group (which in some plays is divided into two sections) that sings, chants, speaks, and dances together to musical accompaniment. It may be broken into smaller groups of different kinds of people or of various voice qualities. Some directors strive for realism by individualizing the chorus, dividing the choral lines among people of varying ages and types; others try for an unnatural quality by having the chorus recite with unrealistic inflections. The choral lines may be given to a single invisible voice, perhaps amplified by a microphone; or all actors may be in the chorus, leaving it to become a character and then returning to the chorus.

Some directors have the chorus stand still in one location; others give small realistic movements to the chorus; some use unison gestures to illustrate the lines; and others prefer to have the chorus members dance as they speak or to have one group dance while another section chants or sings.

**Costumes.** Costuming may be modern dress (to emphasize the timelessness of these plays); theatrical garments of no particular period; ancient Greek clothing without masks or with mask-like makeups; or a recreation of what the director believes to be an authentic Greek production with masks and larger-than-life costumes.

Of course, any good costume is a compromise. It must express the mood and style of the play, reinforce the meaning, express the personality of the character, and be adapted to the taste of the spectators and their idea of the period. Above all, it should be imaginative and theatrical.

**Customs.** When two people meet in a Greek play, do they bow? kiss? kneel? Unfortunately, little is known about the manners and customs of this era. Probably friends greeted each other with a smile and, perhaps, a kiss. Herodotus left a description of Persians of the fifth century B.C. kissing one another: if equal, they kissed on the mouth; if one was inferior, on the cheek. The Greeks might kiss the hand, breast, or knee of a superior; and a hand clasp was the symbol of a pledge.

**Scenery.** For scenery, the production style of formalism is often seen today with steps, levels, ramps, columns, screens, ladders, and tubular constructions. Some, however, prefer a setting that suggests the original Greek facade with three doors. Others may like an impressionistic, symbolistic, or expressionistic type.

**Music.** Music is often used in the background to set the mood or to provide an accompaniment. Ancient instruments, such as the kithara, or modern electronic sounds may be used. Flutes, clarinets, oboes, and percussion instruments seem especially appropriate for these plays.

## SUGGESTED READING

Arnott, Peter D. *The Ancient Greek and Roman Theatre.* New York: Random House, Inc., 1971.

Bieber, Margarete. *The History of the Greek and Roman Theater.* 2d ed. Princeton, N.J.: Princeton University Press, 1961.

Brooke, Iris. *Costume in Greek Classic Drama.* New York: Theatre Arts Books, 1962.

Flickinger, R. C. *The Greek Theatre and Its Drama.* 4th ed. Chicago: University of Chicago Press, 1960.

Hamilton, Edith. *The Greek Way.* New York: W. W. Norton & Company, 1952.

Webster, T.B.L. *Greek Theatre Production.* 2d ed. London: Methuen & Co., Ltd., 1970.

## EXERCISES

To understand better what it was like to act in the fifth century B.C., find or make full-face masks to wear in the following exercises:

1. Wearing a mask appropriate for Oedipus or his wife, Jocasta, to use in Sophocles' *Oedipus Rex*, practice walking with an erect bearing and a stately, dignified manner. Improvise a conversation between the two as you imagine that you are on a platform stage in an amphitheatre seating thousands. Chant or intone the lines.

2. Imagine how Oedipus and Jocasta would move if they were to pray to Zeus. Raise your arms in large, reverent gestures. Improvise and chant a suitable prayer.

3. Improvise a scene that happens in *Hippolytus*, a tragedy by Euripides: Phaedra, wife of King Theseus, confides to the Nurse, her faithful servant, that she is in love with her stepson, Hippolytus. Torn between duty to her husband, who is away, and desire for Hippolytus, Phaedra is near death.

4. Improvise a famous "recognition" scene that occurs in Sophocles' tragedy *Electra*: Orestes and his sister, Electra, do not recognize each other at first because they have been separated for a long time and Orestes has been falsely reported to be dead. When Orestes arrives with a funeral urn, which supposedly contains his remains, and Electra mourns over it, he realizes that this is his sister and reveals his true identity to her.

5. Imagine that you are in the chorus of frogs for Aristophanes' comedy *The Frogs*. Use comic frog-like movements as you make appropriate sounds.

6. Imagine that you are a part of the chorus of different kinds of birds for Aristophanes' comedy *The Birds*. Use bird-like movements and sounds as the chorus attacks two scared Athenians.

---

### SCENE FOR TWO WOMEN
### FROM THE PROLOGUE OF *ANTIGONÊ*
### (c. 440 B.C.)

*By Sophocles*

An English Version by Dudley Fitts and Robert Fitzgerald

CHARACTERS: Antigonê, daughter of Oedipus, late king of Thebes
Ismenê, her sister.

SETTING: The scene takes place before the palace of Creon, king of Thebes, uncle of Antigonê and Ismenê. Three doors are upstage.

TIME: Dawn of the day after the flight of the defeated Argive army.

SITUATION: Because of the curse that their father, Oedipus, laid upon them, Eteocles and Polyneices, brothers of Antigonê and Ismenê, quarrelled about the royal power; and Polyneices was driven from Thebes to Argos. Returning with the Argive army to recover his throne, he and Eteocles killed each other in battle. Creon assumed the vacant throne and issued a proclamation that Eteocles should be given a soldier's funeral with full honors while Polyneices must lie in the fields unburied. The penalty for disobeying his order is death, but Antigonê has decided that she must bury her brother. The following excerpt is the first scene of the play.

COMMENTS: Antigonê is a strong woman, not necessarily in physique but in determination. Ismenê is much weaker: she believes that women cannot fight men. Antigonê is fiery in her passion; Ismenê is resigned to their fate.

[Antigone and Ismene enter from the central door of the Palace.]

**Antig:** Ismenê, dear sister,
    You would think that we had already suffered enough
    For the curse on Oedipus:
    I cannot imagine any grief
    That you and I have not gone through. And now—
    Have they told you the new decree of our King Creon?
**Ismene:** I have heard nothing: I know
    That two sisters lost two brothers, a double death
    In a single hour; and I know that the Argive army
    Fled in the night; but beyond this, nothing.
**Antig:** I thought so. And that is why I wanted you
    To come out here with me. There is something we must do.
**Ismene:** Why do you speak so strangely?
**Antig:** Listen, Ismenê:
    Creon buried our brother Eteoclês
    With military honours, gave him a soldier's funeral,
    And it was right that he should; but Polyneicês,
    Who fought as bravely and died as miserably,—
    They say that Creon has sworn
    No one shall bury him, no one mourn for him,
    But his body must lie in the fields, a sweet treasure
    For carrion birds to find as they search for food.
    That is what they say, and our good Creon is coming here
    To announce it publicly; and the penalty—
    Stoning to death in the public square!
    There it is,
    And now you can prove what you are:
    A true sister, or a traitor to your family.
**Ismene:** Antigonê, you are mad! What could I possibly do?
**Antig:** You must decide whether you will help me or not.
**Ismene:** I do not understand you. Help you in what?

**Antig:** Ismenê, I am going to bury him. Will you come?

**Ismene:** Bury him! You have just said the new law forbids it.

**Antig:** He is my brother. And he is your brother too.

**Ismene:** But think of the danger! Think what Creon will do!

**Antig:** Creon is not strong enough to stand in my way.

**Ismene:** Ah sister!
Oedipus died, everyone hating him
For what his own search brought to light, his eyes
Ripped out by his own hand; and Iocastê died,
His mother and wife at once: she twisted the cords
That strangled her life; and our two brothers died,
Each killed by the other's sword. And we are left:
But oh, Antigonê,
Think how much more terrible than these
Our own death would be if we should go against Creon
And do what he has forbidden! We are only women,
We cannot fight with men, Antigonê!
The law is strong, we must give in to the law
In this thing, and in worse. I beg the Dead
To forgive me, but I am helpless: I must yield
To those in authority. And I think it is dangerous business
To be always meddling.

**Antig:** If that is what you think,
I should not want you, even if you asked to come.
You have made your choice, you can be what you want to be:
But I will bury him; and if I must die,
I say that this crime is holy: I shall lie down
With him in death, and I shall be as dear
To him as he to me.
It is the dead,
Not the living, who make the longest demands:
We die for ever. . .
You may do as you like,
Since apparently the laws of the gods mean nothing to you.

**Ismene:** They mean a great deal to me; but I have no strength
To break laws that were made for the public good.

**Antig:** That must be your excuse, I suppose. But as for me,
I will bury the brother I love.

**Ismene:** Antigonê,
I am so afraid for you!

**Antig:** You need not be:
You have yourself to consider, after all.

**Ismene:** But no one must hear of this, you must tell no one!
I will keep it a secret, I promise!

**Antig:** Oh tell it! Tell everyone!
Think how they'll hate you when it all comes out
If they learn that you knew about it all the time!

**Ismene:** So fiery! You should be cold with fear.

**Antig:** Perhaps. But I am doing only what I must.

**Ismene:** But can you do it? I say that you cannot.

**Antig:** Very well: when my strength gives out, I shall do no more.

**Ismene:** Impossible things should not be tried at all.

**Antig:** Go away, Ismenê:
I shall be hating you soon, and the dead will too,
For your words are hateful. Leave me my foolish plan:
I am not afraid of the danger; if it means death,
It will not be the worst of deaths—death without honour.

**Ismene:** Go then, if you feel that you must.
You are unwise,
But a loyal friend indeed to those who love you.
[Exit into the Palace. Antigone goes off, L.]

---

## SCENE FOR ONE MAN, ONE WOMAN
## FROM ACT II OF *MEDEA*
### (431 B.C.)

### By *Euripides*

Adapted by Robinson Jeffers

CHARACTERS: Medea, former wife of Jason
Jason, now married to Creusa, the daughter of King Creon
Nurse (no lines)
Chorus of Corinthian women (no lines)
Two sons of Medea and Jason (no lines)

SETTING: Before Medea's house in Corinth.

TIME: The day King Creon banished Medea from Corinth.

SITUATION: Medea is distressed at the news of Jason's marriage and her banishment. Mad with anger and jealousy, she has prepared wedding gifts for Creusa. She has then sent the Nurse to tell Jason that she wants peace and wishes to send some presents to the bride.

COMMENTS: Wild with passion and grief, Medea is determined to have revenge, and her wedding gifts will eventually kill Creusa and Creon. Jason, the famous hero, is now of middle age; and in the following scene he is concerned about the safety of his sons.

**Medea:** Stand away from me, women,
While I make my sick peace.
[She goes across the scene to meet Jason, but more and more slowly, and stops. Her attitude indicates her aversion.]

**Jason:** *entering* Well, I have come. I tell you plainly,
Not for your sake: the children's. Your woman says that you have your wits again, and are willing
To look beyond your own woes.

*[Medea is silent. Jason observes her and says:]*
It appears doubtful.
—Where are the boys? I have made inquiry: I can find fosterage for them
In Epidaurus; or any other of several cities
That are Creon's friends. I'll visit them from time to time, and watch
That they're well kept.

**Medea:** *with suppressed violence* You mean . . . take them from me!
Be careful, Jason, I am not patient yet. *[more quietly]* I am the one who labored
  in pain to bear them, I cannot
Smile while I lose them. But I am learning; I am learning.—
No, Jason: I will not give up my little ones
To the cold care of strangers. It would be better for them to be drowned in the
  sea than to live with those
Who do not love them, hard faces, harsh hands. It will be far better for them to
  share
My wandering ocean of beggary and bleak exile:—they'll still be loved;
And when the sky rages I'll hold them warm
Against my heart. I love them, Jason. Only if you would keep them and care for
  them here in Corinth,
I might consent.

**Jason:** Gladly—but they are exiled.

**Medea:** —In your own house.

**Jason:** Gladly I'd do it—but you understand
  They are exiled, as you are.

**Medea:** Innocent; for my rebellion. That's black.
*[She reaches her hands toward him.]*
Forgive me, Jason,
As I do you. We have had too much wrath, and our acts
Are closing on us. On me I mean. Retribution is from the gods, and it breaks
  our hearts: but you
Feel no guilt, you fear nothing, nothing can touch you. It is wonderful to
  stand serene above fate
While earthlings wince. If it lasts. It does not always last.—
Do you love them, Jason?

**Jason:** Ha? Certainly. The children? Certainly!
I am their father.

**Medea:** Oh, but that's not enough. If I am to give them up to you—be patient
  with me,
  I must question you first. And very deeply; to the quick. If anything hap-
    pened to them,
  Would you be grieved?

**Jason:** Nothing will happen to them, Medea, if in my care. Rest your mind on
  it.

**Medea:** You must pardon me: it is not possible to be certain of that.
  If they were . . . killed and their blood
  Ran on the floor of the house or down the deep earth—
  Would you be grieved?

**Jason:** You have a sick mind. What a weak thing a woman is, always dreaming
  of evil.

Medea: Answer me!

Jason: Yes, after I'd cut their killer into red collops—
I'd be grieved.

Medea: That is true: vengeance
Makes grief bearable.—And knowing that. . . Creon's daughter, your
wife . . . no doubt will breed
Many other boys.—But, if something should happen to . . . Creon's
daughter . . . .

Jason: Enough, Medea. Too much.
Be silent!

Medea: I am to conclude that you love . . . Creon's daughter . . .
More than your sons. They'll have to take the sad journey with me.
[to the Nurse]
Tell the boys to come out
And bid their father farewell.
[The Nurse goes into the house.]

Jason: I could take them from you
By force, Medea.

Medea: violently
Try it, you!
[controlling herself]
No, Creon decided otherwise: he said they will share my exile.—Come,
Jason,
Let's be friends at last! I know you love them. If they could stay here in Cor-
inth I'd be content.

Jason: I asked it,
And he refused it.

Medea: You asked him to take
My children from me!
[The children come out with their tutor, followed by the Nurse.]
I am quite patient now; I have learned.—
Come, boys: come,
Speak to your father.

---

### SCENE FOR THREE MEN
### FROM EPISODE FOUR OF *OEDIPUS REX*
### (c. 430 B.C.)

#### By Sophocles

An English Version by Dudley Fitts and Robert Fitzgerald

CHARACTERS: Oedipus, king of Thebes
Messenger
Shepherd
Servants (no lines)
Choragos, leader of the chorus (no lines)
Chorus of Theban elders (no lines)

SETTING: Before the palace of Oedipus, king of Thebes. Three doors are upstage.

TIME: Day.

SITUATION: Oedipus has been waiting impatiently for an elderly shepherd, hoping that he will be able to tell him who are his parents and who killed King Laïos.

COMMENTS: Both the Shepherd and the Messenger are elderly; Oedipus is middle-aged. This play tells the famous story of Oedipus who, unknowingly, killed his father and married his mother. Oedipus is upset at the beginning of this excerpt and becomes more emotional as the scene progresses. As he realizes his guilt, his intense despair and disgust culminate in an agonizing cry in the last speech of this scene.

**Oedipus:** Tell me first, you from Corinth: is this the shepherd
  We were discussing?
**Messenger:** This is the very man.
**Oedipus:** *[to Shepherd]* Come here. No, look at me. You must answer
  Everything I ask.—You belonged to Laïos?
**Shepherd:** Yes: born his slave, brought up in his house.
**Oedipus:** Tell me: what kind of work did you do for him?
**Shepherd:** I was a shepherd of his, most of my life.
**Oedipus:** Where mainly did you go for pasturage?
**Shepherd:** Sometimes Kithairon, sometimes the hills near-by.
**Oedipus:** Do you remember ever seeing this man out there?
**Shepherd:** What would he be doing there? This man?
**Oedipus:** This man standing here. Have you ever seen him before?
**Shepherd:** No. At least, not to my recollection.
**Messenger:** And that is not strange, my lord. But I'll refresh
  His memory: he must remember when we two
  Spent three whole seasons together, March to September,
  On Kithairon or thereabouts. He had two flocks;
  I had one. Each autumn I'd drive mine home
  And he would go back with his to Laïos' sheepfold.—
  Is this not true, just as I have described it?
**Shepherd:** True, yes; but it was all so long ago.
**Messenger:** Well, then: do you remember, back in those days,
  That you gave me a baby boy to bring up as my own?
**Shepherd:** What if I did? What are you trying to say?
**Messenger:** King Oedipus was once that little child.
**Shepherd:** Damn you, hold your tongue!
**Oedipus:** No more of that!
  It is your tongue needs watching, not this man's.
**Shepherd:** My King, my Master, what is it I have done wrong?
**Oedipus:** You have not answered his question about the boy.
**Shepherd:** He does not know . . . He is only making trouble . . .
**Oedipus:** Come, speak plainly, or it will go hard with you.

Shepherd: In God's name, do not torture an old man!

Oedipus: Come here, one of you; bind his arms behind him.

Shepherd: Unhappy king! What more do you wish to learn?

Oedipus: Did you give this man the child he speaks of?

Shepherd: I did.

And I would to God I had died that very day.

Oedipus: You will die now unless you speak the truth.

Shepherd: Yet if I speak the truth, I am worse than dead.

Oedipus: Very well; since you insist upon delaying—

Shepherd: No! I have told you already that I gave him the boy.

Oedipus: Where did you get him? From your house? From somewhere else?

Shepherd: Not from mine, no. A man gave him to me.

Oedipus: Is that man here? Do you know whose slave he was?

Shepherd: For God's love, my King, do not ask me any more!

Oedipus: You are a dead man if I have to ask you again.

Shepherd: Then . . . Then the child was from the palace of Laïos.

Oedipus: A slave child? or a child of his own line?

Shepherd: Ah, I am on the brink of dreadful speech!

Oedipus: And I of dreadful hearing. Yet I must hear.

Shepherd: If you must be told, then . . .

They said it was Laïos' child;

But it is your wife who can tell you about that.

Oedipus: My wife!—Did she give it to you?

Shepherd: My lord, she did.

Oedipus: Do you know why?

Shepherd: I was told to get rid of it.

Oedipus: An unspeakable mother!

Shepherd: There had been prophecies . . .

Oedipus: Tell me.

Shepherd: It was said that the boy would kill his own father.

Oedipus: Then why did you give him over to this old man?

Shepherd: I pitied the baby, my King,

And I thought that this man would take him far away

To his own country.

He saved him—but for what a fate!

For if you are what this man says you are,

No man living is more wretched than Oedipus.

Oedipus: Ah God!

It was true!

All the prophecies!

—Now,

O Light, may I look on you for the last time!

I, Oedipus,

Oedipus, damned in his birth, in his marriage damned,

Damned in the blood he shed with his own hand!

[He rushes into the palace.]

## SCENE FOR ONE MAN, ONE WOMAN
## FROM *LYSISTRATA*
### (411 B.C.)

### By *Aristophanes*

Translator Anonymous

CHARACTERS: Myrrhiné
                Cinesias, her husband

SETTING: Before the house of Lysistrata and the entrance to the Acropolis. Between the two buildings is the opening of the Cave of Pan.

TIME: Seven months after Cinesias left for war.

SITUATION: Under the leadership of Lysistrata, the women of Athens and other Greek states have taken an oath that they will not make love to their husbands until the men decide to stop fighting. The women have captured the Acropolis and have not permitted men to enter. Cinesias, unhappy about the state of himself and his household with his wife away, has demanded to see Myrrhiné; and Lysistrata has agreed to a meeting.

COMMENTS: Myrrhiné in this excerpt is torn between her oath and her desire for Cinesias. She tantalizes him by being alternately cold and ardent. Both Myrrhiné and Cinesias are attractive young people.

Cinesias: There, you see, the child is gone; there's nothing to hinder us; won't you lie down now?

Myrrhiné: But, miserable man, where, where?

Cinesias: In the cave of Pan; nothing could be better.

Myrrhiné: But how shall I purify myself before going back into the citadel?

Cinesias: Nothing easier! you can wash at the Clepsydra.

Myrrhiné: But my oath? Do you want me to perjure myself?

Cinesias: I'll take all responsibility; don't worry.

Myrrhiné: Well, I'll be off, then, and find a bed for us.

Cinesias: There's no point in that; surely we can lie on the ground.

Myrrhiné: No, no! even though you are bad, I don't like your lying on the bare earth.

   *(She goes back into the Acropolis.)*

Cinesias: *(enraptured)* Ah! how the dear girl loves me!

Myrrhiné: *(coming back with a cot)* Come, get to bed quick; I am going to undress. But, oh dear, we must get a mattress.

Cinesias: A mattress? Oh! no, never mind about that!

Myrrhiné: No, by Artemis! lie on the bare sacking? never! That would be squalid.

Cinesias: Kiss me!

Myrrhiné: Wait a minute!

   *(She leaves him again.)*

Cinesias: Good god, hurry up!

**Myrrhiné:** *(coming back with a mattress)* Here is a mattress. Lie down, I am just going to undress. But you've got no pillow.

**Cinesias:** I don't want one either!

**Myrrhiné:** But *I* do.

*(She leaves him again.)*

**Cinesias:** Oh god, oh god, she treats my tool just like Heracles!

**Myrrhiné:** *(coming back with a pillow)* There, lift your head, dear! *(Wondering what else to tantalize him with; to herself)* Is that all, I wonder?

**Cinesias:** *(misunderstanding)* Surely, there's nothing else. Come, my treasure.

**Myrrhiné:** I am just unfastening my girdle. But remember what you promised me about making peace; mind you keep your word.

**Cinesias:** Yes, yes, upon my life I will.

**Myrrhiné:** Why, you have no blanket!

**Cinesias:** My god, what difference does *that* make? What I want is to make love!

**Myrrhiné:** *(going out again)* Never fear—directly, directly! I'll be back in no time.

**Cinesias:** The woman will kill me with her blankets!

**Myrrhiné:** *(coming back with a blanket)* Now, get yourself up.

**Cinesias:** *(Pointing)* I've got *this* up!

**Myrrhiné:** Wouldn't you like me to scent you?

**Cinesias:** No, by Apollo, no, please don't!

**Myrrhiné:** Yes, by Aphrodité, but I will, whether you like it or not.

*(She goes out again.)*

**Cinesias:** God, I wish she'd hurry up and get through with all this!

**Myrrhiné** *(coming back with a flask of perfume)* Hold out your hand; now rub it in.

**Cinesias:** Oh! in Apollo's name, I don't much like the smell of it; but perhaps it will improve when it's well rubbed in. It does not somehow smack of the marriage bed!

**Myrrhiné:** Oh dear! what a scatterbrain I am; if I haven't gone and brought Rhodian perfumes!

**Cinesias:** Never mind, dearest, let it go now.

**Myrrhiné:** You don't really *mean* that.

*(She goes.)*

**Cinesias:** Damn the man who invented perfumes!

**Myrrhiné:** *(coming back with another flask)* Here, take this bottle.

**Cinesias:** I have a better one all ready for you, darling. Come, you provoking creature, to bed with you, and don't bring another thing.

**Myrrhiné:** Coming, coming; I'm just slipping off my shoes. Dear boy, will you vote for peace?

**Cinesias:** I'll think about it. *(Myrrhiné runs away.)* I'm a dead man, she is killing me! She has gone, and left me in torment!

# Chapter Three

# Classicism
# of Ancient Rome

When Rome began to expand in the third century B.C., the Romans discovered the Greek theatre and started to copy it at home. From 240 B.C. on, professional male actors presented Latin tragedies and comedies at festivals, games, religious events, funerals, and celebrations of victories.

## PLAYS

The New Comedy of Menander and others had a great effect on Roman playwrights. Some, like Plautus and Terence, wrote Latin imitations using Greek characters and locales; other playwrights used Roman characters in plays about contemporary life and Roman history, but their works are not extant. Twenty-one comedies by Plautus (c. 254–184 B.C.) and six by Terence (c. 190–159 B.C.) exist today. All deal with the domestic affairs of well-to-do city people in Greece, use as the locale a street in Greece, and have the same types of Greek characters as are found in New Comedy.

There is no chorus, however, in Roman comedies; but music accompanied some of the scenes, and there are songs and dances in the plays of Plautus. Plots involve mistaken identity, the machinations of slaves, complicated intrigue, and the reuniting of long-lost relatives. Plautus used the single plot in farcical situation comedies, but Terence (unlike the Greeks) used an intricate double plot as he wrote more senti-mental comedies of lovers and romance.

There was also one famous Roman writer of tragedies—Seneca (c. 4 B.C.-A.D. 65). Nine of his plays are extant, some of which show the influence of Euripides. Probably his works were recited but never given a stage production in his time; however, his tragedies are important histor-ically because of the effect they had on Renaissance writers. The struc-ture of Seneca's plays caused later writers to keep to the three unities of time, place, and action and to try a five-act division. They also copied Seneca's use of cruelty, violence, ghosts, evil characters, moral philosophizing, imagistic poetry, asides, soliloquies, and the *confidant* (a person to whom secrets are confided).

Some of the most famous Roman plays are: Plautus' *Amphitryon, The Haunted House, The Pot of Gold, The Captives, The Braggart Warrior,* and *The Menaechmi;* Terence's *The Woman of Andros, The Self-Tormentor, The Eunuch, Phormio, The Mother-in-Law,* and *The Brothers;* and Seneca's *Oedipus, Thyestes, Medea,* and *Phaedra.*

## PRODUCTIONS THEN

**Theatres.** Plays in Rome were presented in temporary theatres that be-came more and more magnificent through the years. Theatres varied, of course, but usually actors performed on a long, narrow platform stage, backed by a cloth or wall (about three stories high in some theatres) that had three entrances into the stage house. These openings resembled houses on a street or sometimes a side street. There was also an entrance into the stage house at each end of the platform that supposedly led to the harbor, marketplace, or other parts of town. In front of the stage was a semicircular orchestra surrounded by banked seats. Performances took place outdoors in the daylight, but an awning may have covered the au-dience. In the second century B.C., a curtain was first used in a theatre by being dropped into a slot at the front of the stage at the beginning of a performance and raised at the end. Stone theatres were built outside of Rome earlier, but it was 55 B.C. before a stone theatre, seating about ten thousand, was built in Rome.

**Scenery.** Vitruvius, a Roman architect in the first century B.C., de-scribed comedy settings as private dwellings with balconies. He wrote that tragedies used columns, roofs, statues, and other objects suited to kings and that satyric scenes were decorated with trees, caverns, moun-tains, and other rustic objects.

**Costumes.** Greek clothing, with tights underneath, was worn for the comedies of Plautus and Terence because the characters are supposed to be Greek. The actors wore masks and wigs and a sandal called a *socc us*. Some colors may have been associated with certain types, such as red for slaves and purple for nobles.

Roman actors portraying Greek characters in tragedies wore long-sleeved cloaks, high boots, enormous wigs, and masks. Actors portraying Roman characters in tragedies and comedies wore typical Roman clothing of the period plus masks and wigs.

**Acting.** Unlike Greek actors, who were highly respected members of the community, Roman actors were primarily lowly slaves, freedmen, or foreigners. Their acting was highly presentational. With the noisy, unruly Roman spectators, the actors had to try to command the audience's attention by acting directly to them most of the time and by being lively and entertaining. In the comedies, the actors, who had to sing and dance as well as act, used crude horseplay and slapstick as they played with verve and abandon.

Tragic acting was more oratorical than comic acting. In fact, one Roman actor, Roscius, wrote a book in which he compared acting to oratory. In tragedies, the crude, uneducated Roman audiences apparently liked melodramatic effects, vice, spectacle, and violent action. The actors were sometimes accused of ranting and using extravagant facial expressions and gestures, but actually they were probably doing the best they could to please the large, illiterate crowds.

## PRODUCTIONS NOW

**Acting Comedies.** When producing Plautus' farces, the acting should be mainly presentational with a rapid, lively pace. The characters are types that stem from Greek New Comedy, such as scheming slaves, the old father, the young lovers, the braggart but cowardly soldier, the hungry parasite, the sensual courtesan, the slave dealer, the quack doctor, the moneylender, and the cook. Most parts should be played broadly and exuberantly, exaggerating character traits that are funny. Actors must speak distinctly, point key words, and use great vocal variety. There should be a lot of fast actions, gesturing, and energy onstage. Actors should remember, though, that while slaves run most of the time, gentlemen should never run. Comic business, clowning, and horseplay must be used for this style of playing, which may be called low comedy acting.

In addition, performers in a Plautus play often need to sing and dance. A 1962 musical *A Funny Thing Happened on the Way to the Forum* by Stephen Sondheim, Burt Shevelove, and Larry Gelbart offers a combination of several plots by Plautus and demonstrates well the vivacity, fun, and slapstick of the original shows.

Terence's comedies do not have the farcical situations and exaggerated characters that Plautus used; they are more serious and sentimental. While these plays still require a presentational approach, the actors can use more subtle characterizations, movements, and stage business.

Today's scenery can be a modern reproduction of the Greek street used in the original Roman productions or a funny, exaggerated version of the same. Greek costumes similar to those worn originally are often selected, with or without masks.

**Acting Tragedies.** Seneca's tragedies have for years been considered unactable, but Peter Brook's production of Seneca's *Oedipus* in 1968 in London, with John Gielgud and Irene Worth, brought attention to these ancient tragedies. Clothing the chorus in brown sweaters and trousers, Miss Worth in a simple, long black dress, and Gielgud in black trousers and turtle-necked sweater, Brook used an immense, revolving golden cube to dominate the stage. The dramatic action was intense and varied as the players used expressive movements to emphasize the meaning of the lines. Those who are interested in the modern theatre of cruelty might well consider a production of a play by the old master of cruelty—Seneca.

## SUGGESTED READING

Arnott, Peter D. *The Ancient Greek and Roman Theatre*. New York: Random House, 1971.

Beare, William. *The Roman Stage: A Short History of Latin Drama in the Time of the Republic*. 3d ed. London: Methuen & Co., Ltd., 1963.

Bieber, Margarete. *The History of the Greek and Roman Theater*. 2d ed. Princeton, N.J.: Princeton University Press, 1961.

Duckworth, George E. *The Nature of Roman Comedy*. Princeton, N.J.: Princeton University Press, 1952.

Hamilton, Edith. *The Roman Way*. New York: W. W. Norton, 1932.

Highet, Gilbert. *The Classical Tradition*. New York: Oxford University Press, 1949.

Nicoll, Allardyce. *Masks, Mimes, and Miracles*. New York: Harcourt Brace Jovanovich, Inc., 1931.

## EXERCISES

Find or make full-face or half-masks to wear in the following exercises:

1. Walk and talk like an old, irate father; a scheming slave; a hungry parasite; an erotic courtesan; a braggart but cowardly soldier; a bumbling doctor; or young lovers.

2. Imagine that you are the Roman actor who must deliver the prologue of *The Menaechmi* to a noisy audience of thousands. Try to capture their attention by humor and funny business as you give them the exposition they need to understand this comedy. Explain to them how twin brothers were separated when they were seven years old, how one boy was raised in Syracuse and the other in Epidamnus, and how they both were named Menaechmus. When grown, Menaechmus II of Syracuse has decided to try to find his twin, and so he has come to Epidamnus to search for his brother.

3. Improvise a comic scene from *The Haunted House.* Philolaches has been having a great time at a party in his house, which is full of strangers and women; but when his slave, Tranio, warns him that his father is returning home, he is terrified because he knows his father will disapprove. The clever Tranio says that he will take care of everything, and he does by meeting the father at the door and telling him a wild story about the house being haunted.

4. Improvise a comic scene in which a braggart warrior tells his disbelieving servant about his recent battle experience.

5. Improvise a comic scene that happens in *The Menaechmi.* Menaechmus I steals a cloak from his wife, talks about this with Peniculus, a parasite who is always hungry, and then gives the cloak to Erotium, a seductive courtesan who lives nearby. He asks her to have lunch prepared for the three of them and then leaves with Peniculus to get a drink. Erotium calls her cook, Culindrus, and sends him to buy food. A short time later, Culindrus, returning with the provisions, meets Menaechmus II, who has arrived in Epidamnus to look for his long-lost twin brother. Thinking that he is Menaechmus I, Culindrus talks to him about the lunch with Erotium. Menaechmus II does not understand what he is talking about and is completely confused.

6. Improvise a serious scene in which Medea, who is furious because her husband, Jason, left her to marry Creusa, prepares wedding gifts for the bride. The presents will kill Creusa and her father, King Creon. (See Seneca's *Medea.*)

---

### SCENE FOR TWO MEN, ONE WOMAN
### FROM ACT IV OF *THE MENAECHMI*
### (c. 184 B.C.)

*By Plautus*

Translated by Richard W. Hyde and Edward C. Weist

CHARACTERS: Father-in-law of Menaechmus I
Wife of Menaechmus I
Menaechmus II, of Syracuse

SETTING: A street in Epidamnus on which stand the houses of Menaechmus I and Erotium, a courtesan.

TIME: Afternoon.

SITUATION: Menaechmus II of Syracuse has come to Epidamnus to look for his twin brother, from whom he has been separated since they were seven years old. He has been mistaken for Menaechmus I by various people including the latter's wife, who has become so upset that she has called in her father to help her.

COMMENTS: This excerpt is an example of the "mistaken identity" situation that is frequent in Roman comedies. The wife is a scolding type who wants to reform her husband. Her father is an elderly gentleman who tries to keep peace in the family. Menaechmus II is so mystified by the queer actions of these two that he takes refuge in pretending that he is mad.

**Father:** I'll find out from him just what has happened. I'll go speak to him. *[goes over to Menaechmus II and taps him with staff]* Menaechmus, for my enlightenment tell me what you are quarreling about. Why are you sad? Why does she stand apart from you, in anger?

**Menaechmus II:** Whoever you are, whatever your name is, old man, I call as my witnesses great Jupiter and the gods—

**Father:** Why? Wherefore? And for what?

**Menaechmus II:** That I have neither wronged this woman, who accuses me of stealing this cloak from her house—

**Wife:** Perjury, eh?

**Menaechmus II:** If I have ever set my foot inside the house in which she lives, may I be the most accursedly accursed!

**Father:** Are you in your right mind, to make such a wish? Do you deny that you have ever set foot in the house you live in, you utter madman?

**Menaechmus II:** Old man, do you say I live in that house?

**Father:** Do you deny it?

**Menaechmus II:** I' faith, I do deny it.

**Father:** No; you deny not "in faith" but in joke—unless, of course, you have moved out overnight *[motions wife to C.]* —Come here, please, daughter. What do you say? You haven't moved from the house, have you?

**Wife:** Why should we, or where should we move to, I ask you?

**Father:** By heaven, I don't know.

**Wife:** It's clear that he is making fun of you. Don't you get that?

**Father:** Menaechmus, you have joked long enough; now attend to business.

**Menaechmus II:** I ask you, what business have I with you? Or who are you? Are you sane? And this woman, who has been plaguing me this way and that—is she sane? *[tears his hair in exasperation]*

**Wife:** *[to Father, frightened]* Do you see the color of his eyes? See how a green color is coming over his temples and forehead! How his eyes shine!

**Menaechmus II:** *[to audience]* Alack, they say I'm crazy, whereas it is they who are really that way themselves. What could be better for me, since they say I am mad than to pretend to be insane, to scare them off? *[begins to jump about madly]*

**Wife:** How he stretches and gapes! What shall I do, father?

**Father:** Come over here, my child, as far as you can from him. *[Retreating L.]*

**Menaechmus II:** *[pretending madness]* Ho, Bacchus! Ho, Bromius! Where in this forest do you bid me to the hunt? I hear, but cannot leave this place, so closely am I guarded by that rabid bitch upon my left. And behind there is that bald goat, who often in his time has ruined innocent citizens by his false testimony.

**Father:** Curse you!

**Menaechmus II:** Lo, Apollo from his oracle bids me to burn out the eyes of that woman with flaming torches. [*Charges at wife, then immediately retreats*]

**Wife:** I am lost, father! He threatens to burn out my eyes.

**Father:** [*to wife, aside*] Hist, daughter!

**Wife:** What? What shall we do?

**Father:** Suppose I summon the slaves? I'll go bring some people to take this man away and chain him up indoors before he makes any more disturbance.

**Menaechmus II:** [*aside*] I'm stuck; if I don't hit upon a scheme, they'll take me into the house with them. [*aloud*] Apollo, you forbid me to spare her face with my fists unless she leaves my sight and goes utterly to the devil? [*advances threateningly*] I'll do your bidding, Apollo!

**Father:** Run home as fast as you can, before he thumps you.

**Wife:** I am running. Watch him father; don't let him get away! Oh! am I not a miserable woman to have to listen to such things! [*Exit into her house.*]

**Menaechmus II:** [*aside*] I got rid of her rather well. [*aloud, threatening Father*] Now, Apollo, as for this most filthy wretch, this bearded tremulous Tithonus, who is called the son of Cygnus, you bid me break his limbs and bones and joints with that staff which he holds?

**Father:** [*retreats, shaking his staff*] You'll get a beating if you touch me or come any closer.

**Menaechmus II:** I'll do your bidding! I'll take a double-edged axe and chop the flesh of this old man to mince meat, down to the very bones!

**Father:** [*aside*] Well then, I must beware and take care of myself. Really, I am afraid, from the way he threatens, that he may do me harm. [*Menaechmus retreats C.*]

**Menaechmus II:** You give me many commands, Apollo! Now you bid me take my fierce untamed yoked horses and mount my chariot, to crush this old stinking toothless lion. Now I've mounted! [*business*] Now I hold the reins! Now the goad is in my hand! Forward, my steeds, make loud the clatter of your hooves! And in swift flight make undiminished the fleetness of your feet. [*Gallops about the stage.*]

**Father:** Do you threaten me with yoked horses?

**Menaechmus II:** Lo, Apollo, again you bid me make a charge at him, this fellow who stands here, and slay him. [*rushes forward, then suddenly stops*] But who is this, who drags me from my chariot by the hair? He alters your commands, even the commands of Apollo! [*pretends to fall senseless to the ground*]

**Father:** [*advances cautiously*] Alas, by heaven, it is a severe disease! O gods, by your faith, what sudden changes do ye work! Take this madman—how strong he was a little while before. This disease has smitten him all of a sudden. I'll go get a doctor as quick as I can. [*Exit, L.*]

**Menaechmus II:** [*getting up*] Lord! These idiots who compel me, a sane man, to act like a madman! Have they got out of my sight now, I wonder? Why don't I go straight back to the ship while the going is good? [*as he starts to* *go, R., to audience]* I beg of all of you, if the old man comes back don't tell him what street I've taken. *[Exit, R.]*

---

## SCENE FOR ONE MAN, ONE WOMAN
## FROM ACT V, SCENE 2 OF *MEDEA*
## (c. 40 to 65)

### By *Seneca*

Translated by Frank Justus Miller

CHARACTERS: Medea, former wife of Jason
                 Jason
                 Their son (no lines)
                 Citizens of Corinth (no lines)

SETTING: Before the house of Jason in Corinth.

TIME: Shortly after Medea has killed one of her and Jason's two children.

SITUATION: Jason has found it politically expedient to abandon Medea and marry Creusa, daughter of King Creon of Corinth. Angry and jealous, Medea has sent wedding gifts to Creusa that have resulted in the deaths of Creusa and Creon. Next, in madness, Medea has slain one of her and Jason's two sons. Jason and a group of citizens have entered to capture Medea.

COMMENTS: Medea in this excerpt is in an ecstasy of madness, bent upon revenge. Jason unsuccessfully tries to reason with her. Compare Seneca's version of this legend with Euripides' *Medea.*

*(Enter Jason)*

**Jason:** *(shouting to citizens)* Ho, all ye loyal sons, who mourn the death of kings!
  Come, let us seize the worker of this hideous crime.
  Now ply your arms and raze her palace to the ground.
  *(Medea appears on the housetop with her two sons.)*
**Medea:** Now, now have I regained my regal state, my sire,
  My brother! Once again the Colchians hold the spoil
  Of precious gold! And by the magic of this hour
  I am a maid once more. O heavenly powers, appeased
  At length! O festal hour! O nuptial day! On, on!
  Accomplished is the guilt, but not the recompense.
  Complete the task while yet thy hands are strong to act!
  Why dost thou linger still? Why dost thou hesitate
  Upon the threshold of the deed? Thou canst perform it.
  Now wrath has died within me, and my soul is filled
  With shame and deep remorse. Ah me, what have I done,
  Wretch that I am? Wretch that thou art, well mayst thou mourn,
  For thou hast done it!
  At that thought delirious joy
  O'ermasters me and fills my heart which fain would grieve.
  And yet, methinks, the act was almost meaningless,

32

Since Jason saw it not; for naught has been performed
If to his grief be added not the woe of sight.

**Jason:** (*discovering her*) Lo, there she stands upon the lofty battlements!
Bring torches! Fire the house, that she may fall ensnared
By those devices she herself hath planned.

**Medea:** (*derisively*) Not so,
But rather build a lofty pyre for these thy sons;
Their funeral rites prepare. Already for thy bride
And father have I done the service due the dead;
For in their ruined palace have I buried them.
One son of thine has met his doom; and this shall die
Before his father's face.

**Jason:** By all the gods, and by the perils of our flight,
And by our marriage bond which I have ne'er betrayed,
I pray thee spare the boy, for he is innocent.
If aught of sin there be, 'tis mine. Myself I give
To be the victim. Take my guilty soul for his.

**Medea:** 'Tis for thy prayers and tears I draw, not sheathe the sword.
Go now, and take thee maids for wives, thou faithless one;
Abandon and betray the mother of thy sons.

**Jason:** And yet, I pray thee, let one sacrifice atone.

**Medea:** If in the blood of one my passion could be quenched,
No vengeance had it sought. Though both my sons I slay,
The number still is all too small to satisfy
My boundless grief. If in my womb there still should lurk
A pledge of thee, I'll search my vitals with a sword
And hale it forth.

**Jason:** Then finish what thou hast begun—
I ask no more—and grant at least that no delay
Prolong my helpless agony.

**Medea:** (*to herself*) Now hasten not,
Relentless passion, but enjoy a slow revenge.
This day is in thy hands; its fertile hours employ.

**Jason:** Oh, take my life, thou heartless one.

**Medea:** Thou bid'st me pity—
Well! (*Slays the second child*) —'Tis done!
No more atonement, passion, can I offer thee.
Now hither lift thy tearful eyes, ungrateful one.
Dost recognise they wife? 'Twas thus of old I fled.
The heavens themselves provide me with a safe retreat.
(*A chariot drawn by dragons appears in the air*)
Twin serpents bow their necks submissive to the yoke.
Now, father, take thy sons; while I, upon my car,
With wingéd speed am borne aloft through realms of air.
(*Mounts her car and is borne away.*)

**Jason:** (*calling after her*) Speed on through realms of air that mortals never see:
But, witness heaven, where thou art gone no gods can be!

# Chapter Four

# Italian Renaissance Theatre

The Roman theatre degenerated under the Roman Empire and Teutonic conquerors until the immorality of mimes (short, topical farce comedies that usually dealt with immoral subject matter) aroused the ire of the early Christian church. In the fifth century A.D., performers in mimes were excommunicated; and in the sixth century, the theatres were closed.

During the Dark Ages, there were strolling entertainers in Europe, but there was little organized theatrical activity. Curiously, when drama was "reborn" in Europe in the tenth century, it took place in the church that had helped to obliterate it. The clergy turned to plays to assist them in teaching about the Bible, church events, and the lives of saints.

The writing in these anonymous, medieval, religious plays is crude. Unlike the Greek and Roman classical drama, the plots are not well constructed; they do not observe the three unities (they span long periods of time, use many locales, and have a variety of events that show little relationship to one another); and there is no separation of comedy and tragedy because funny things were mixed into serious plays to make them more entertaining to the people.

At first, these plays were acted in Latin by the clergy inside European cathedrals and monasteries. As the productions became larger, they were sometimes presented outside on the church steps or on a platform in the churchyard, town square, or streets, or on pageant-wagons. Gradually local languages replaced Latin, nonclerics took over the acting, and productions became more elaborate as they were sponsored by trade guilds or special societies. For scenery, simple fragmentary set pieces were used to suggest locales; for example, a throne chair might be used to indicate a palace while nearby other scenic pieces might suggest heaven and hell. This is similar to what is called today a simultaneous set.

In Italy from the fourteenth to the seventeenth centuries, many factors caused that great period known as the Renaissance, a time in which there was a tremendous revival of interest in learning, literature, and the arts. Although religious drama continued to be popular in some other countries, by the fifteenth century in Italy it was gradually supplanted by the secular.

Although not known for its plays, the Italian Renaissance period is important theatrically for the development of ideas about neoclassicism, theatres with proscenium-arch stages, perspective scenery, elaborate stage machinery, the *commedia dell'arte*, and opera.

## PLAYS

In the Italian Renaissance, there were productions of classical plays, especially those of Plautus, Terence, and Seneca, because more scholars knew Latin than Greek. Amateur actors at courts and academies in Rome, Ferrara, Mantua, Urbino, and other cities performed the old plays in Latin. The next step was for Italian scholars to write Latin imitations of the classics and then plays in the local language.

Italy produced no drama of great worth during the Renaissance probably because of the emphasis on elaborate scenery and the scholars' insistence on following rigid rules for playwriting that they gleaned from reading Aristotle and the ancient Greek and Latin plays. Although the Greeks had not adhered to the three unities consistently, Renaissance Italian scholars believed that their neoclassical plays must follow the three unities of time, place, and action (one day, one locale, and one plot) and that there should be no mixture of comedy and tragedy.

## PRODUCTIONS THEN

**Theatres and Scenery.**   The oldest surviving indoor theatre built in the Renaissance is the Teatro Olimpico at Vicenza, Italy, which was opened in 1585 with a cast of 108 playing *Oedipus Rex* in Italian. It has a stage that is similar to Roman stages, with three entrances in the ornate back wall and one at each end.

Although temporary proscenium arches were used earlier, the first theatre known to have a permanent proscenium arch was the Teatro

Farnese built at Parma in 1618. Earlier, some theatres, copying the Roman practice, had used curtains that fell into a trough; but eventually at the Teatro Farnese a large curtain was added that rose to reveal elaborate perspective scenery.

By the middle of the seventeenth century, flat wings, borders, and backdrops, arranged on a raked stage to emphasize the forced perspective, came to be the standard; machines to shift them were available; and elaborate stage effects were common. The auditorium was usually in the shape of a horseshoe with pit, boxes, and galleries.

**Acting.** Actors in the classical and neoclassical plays who performed for the upper class were mainly amateurs. It is believed that they worked primarily downstage so they would not ruin the perspective effect of the scenery and that the acting was probably formal, decorous, oratorical, staid, and presentational.

While the upper class enjoyed watching amateurs perform plays, opera, and spectacular entertainments of dance, song, and pageantry in their elegant theatres, the common people could see professional actors in the *commedia dell'arte*.

**Commedia dell'Arte.** Starting about the middle of the sixteenth century, *commedia dell'arte* troupes (a typical one might have seven men and three women) were popular in Italy and other European countries for more than two hundred years. Their productions could be done almost anywhere: on outdoor platforms backed by a simple curtain, in banquet halls, or in theatres.

There were no written scripts, only scenarios (outlines of plays). The actors improvised their lines after studying the scenario, which gave the basic plot and perhaps some *lazzi* (comic business). These farcical plots, which usually involved stock characters in complicated love affairs, show the influence of Plautus, Terence, and ancient mimes. Each character had a standard characterization, costume, and mask, except for the young lovers, who wore contemporary clothing without masks. Some of the characters who appeared regularly were:

- Pantalone, a foolish old miser, who traditionally wore a long red or black cloak with a red cap and a mask with a large nose and pointed beard.
- Capitano, a braggart warrior, who wore a funny uniform and plumed hat, carried a large wooden sword, and had a mask with a big nose and a long mustache.
- Dottore, a bookish, doddering, old bore, who was garbed in a scholarly black robe and hat and wore a mask with red cheeks and a short beard.
- Zany servants (*zannis*) named Arlecchino (or Harlequin in France), who was originally dressed in a black half-mask and a patched costume; Pedrolino (later Pierrot in France), who appeared in a loose white costume

with white makeup on his face; Pulcinella (changed to Punch in England); Brighella; Scapini; Coviello; or Scaramuccia.
- Columbina and Franceschina, flippant female servants.
- Good-looking young lovers.

An actor usually played only one stock character in his or her lifetime, developing comic business (*lazzi*) to use over and over again. Rehearsals were few; actors read the scenario, rehearsed enough to be sure of names and places, then hung the scenario backstage and depended on their imaginations to improvise the play.

It is thought that the acting was lively, filled with funny horseplay and slapstick. *Lazzi* used by the comedians included pratfalls; tripping oneself and others; slipping and falling; tumbling down steps; catching and eating imaginary flies; hitting with swords, slapsticks, and boards; squirting water; chasing another around the stage; disguising as another character; imitating another's voice; and doing magic, juggling, and acrobatic tricks.

Verbally, they used puns, ridiculous phrases, epigrams, and satire; however, since the plots were trite and used repeatedly the same characters in the same basic situations, the words were relatively unimportant. Actors relied on their skills in pantomiming, dancing, singing, juggling, playing musical instruments, and acrobatics to entertain audiences. At intermissions, these skills were also used as they passed hats for money.

## PRODUCTIONS NOW

*Commedia dell'arte* characters and gags are still with us in Punch and Judy puppet shows, mimes, pantomimes, circus clowns, burlesque and vaudeville sketches, and the slapstick comedy of the Keystone Kops, the Three Stooges, Laurel and Hardy, and others. With interest today growing in improvisation, productions are being done again of old *commedia dell'arte* scenarios, of which about eight hundred are in existence.

To prepare for such an improvisation, actors should study the descriptions of the characters and practice appropriate *lazzi*, which modern comedians would term *shticks*. Singing, dancing, acrobatic tricks, juggling, and playing musical instruments should be used. Working to the audience most of the time with many asides and soliloquies, the actors should exhibit great vitality and a joyous comic spirit as they clown their way through these fast-paced farces. Voices should have extreme variations of pitch, loudness, and rate. Characterizations must be exaggerated: these characters are clowns and buffoons. Only the young lovers show any realistic qualities. The humor is not subtle and intellectual; the comedy is broad, physical, and presentational. This is low comedy acting.

Authentic costumes with masks or mask-like makeup will add greatly to a production, but mere suggestions of these or exaggerated versions may also work well. Sets and props can be as simple as they were with the early *commedia dell'arte* troupes; that is, almost nonexistent.

## SUGGESTED READING

Beaumont, Cyril V. *The History of Harlequin.* New York: Benjamin Blom, 1967.

Herrick, Marvin T. *Italian Comedy in the Renaissance.* Urbana, Ill.: University of Illinois Press, 1966.

Hewitt, Barnard (ed.). *The Renaissance Stage: Documents of Serlio, Sabbattini, and Furttenbach.* Coral Gables, Fla.: University of Miami Press, 1958.

Nicoll, Allardyce. *Masks, Mimes, and Miracles.* New York: Harcourt Brace Jovanovich, Inc., 1931.

————. *Stuart Masques and the Renaissance Stage.* London: George G. Harrap & Co., Ltd., 1937.

Smith, Winifred. *The Commedia dell'Arte.* Rev. ed. New York: Benjamin Blom, 1965.

## EXERCISES

Find or make masks to wear in the following exercises (all wear masks except the young lovers):

1. Walk and talk as Pantalone, Capitano, Dottore, Harlequin, Pierrot, or the young lovers. (See the descriptions in this chapter.)
2. Practice some of the *lazzi* mentioned in this chapter.
3. Improvise on these situations:
   a. Pantalone believes that he is to dine alone with a beautiful woman, but she arranges for her male servant, Harlequin, to impersonate her at the dinner.
   b. A lovely young girl, who has been abducted by Capitano, plots with Columbina and Harlequin to escape to see her handsome lover.
   c. A man enters a strange city and is handed gifts by a courtesan whom he has never seen before and berated by another woman who says she is his wife, although he has never known her either. In time, his long-lost twin brother arrives for a reconciliation and explanation of the confusion.
   d. While Dottore attempts to speak to the audience on a serious subject, Harlequin dances about with a slapstick upstage, mugging, imitating, and making fun of Dottore, who is not aware of his presence.

SCENARIO FOR THREE MEN, THREE WOMEN
FROM ACT I OF *THE TWIN CAPTAINS*
(WRITTEN EARLIER, PUBLISHED 1611)

*By Flaminio Scala*

Translated by Henry F. Salerno

CHARACTERS: Pantalone, a Venetian
Flaminia, his daughter
Doctor Gratiano
Isabella, his daughter, wife of Captain Spavento
Franceschina, his servant
Oratio, a gentleman

SETTING: Rome.

TIME: Seven years since Isabella married Captain Spavento; six and one-half years since Captain Spavento left Rome to go to Naples to find his twin brother.

SITUATION: While Captain Spavento has been searching for his twin in Naples, his wife, Isabella, has fallen in love with Oratio. The following excerpt from the scenario is the beginning of the play.

COMMENTS: Unlike the other scenes in this text, you will have to improvise your lines for this one. Follow the suggestions given in this chapter. Compare this plot with Plautus' *The Menaechmi* and Shakespeare's *The Comedy of Errors*.

**Isabella and Franceschina:** Isabella enters with Franceschina, complaining to her servant that she is neither widowed nor married, for it is seven years since her father, Gratiano, married her to a captain. After six months, she says, the Captain left, saying he was going to Naples to find his brother. From that time she has heard nothing of him. She has become melancholy because of that, and because she has fallen in love with a gentleman named Oratio. Franceschina commends her love and praises Oratio, saying she knows him well.

**Flaminia:** Just then, Flaminia, who has heard all, comes out and says, "Signora Isabella, I advise you for your own good to put all thoughts of Oratio out of your mind." When Franceschina scolds her, Flaminia angrily calls her a slut, and after exchanging angry words, they come to blows.

**Oratio:** At that, Oratio enters and forces them apart, showing tender feeling for Isabella. When Flaminia angrily turns on Oratio and gives him a tongue lashing, he reproves her, but she, only made more angry, says to him, "Oh, traitor, so you leave me for a slut." Franceschina calls her a liar and attacks her again.

**Pantalone:** Then Pantalone, Flaminia's father, arrives, and Flaminia tells him she has been fighting with that crazy Isabella. Isabella responds that Flaminia herself is crazy, and full of rage, she turns on Flaminia, striking her repeatedly like a mad woman. All the others standing about are dumbfounded. Finally, Flaminia escapes into the house, and Isabella, nearly out of her mind, goes into her house. Franceschina, as if possessed, also goes into the house. The frightened Oratio goes off up the street, leaving only the thunderstruck Pantalone.

**Dr. Gratiano:** Gratiano, Isabella's father, enters, and Pantalone immediately tells him to go for a physician to cure his daughter, who has gone mad. Gratiano thinks he is joking, and tells him to mind his own business.

**Franceschina:** At that, Franceschina comes out and tells Gratiano that Isabella has smashed all the dishes, the glassware, and whatever was breakable in the house. Gratiano, desperate, goes into the house. Franceschina makes a face at Pantalone, and she goes into the house. Pantalone goes into his own house to find out from Flaminia the cause of all the trouble.

# Chapter Five

# Elizabethan
# and Jacobean Theatre

Queen Elizabeth I ruled England from 1558 to 1603; James I was king from 1603 to 1625; and during their reigns many of the world's greatest plays were written. The two chief influences on the playwriting of this period were the medieval religious plays and the classical drama.

## PLAYS

From the medieval drama, the Elizabethans inherited plays that had a loose construction, intermingled comedy and tragedy, had a didactic and moral purpose, did not adhere to the unities of time, place, and action, and were staged using simultaneous sets.

As for the classical influence, the Renaissance, which started in Italy, spread to other countries. By the sixteenth century, there was a great interest in England in the ancient classics among scholars in the schools, universities, and Inns of Court (training places for lawyers). They studied Plautus, Terence, and Seneca and performed their plays in Latin. Next they wrote imitations of them in Latin and eventually in English.

From Plautus and Terence, Elizabethan scholars learned to make use of certain stock characters, plots of mistaken identity and intrigue, love stories, and witty dialogue. From Terence, they discovered how to weave two plots together.

By studying Seneca, they saw how to write plays of violence and cruelty with mad characters and ghosts. They followed his five-act structure and use of imagistic poetry. However, while Elizabethan drama showed certain classical influences, neoclassicism was never as popular in England as it was on the continent. Most Elizabethan dramatists liked the freedom of medieval drama, not the restrictions of classicism.

Other influences in shaping the plays of this period were:

1. The structure of the theatres. A platform stage, a few properties to indicate the settings, trap doors, and balconies left the writers free to shift locales as they wished.
2. The composition of the acting companies. The fact that most playwrights were writing for a definite acting company meant that they tailored certain parts for specific actors. Because no women acted in England at this time, authors limited their female roles to parts that a few young lads could play.
3. Plays and literature from the continent. Ideas from the *commedia dell'arte*, pastoral drama, comedies, and novella were used.
4. The tastes of Elizabethan audiences. All types of people from the wealthy to the poor attended the outdoor public theatres, which may have held as many as two to three thousand. Small indoor private theatres were also in use, but since they charged higher prices, their audiences were more elite. Some acting companies, such as Shakespeare's, played in both outdoor and indoor theatres as well as at court.

The result of all of these influences was a style of playwriting that may be termed romantic. Characterized by freedom of spirit, imagination, and emotions, this period was not hampered by classical restraint, decorum, and dignity. Most Elizabethan writers did not feel obliged to adhere to the separation of comedy and tragedy and to the unities of time, place, and action (often one and sometimes two subplots are used). Plots are not tightly organized but are in a loose construction requiring many scenes that depict a succession of events in chronological order. Love stories are prominent, often set in remote, romantic places, and the language is emotional and imagistic. There is much movement involving dancing, fencing, and fighting; and the ancient Greeks, who abhorred the sight of violence in a play, would have been shocked to see the bodies littering the stage at the end of a typical Elizabethan tragedy.

The principal dramatists among Shakespeare's contemporaries were: Thomas Kyd (1558–1594), who used many Senecan devices in his popular work *The Spanish Tragedy* (c. 1587), including a theme of revenge; Christopher Marlowe (1564–1593), who taught Elizabethans how to write poetic drama in *Tamburlaine the Great* (1587), *The Tragical History of Doctor Faustus* (c. 1589), *The Jew of Malta* (c. 1590), and *Edward*

*II* (1591); Ben Jonson (c. 1573–1637), who showed the Greek classical influence in comedies of humours such as *Every Man in His Humour* (1598), *Volpone* (1606), *The Alchemist* (1610), and *Bartholomew Fair* (1614); and Francis Beaumont (1584–1616) and John Fletcher (1579–1625), who popularized tragicomedies and romantic tragedies with *Philaster* (c. 1610) and *The Maid's Tragedy* (c. 1611).

William Shakespeare (1564–1616) is credited with thirty-seven of the finest plays ever written. His best historical plays are *Richard III* (c. 1593), *Richard II* (c. 1595), *Henry IV*, Parts I and II (c. 1597), and *Henry V* (c. 1598). His farce comedies include *The Comedy of Errors* (c. 1589), *The Taming of the Shrew* (c. 1594), and *The Merry Wives of Windsor* (c. 1597). His popular romantic comedies are *A Midsummer Night's Dream* (c. 1595), *The Merchant of Venice* (c. 1595), *Much Ado About Nothing* (c. 1598), *As You Like It* (c. 1600), and *Twelfth Night* (c. 1601). His serious comedies, often called dark comedies, are *Troilus and Cressida* (c. 1601), *All's Well That Ends Well* (c. 1602), and *Measure for Measure* (c. 1604). His greatest tragedies are *Romeo and Juliet* (c. 1596), *Julius Caesar* (c. 1599), *Hamlet* (c. 1601), *Othello* (c. 1604), *King Lear* (c. 1605), *Macbeth* (c. 1606), and *Antony and Cleopatra* (c. 1607). Two of the plays written late in his career, *The Winter's Tale* (c. 1611) and *The Tempest* (c. 1611), followed the vogue for tragicomedies.

## PRODUCTIONS THEN

**Theatres.**    Not much is known about the open-air public theatres in the days of Queen Elizabeth I, but probably in most of them there was a large stage that projected into the unroofed yard so that standing spectators surrounded the actors on three sides. Around the yard were several tiers of galleries, roofed with thatch or tile, for seated playgoers. To the rear of the stage was a wall that may have had one door on each side and a large opening in the center that could be opened by doors or curtains to reveal an inner stage. On the second level was probably an upper acting area with curtains in back that could be drawn aside to reveal another inner stage. The third level may have been used by actors for some scenes but was ordinarily for the musicians.

**Scenery, Props, and Sound.**    As in the medieval religious drama, these productions used few properties and little or no painted scenery. To establish a locale, the playwright could name the place in a line of dialogue or visible scene shifters could put a simple prop or two onstage. The Elizabethans also used trap doors and a machine for lowering gods. To add excitement to their plays, they created thunder, lightning, rain, rising mists, and blazing stars; actors carried bloody sponges to use when they were stabbed; the sound-effects man shot off a cannon in the hut at the top of the theatre; and musicians accompanied songs and dances, provided fanfares, and added mood music.

**Costumes.** Little attempt was made at historical costuming. For the most part, elaborate and beautiful contemporary clothing was worn; however, some special costumes were used for animals, fairies, witches, ghosts, royalty, religious people, and certain foreigners, such as Romans and Greeks.

**Lighting.** Plays in the public theatres were presented in the open air under the afternoon sun. There was no way to make the stage dark even when it was necessary for Macbeth to perpetrate a midnight murder. When an actor entered carrying a lighted candle or lantern, the audience knew that the stage was then supposed to be dark.

**Acting.** A typical acting company of this period may have had about twenty members, all of whom were men. About half were shareholders who divided the profits, and about half were hired men who received a salary. In addition, there were young male apprentices who played pages, children, and women's parts. We know very little about the acting of this period, but certain assumptions can be made from a study of the plays and the theatres:

1. The actors must have been versatile because, in addition to acting, the plays call for them to sing, dance, fence, and play musical instruments.
2. Actors must have known a great number of parts—some large, some small—that they could play on short notice because, with the repertory system, there was a different bill each playing day.
3. Working in outdoor theatres on a thrust stage with a large, noisy audience surrounding them on three sides would demand that the actors' voices be well developed and that they project their lines to the spectators most of the time to try to hold their attention.
4. The great number of soliloquies, asides, and speeches to the audience found in the plays would indicate also that the acting was mainly presentational.

Shakespeare, who was an actor as well as a playwright, commented on the acting of the day when he had Hamlet say to the players in Act III, Scene 2 of *Hamlet*: "O, it offends me to the soul to hear a robustious periwig-pated fellow tear a passion to tatters, to very rags, to split the ears of the groundlings, who for the most part are capable of nothing but inexplicable dumb-shows and noise." Hamlet's advice, which we may assume was also Shakespeare's coaching, was:

44

1. Speak the speech "trippingly on the tongue"; do not mouth the words.
2. Do not "saw the air too much with your hand," but gesture gently.
3. Actors' passion onstage should be controlled and smooth and not get out of hand.
4. However, actors should not be too tame but should "suit the action to the word, the word to the action."
5. Be natural; do not overact. Your job is to hold the "mirror up to nature" and to give an accurate picture of the age.
6. Do not strut or bellow, but imitate humanity well.
7. Do not ad lib; stick to the script.
8. Do not laugh at your own jokes to get the audience to laugh.

You should study the complete passage, which you will find in the exercises in this chapter. It contains excellent advice for all actors.

## PRODUCTIONS NOW

**Acting.** When you are given a role from an Elizabethan or Jacobean play, one of the first things you must do is study the words. Since many of these words are unfamiliar to us today, you must get an annotated copy of the work, study the explanations of words and phrases, and read critical comment on the meanings of scenes and the entire play.

When you have archaic words to say, speak them distinctly and hope that the context of the sentence plus appropriate actions will communicate the meaning to the audience. For example, when Romeo greets a servant in Act I, Scene 3 of *Romeo and Juliet* with "God-den, good fellow," he means "God give you good-even, good fellow." If Romeo nods to the servant as he says the Shakespearean line, the meaning should be clear.

Next you should analyze the figurative language: the allusion or reference; the simile (a comparison that is often introduced by *like* or *as*); the metaphor (a comparison that is made when a word or phrase is used in place of another); the personification (attribution of human qualities to an object or abstraction); and other figures of speech.

When Romeo says the following in Act I, Scene 1, he is alluding to an ancient god and goddess:

. . . she'll not be hit
With Cupid's arrow; she hath Dian's wit; . . .

By doing research, you should discover that Cupid was the Roman god of erotic love and that Diana was an Italian goddess of the forest and of childbirth.

Romeo uses a simile and an allusion in the following passage from
Act II, Scene 2:

> . . . for thou art
> As glorious to this night, being o'er my head,
> As is a wingèd messenger of heaven
> Unto the white-upturnèd wonde'ring eyes
> Of mortals that fall back to gaze on him
> When he bestrides the lazy-pacing clouds
> And sails upon the bosom of the air.

Romeo is comparing Juliet to the god Mercury, who was the winged messenger to the gods. (Please note that when you see an accent mark on a
final syllable, as in *wingèd* and *upturnèd,* you should sound that syllable;
therefore, *wingèd* is pronounced with two syllables and *upturnèd* with
three.)

In the same scene, Romeo uses a metaphor and personification
when he exclaims:

> But, soft! what light through yonder window breaks?
> It is the east, and Juliet is the sun.
> Arise, fair sun, and kill the envious moon,
> Who is already sick and pale with grief,
> That thou her maid art far more fair than she: . . .

To interpret a figure of speech well, you first must understand it; then
visualize it. If you cannot, try acting out the imagery (with the aid of
some fellow actors) to get a vivid picture in your mind. (See Exercise 3 in
this chapter.) Once you can see the image in your mind's eye, you should
be able to interpret the lines meaningfully.

Shakespeare was also fond of using puns (the humorous use of words
having the same or nearly the same sound but different meanings or the
use of a word in such a way as to suggest different meanings). Be sure you
understand the joke when you have lines such as the following from Act
I, Scene 1 of *Romeo and Juliet* to say:

> **Sampson:**   Gregory, o' my word, we'll not carry coals.
> **Gregory:**   No, for then we should be colliers.
> **Sampson:**   I mean, an' we be in choler, we'll draw.
> **Gregory:**   Ay, while you live, draw your neck out o' the collar.

Many playwrights of this period, including Shakespeare, wrote in poetry.
Shakespeare has some low comedy characters talk in prose (note the
prose used by Sampson and Gregory above), and when characters such as
King Lear and Hamlet act insane, they may speak prose; but most of his
plays are in blank verse. This means that the lines are unrhymed and in

iambic pentameter. (An *iamb* is a metrical foot consisting of one unstressed syllable followed by a stressed syllable. *Pentameter* means that a line has five metrical feet.) As an example of blank verse, look at the following lines from Act II, Scene 2 of *Romeo and Juliet.* The lines are marked using ˘ for unaccented syllables and ´ for accented syllables. A straight line is at the end of each foot.

> Juliet: Thŏu knŏw'st| tħe másk| ŏf night| iš ŏn| mў fáce;|
> Elše wóuld| ă ṁai|dĕn blúsh| ḃepáint| ṁy chéek|
> Fŏr tħat| wħich thŏu| hăst héard| ṁe spéak| tŏníght.|

At times, Shakespeare wrote two or more lines to make five metrical feet, as in the following passage from Act I, Scene 4 of *Hamlet:*

> Marcellus: You shall not go, my lord.
> Hamlet:                              Hold off your hands.
>
> Horatio: Be ruled; you shall not go.
> Hamlet:                              My fate cries out, . . .

You should analyze your lines to see how you want to phrase them. You should, of course, pause only at the end of a thought. As mentioned in Chapter 2, punctuation may be a guide in most cases to pausing, but not always; for example, consider the opening lines of Hamlet's soliloquy from Act III, Scene 1:

> Hamlet: To be, or not to be—that is the question:
> Whether 'tis nobler in the mind to suffer
> The slings and arrows of outrageous fortune
> Or to take arms against a sea of troubles,
> And by opposing end them.

In this passage you will probably not want to pause at the end of line 2 because the thought continues to line 3; however, even though there is no punctuation mark at the end of line 3, you will most likely take a slight pause there before going to line 4. You must analyze the lines and make your own decisions.

When speaking blank verse, though, actors cannot hem or haw or stumble over words, as in some modern plays. The poetry must be clear, distinct, and musical, yet it cannot sound "hammy" or "sing-song." The best advice is to concentrate on being the character and expressing the thoughts and feelings of the lines, and the beauty and rhythm of the poetry should come through automatically.

Two devices used in this and other time periods need special attention: these are the soliloquy and the aside. A *soliloquy* is a speech in which a character expresses ideas and emotions while alone onstage, such as the excerpt quoted above from *Hamlet.* Should these speeches be delivered directly to the audience, or should they be said as though speaking aloud one's thoughts? To arrive at your interpretation, you must make a careful analysis of the meanings of the words. Probably some lines should be delivered one way and some the other.

An *aside* is a brief remark to the audience that other characters onstage pretend not to hear. The person making the aside may simply turn toward the audience no matter where he or she is located onstage, or the actor may move closer to the spectators to speak directly to them. Other actors onstage should turn away, freeze, or engage in some action so that they seem not to hear the aside. In the exercises in this chapter, you will find both asides and soliloquies for practice.

Elizabethan lines, which contain many poetic images and profound ideas, demand that you have a voice and body that can respond to them with sensitivity. Your voice should have excellent articulation and variation to convey the beauty, the meaning, and the intensity of the lines.

To express the freedom of spirit inherent in these romantic plays, there should be a great deal of stage action. Most of the movements and gestures of young, healthy characters may be graceful and sweeping, yet controlled. Some plays demand period dancing and fighting of various kinds (Elizabethan men took pride in their abilities in both), and these will take many hours of rehearsal. Some characters will also have to sing and others play musical instruments. To perform these plays, one must be versatile.

Shakespeare and other writers of this period created some of the finest three-dimensional characters ever written; and all actors should find these romantic plays an exciting challenge.

**Costumes.**    Costuming may vary according to the wishes of the director or the amount of money available. It may be authentic for the time and locale of the play; it may be Elizabethan or Jacobean; it may be of no particular period; it may be in modern dress; or it may be in another era that is thought to be compatible with the tone of the play. An example of the last type was Joseph Papp's production in 1973 of *Much Ado About Nothing*, which was changed from sixteenth-century Sicily to a small American town in the early twentieth century.

If Elizabethan or Jacobean costumes are selected, actors will need time to become accustomed to the clothing. Women will find that the farthingale (a support worn under a large skirt to make it stand out) can be tricky to move and sit in. The tight bodice, stomacher, and ruff at the neck mandate an erect posture. Important accessories for a woman may be a fan, a pomander, jewelry, a small hand mirror hanging from the waist, and high heels. Outside clothes might include a hooded cloak, a veil, or a half-mask. Men may find it difficult to wear doublet, breeches, hose, ruff, sword, dagger, cape, gloves, and hat. Men also had handkerchiefs, rings, lockets, pocket watches, and other jewelry.

**Customs.** The clothes described above made it necessary for both sexes to sit upright on the edge of the chair. Crossing your legs was not done in high society; only those of the lower classes who wore loose clothing could do this.

Men wore their hats most of their waking day, both outdoors and indoors, even while eating. They removed them only while in church, in the presence of royalty or a lady, or while saying a prayer and put them back on as soon as possible. Tobacco became available in England in the early seventeenth century, and this was chewed or smoked in clay pipes. When men greeted a male friend, they might bow, clasp hands, or grip arms above the wrists or above the elbows. When they fought, it was likely to be with both a rapier and dagger.

When ladies greeted other women who were friends, they might kiss on the cheek. They usually curtsied to men and older ladies. When a lady walked with a gentleman, they might hold hands or she might place her hand on his sleeve as he held his arm, palm down, at a comfortable height for her. Ladies wore makeup and plucked their eyebrows, and they often carried fans that had small mirrors so that they could check on their appearance.

**Bows and Curtsies.** To bow, a man may keep his feet parallel, with one foot slightly in back of the other as he bends both knees and nods his head or bends forward from the waist. His hat may be placed over his heart or brought back low to one side, and it may be returned to his head as the knees are straightened. In a more formal bow, a man may step back with the toes slightly turned out on the rear foot. He should transfer his weight to the back leg as he bends his rear knee and nods his head or bends forward.

To curtsy, a woman should place the ball of one foot in back of the other, keeping the weight on both feet. She should bend her knees while nodding her head or bending forward from the waist. If the design of the dress permits, she may step back with one foot, putting all of her weight on it as she bends the rear knee. She should point the toe of the front foot as she bends forward. The depth of the curtsy depends on whom she is greeting, with royalty receiving the deepest. Hands may rest on her dress, may be crossed over her breast, or may be held out and back with palms turned to the front.

Maids make only a slight "bob" curtsy as they enter and leave rooms. This is done by bending the knees slightly and nodding the head.

**Scenery.** In the colleges, universities, and regional theatres of the United States, more plays by Shakespeare are produced than by any other playwright. Production styles vary, of course, but most choose a variation of the formalistic (levels, steps, screens, ramps, and columns); constructivistic; projected scenery; a modified version of the Elizabethan stage; or a recreation of what the director and designer believe to be an authentic Elizabethan stage. With so many different locales in each play, the main objective of any designer should be a set that provides enough playing space so that actors can move quickly from one scene to the next.

**Music.** Just as music added to the original Elizabethan and Jacobean productions, so music can be used today to provide "flourishes," accompany songs and dances, and add mood and transitional music. Authentic instruments, such as the virginal, spinet, lute, recorder, oboe, trumpet, drum, organ, and viol de gamba, or recordings of these are often used.

## SUGGESTED READING

Aykroyd, J. W. *Performing Shakespeare.* New York: Samuel French, Inc., 1979.

Hodges, C. Walter. *The Globe Restored.* 2d ed. London: Oxford University Press, 1968.

Hotson, Leslie. *Shakespeare's Wooden O.* New York: The Macmillan Company, 1960.

Joseph, Bertram. *Elizabethan Acting.* 2d ed. London: Oxford University Press, 1964.

Nagler, Alois M. *Shakespeare's Stage.* New Haven, Conn.: Yale University Press, 1958.

Nicoll, Allardyce. *Stuart Masques and the Renaissance Stage.* London: George G. Harrap & Co., Ltd., 1937.

Webster, Margaret. *Shakespeare Without Tears.* Greenwich, Conn.: Fawcett Publications, Inc., 1966.

## EXERCISES

Roles in Elizabethan and Jacobean plays demand meticulous preparation. The following are exercises to help you get ready to act in scenes from these works:

1. To practice the bows and curtsies described in this chapter, imagine that you are a member of the court of Queen Elizabeth I. Accompany the queen on a walk and reenact the famous incident in which the queen was helped across a mudhole by Sir Walter Raleigh, who put down his cloak so that she would not soil her shoes.

2. Improvise a scene in which three witches meet in a deserted place. (See Act I, Scene 1 of *Macbeth*.)

3. Shakespeare's lines are filled with poetic images, some of which may be difficult for you to interpret meaningfully. When this happens, try acting out the image with the help of some other actors. Take, for example, the following simile in a speech by Romeo from Act II, Scene 2:

> O, speak again, bright angel! for thou art
> As glorious to this night, being o'er my head,
> As is a wingèd messenger of heaven
> Unto the white-upturnèd wondering eyes
> Of mortals that fall back to gaze on him
> When he bestrides the lazy-pacing clouds
> And sails upon the bosom of the air.

The messenger may be played by one actor while two others may act as the mortals who watch him. Find other poetic images and act them out.

4. Imagine that you are Romeo and Juliet meeting for the first time at a dance in Verona. Find suitable recorded music for the century you favor (directors usually set this play in the fourteenth, fifteenth, or sixteenth century) and, by consulting books on period dances, devise a suitable dance. Look at Act I, Scene 5 of *Romeo and Juliet*.

5. To practice delivering an effective soliloquy, study two of the best ever written: Hamlet's soliloquy beginning "To be, or not to be" or Ophelia's soliloquy starting "O, what a noble mind is here o'erthrown!" Both are in the excerpt from Act III, Scene 1 of *Hamlet* in this chapter.

6. To practice asides, look at Jaques' three asides in Act III, Scene 3 of *As You Like It*. In this passage, Jaques, a bitter, melancholy critic, is making fun of Touchstone, who is speaking to Audrey:

**Touchstone:** I am here with thee and thy goats as the most capricious poet, honest Ovid, was among the Goths.
**Jaques:** *(aside)* O knowledge ill-inhabited, worse than Jove in a thatched house!

---

**Touchstone:** . . . For honesty coupled to beauty is to have honey a sauce to sugar.
**Jaques:** *(aside)* A material fool!

---

**Touchstone:** . . . I will marry thee, and to that end I have been with Sir Oliver Martext, the vicar of the next village, who hath promised to meet me in this place of the forest and to couple us.
**Jaques:** *(aside)* I would fain see this meeting.

7. Study Hamlet's advice to the players. The following passage is in Act III, Scene 2 of *Hamlet*.

51

**Hamlet:** Speak the speech, I pray you, as I pronounced it to you, trippingly on the tongue: but if you mouth it, as many of your players do, I had as lief the town-crier spoke my lines. Nor do not saw the air too much with your hand, thus, but use all gently; for in the very torrent, tempest, and, as I may say, the whirlwind of passion, you must acquire and beget a temperance that may give it smoothness. O, it offends me to the soul to hear a robustious periwig-pated fellow tear a passion to tatters, to very rags, to split the ears of the groundlings, who for the most part are capable of nothing but inexplicable dumb-shows and noise: I would have such a fellow whipped for o'er-doing Termagant; it out-herods Herod: pray you, avoid it.

**First Player:** I warrant your honour.

**Hamlet:** Be not too tame neither, but let your own discretion be your tutor: suit the action to the word, the word to the action; with this special observance, that you o'er-step not the modesty of nature: for any thing so overdone is from the purpose of playing, whose end, both at the first and now, was and is, to hold, as 't were, the mirror up to nature; to show virtue her own feature, scorn her own image, and the very age and body of the time his form and pressure. Now this overdone, or come tardy off, though it make the unskillful laugh, cannot but make the judicious grieve; the censure of the which one must in your allowance o'erweigh a whole theatre of others. O, there be players that I have seen play, and heard others praise, and that highly, not to speak it profanely, that, neither having the accent of Christians nor the gait of Christian, pagan, nor man, have so strutted and bellowed that I have thought some of nature's journeymen had made men and not made them well, they imitated humanity so abominably.

**First Player:** I hope we have reformed that indifferently with us, sir.

**Hamlet:** O, reform it altogether. And let those that play your clowns speak no more than is set down for them; for there be of them that will themselves laugh, to set on some quantity of barren spectators to laugh too; though, in the mean time, some necessary question of the play be then to be considered: that's villainous, and shows a most pitiful ambition in the fool that uses it. Go, make you ready.

---

SCENE FOR TWO MEN
FROM ACT I, SCENE 3 OF *THE TRAGICAL HISTORY
OF DOCTOR FAUSTUS*
(c. 1589)

By *Christopher Marlowe*

CHARACTERS: Doctor Faustus
               Mephistophilis, a devil
SETTING: A grove in Germany.
TIME: Night; sixteenth century.

SITUATION: While Faustus was born of "base stock," he went to the university at Wittenberg, where he received a doctor's degree. He has become interested in magic, and his friends, Valdes and Cornelius, have encouraged and instructed him in this subject. In this scene, Faustus has entered a dark grove and conjured up a devil, Mephistophilis, who is dressed like a Franciscan friar.

COMMENTS: In 1587, an anonymous German author published a book about Faust, who was a magician who had amazed German audiences in the early 1500s. An English translation was published in 1592, and this inspired Marlowe to write this play about the man who sold his soul to the devil in return for magical powers. Many other writers have also used the Faust story, notably Goethe.

**Meph.:** Now, Faustus, what wouldst thou have me do?
**Faustus:** I charge thee wait upon me whilst I live,
To do whatever Faustus shall command,
Be it to make the moon drop from her sphere
Or the ocean to overwhelm the world.
**Meph.:** I am a servant to great Lucifer,
And may not follow thee without his leave;
No more than he commands must we perform.
**Faustus:** Did he not charge thee to appear to me?
**Meph.:** No, I came now hither of mine own accord.
**Faustus:** Did not my conjuring speeches raise thee? Speak!
**Meph.:** That was the cause, but yet per accident;
For when we hear one rack the name of God,
Abjure the Scriptures and his Savior Christ,
We fly, in hope to get his glorious soul;
Nor will we come, unless he use such means
Whereby he is in danger to be damn'd.
Therefore the shortest cut for conjuring
Is stoutly to abjure the Trinity,
And pray devoutly to the Prince of Hell.
**Faustus;** So Faustus hath
Already done, and holds this principle:
There is no chief but only Belzebub,
To whom Faustus doth dedicate himself.
This word "damnation" terrifies not him,
For he confounds hell in Elysium;
His ghost be with the old philosophers!
But, leaving these vain trifles of men's souls,
Tell me what is that Lucifer, thy lord?
**Meph.:** Arch-regent and commander of all spirits.
**Faustus:** Was not that Lucifer an angel once?
**Meph.:** Yes, Faustus, and most dearly lov'd of God.
**Faustus:** How comes it then that he is prince of devils?
**Meph.:** Oh, by aspiring pride and insolence,
For which God threw him from the face of Heaven.

**Faustus:** And what are you that live with Lucifer?
**Meph.:** Unhappy spirits that fell with Lucifer,
Conspir'd against our God with Lucifer,
And are forever damn'd with Lucifer.
**Faustus:** Where are you damn'd?
**Meph.:** In hell.
**Faustus:** How comes it then that thou are out of hell?
**Meph.:** Why this is hell, nor am I out of it!
Think'st thou that I, who saw the face of God,
And tasted the eternal joys of Heaven,
Am not tormented with ten thousand hells
In being depriv'd of everlasting bliss?
O Faustus, leave these frivolous demands,
Which strike a terror to my fainting soul.
**Faustus:** What, is great Mephistophilis so passionate
For being depriv'd of the joys of Heaven?
Learn thou of Faustus manly fortitude,
And scorn those joys thou never shalt possess.
Go bear these tidings to great Lucifer:
Seeing Faustus hath incurr'd eternal death
By desperate thoughts against Jove's deity,
Say he surrenders up to him his soul,
So he will spare him four-and-twenty years,
Letting him live in all voluptuousness,
Having thee ever to attend on me,
To give me whatsoever I shall ask,
To tell me whatsoever I demand,
To slay mine enemies, and aid my friends,
And always be obedient to my will.
Go, and return to mighty Lucifer,
And meet me in my study at midnight,
And then resolve me of thy master's mind.
**Meph.:** I will, Faustus. (*Exit*)
**Faustus:** Had I as many souls as there be stars,
I'd give them all for Mephistophilis.
By him I'll be great emperor of the world,
And make a bridge through the moving air,
To pass the ocean with a band of men;
I'll join the hills that bind the Afric shore,
And make that country continent to Spain,
And both contributory to my crown.
The Emperor shall not live but by my leave,
Nor any potentate of Germany.
Now that I have obtain'd what I desire,
I'll live in speculation of this art
Till Mephistophilis return again. (*Exit*)

SCENE FOR ONE MAN, ONE WOMAN
FROM ACT II, SCENE 1 OF *THE TAMING
OF THE SHREW*
(c. 1594)

*By William Shakespeare*

CHARACTERS: Katharina, the shrew, daughter to Baptista
                 Petruchio, a gentleman of Verona, a suitor to Katharina

SETTING: A room in Baptista's house in Padua.

TIME: Day; late sixteenth century.

SITUATION: Baptista, a rich gentleman, has two daughters: Bianca, who has beauty and charm and many suitors, and Katharina, who has a shrewish disposition and no admirers. Baptista has stated that until the eldest, Katharina, is married, he will not allow Bianca to marry. The latter's suitors have been in despair until Petruchio has arrived. Told of Katharina's wealth, he has become interested in wooing her; and Baptista has agreed to the marriage, provided Kate accepts him. The following excerpt is their first meeting.

COMMENTS: Petruchio is a handsome, robust, masterly man who knows he can tame Katharina. Katharina, a woman of great vitality and energy, in this scene is petulant, irritable, and shrewish. This play is a farce comedy and must be played broadly and spiritedly. As much funny business as possible should be used.

**Petruchio:** Good morrow, Kate; for that's your name, I hear.
**Katharina:** Well have you heard, but something hard of hearing:
They call me Katharine that do talk of me.
**Petruchio:** You lie, in faith, for you are called plain Kate,
And bonny Kate, and sometimes Kate the Curst;
But Kate, the prettiest Kate in Christendom,
Kate of Kate-Hall, my superdainty Kate,
For dainties are all Kates—and therefore, Kate,
Take this of me, Kate of my consolation:
Hearing thy mildness praised in every town,
Thy virtues spoke of, and thy beauty sounded,
Yet not so deeply as to thee belongs,
Myself am moved to woo thee for my wife.
**Katharina:** Moved! in good time. Let him that moved you hither
Remove you hence. I knew you at the first
You were a movable.
**Petruchio:** Why, what's a movable?
**Katharina:** A joined stool.
**Petruchio:** Thou hast hit it. Come, sit on me.
**Katharina:** Asses are made to bear, and so are you.
**Petruchio:** Women are made to bear, and so are you.
**Katharina:** No such jade as you, if me you mean.
**Petruchio:** Alas, good Kate, I will not burden thee!

For, knowing thee to be but young and light—
**Katharina:** Too light for such a swain as you to catch,
And yet as heavy as my weight should be.
**Petruchio:** Should be! should—buzz!
**Katharina:** Well ta'en, and like a buzzard.
**Petruchio:** O slow-winged turtle! shall a buzzard take thee?
**Katharina:** Ay, for a turtle, as he takes a buzzard.
**Petruchio:** Come, come, you wasp. I' faith, you are too angry.
**Katharina:** If I be waspish, best beware my sting.
**Petruchio:** My remedy is then to pluck it out.
**Katharina:** Aye, if the fool could find it where it lies.
**Petruchio:** Who knows not where a wasp does wear his sting?
In his tail.
**Katharina:** In his tongue.
**Petruchio:** Whose tongue?
**Katharina:** Yours, if you talk of tails; and so farewell.
**Petruchio:** What, with my tongue in your tail? nay, come again,
Good Kate, I am a gentleman.
**Katharina:** That I'll try. (*She strikes him.*)
**Petruchio:** I swear I'll cuff you if you strike again.
**Katharina:** So may you lose your arms.
If you strike me, you are no gentleman,
And if no gentleman, why then no arms.
**Petruchio:** A herald, Kate? O, put me in thy books!
**Katharina:** What is your crest? a coxcomb?
**Petruchio:** A combless cock, so Kate will be my hen.
**Katharina:** No cock of mine. You crow too like a craven.
**Petruchio:** Nay, come, Kate, come. You must not look so sour.
**Katharina:** It is my fashion when I see a crab.
**Petruchio:** Why, here's no crab, and therefore look not sour.
**Katharina:** There is, there is.
**Petruchio:** Then show it me.
**Katharina:** Had I a glass, I would.
**Petruchio:** What, you mean my face?
**Katharina:** Well aimed of such a young one.
**Petruchio:** Now, by Saint George, I am too young for you.
**Katharina:** Yet you are withered.
**Petruchio:** 'Tis with cares.
**Katharina:** I care not.
**Petruchio:** Nay, hear you, Kate. In sooth you scape not so.
**Katharina:** I chafe you, if I tarry. Let me go.
**Petruchio:** No, not a whit. I find you passing gentle.
'Twas told me you were rough and coy and sullen,
And now I find report a very liar;
For thou are pleasant, gamesome, passing courteous,
But slow in speech, yet sweet as springtime flowers.
Thou canst not frown, thou canst not look askance,
Nor bite the lip, as angry wenches will,
Nor hast thou pleasure to be cross in talk,

But thou with mildness entertain'st thy wooers,
With gentle conference, soft and affable.
Why does the world rèport that Kate doth limp?
O slanderous world! Kate like the hazel twig
Is straight and slender, and as brown in hue
As hazel nuts, and sweeter than the kernels.
O, let me see thee walk. Thou dost not halt.
**Katharina:** Go, fool, and whom thou keep'st command.
**Petruchio:** Did ever Dian so become a grove
As Kate this chamber with her princely gait?
O, be thou Dian, and let her be Kate,
And then let Kate be chaste and Dian sportful!
**Katharina:** Where did you study all this goodly speech?
**Petruchio:** It is extempore, from my mother wit.
**Katharina:** A witty mother! Witless else her son.
**Petruchio:** Am I not wise?
**Katharina:** Yes; keep you warm.
**Petruchio:** Marry, so I mean, sweet Katharine, in thy bed.
And therefore, setting all this chat aside,
Thus in plain terms: Your father hath consented
That you shall be my wife, your dowry 'greed on,
And, will you, nill you, I will marry you.
Now Kate, I am a husband for your turn.
For, by this light whereby I see thy beauty,
Thy beauty, that doth make me like thee well,
Thou must be married to no man but me;
For I am he am born to tame you Kate,
And bring you from a wild Kate to a Kate
Conformable as other household Kates.
Here comes your father. Never make denial.
I must and will have Katharine to my wife.

---

## SCENE FOR ONE MAN, ONE WOMAN
## FROM ACT II, SCENE 2 OF *ROMEO AND JULIET*
### (c. 1596)

*By William Shakespeare*

CHARACTERS: Romeo, son to Montague
Juliet, daughter to Capulet
Nurse to Juliet (has one line from offstage)

SETTING: Capulet's orchard in Verona.

TIME: Late at night after a feast has ended at the Capulet house.

SITUATION: At the party, Romeo and Juliet have met and been attracted to each other despite the fact that their families are enemies. Romeo has returned to the Capulet house to try to find Juliet again, and he sees her above at a window.

57

COMMENTS: Juliet is almost fourteen, a lovely, sensitive young lady with a simplicity, innocence, and truthfulness of nature that make her the ideal romantic heroine. Romeo is likewise the ideal romantic hero—a handsome, passionate youth who went to the Capulet party hoping to see his beloved Rosaline and came away thinking only of Juliet.

**Juliet:** Ay me!
**Romeo:** She speaks.
O, speak again, bright angel! for thou art
As glorious to this night, being o'er my head,
As is a wingèd messenger of heaven
Unto the white-upturnèd wond'ring eyes
Of mortals that fall back to gaze on him
When he bestrides the lazy-pacing clouds
And sails upon the bosom of the air.
**Juliet:** O Romeo, Romeo! wherefore art thou Romeo?
Deny thy father and refuse thy name!
Or, if thou wilt not, be but sworn my love,
And I'll no longer be a Capulet.
**Romeo:** *(Aside)* Shall I hear more, or shall I speak at this?
**Juliet:** 'Tis but thy name that is my enemy.
Thou art thyself, though not a Montague.
What's Montague? It is nor hand, nor foot,
Nor arm, nor face, nor any other part
Belonging to a man. O, be some other name!
What's in a name? That which we call a rose
By any other name would smell as sweet.
So Romeo would, were he not Romeo call'd,
Retain that dear perfection which he owes
Without that title. Romeo, doff thy name;
And for that name, which is no part of thee,
Take all myself.
**Romeo:** I take thee at thy word.
Call me but love, and I'll be new baptiz'd;
Henceforth I never will be Romeo.
**Juliet:** What man art thou that, thus bescreen'd in night,
So stumblest on my counsel?
**Romeo:** By a name
I know not how to tell thee who I am.
My name, dear saint, is hateful to myself,
Because it is an enemy to thee.
Had I it written, I would tear the word.
**Juliet:** My ears have yet not drunk a hundred words
Of that tongue's utterance, yet I know the sound.
Art thou not Romeo, and a Montague?
**Romeo:** Neither, fair saint, if either thee dislike.
**Juliet:** How cam'st thou hither, tell me, and wherefore?
The orchard walls are high and hard to climb,

And the place death, considering who thou art,
If any of my kinsmen find thee here.
**Romeo:** With love's light wings did I o'erperch these walls;
For stony limits cannot hold love out,
And what love can do, that dares love attempt.
Therefore thy kinsmen are no let to me.
**Juliet:** If they do see thee, they will murder thee.
**Romeo:** Alack, there lies more peril in thine eye
Than twenty of their swords! Look thou but sweet,
And I am proof against their enmity.
**Juliet:** I would not for the world they saw thee here.
**Romeo:** I have night's cloak to hide me from their sight;
And but thou love me, let them find me here.
My life were better ended by their hate
Than death proroguèd, wanting of thy love.
**Juliet:** By whose direction found'st thou out this place?
**Romeo:** By love, that first did prompt me to enquire.
He lent me counsel, and I lent him eyes.
I am no pilot; yet, were thou as far
As that vast shore wash'd with the farthest sea,
I would adventure for such merchandise.
**Juliet:** Thou know'st the mask of night is on my face;
Else would a maiden blush bepaint my cheek
For that which thou hast heard me speak tonight.
Fain would I dwell on form—fain, fain deny
What I have spoke; but farewell compliment!
Dost thou love me? I know thou wilt say "Ay";
And I will take thy word. Yet, if thou swear'st,
Thou mayst prove false. At lovers' perjuries,
They say Jove laughs. O gentle Romeo,
If thou dost love, pronounce it faithfully.
Or if though think'st I am too quickly won,
I'll frown, and be perverse, and say thee nay,
So thou wilt woo; but else, not for the world.
In truth, fair Montague, I am too fond,
And therefore thou mayst think my 'haviour light;
But trust me, gentleman, I'll prove more true
Than those that have more cunning to be strange.
I should have been more strange, I must confess,
But that thou overheard'st, ere I was ware,
My true love's passion. Therefore pardon me,
And not impute this yielding to light love,
Which the dark night hath so discovered.
**Romeo:** Lady, by yonder blessed moon I swear,
That tips with silver all these fruit tree tops—
**Juliet:** O, swear not by the moon, the inconstant moon,
That monthly changes in her circled orb,
Lest that thy love prove likewise variable.
**Romeo:** What shall I swear by?

Juliet: Do not swear at all;
Or if thou wilt, swear by thy gracious self,
Which is the god of my idolatry,
And I'll believe thee.
Romeo: If my heart's dear love—
Juliet: Well, do not swear. Although I joy in thee,
I have no joy of this contract tonight.
It is too rash, too unadvised, too sudden;
Too like the lightning, which doth cease to be
Ere one can say "It lightens." Sweet, good night!
This bud of love, by summer's ripening breath
May prove a beauteous flower when next we meet.
Good night, good night! As sweet repose and rest
Come to thy heart as that within my breast!
Romeo: O, wilt thou leave me so unsatisfied?
Juliet: What satisfaction canst thou have tonight?
Romeo: The exchange of thy love's faithful vow for mine.
Juliet: I gave thee mine before thou didst request it;
And yet I would it were to give again.
Romeo: Wouldst thou withdraw it? For what purpose, love?
Juliet: But to be frank and give it thee again.
And yet I wish but for the thing I have.
My bounty is as boundless as the sea,
My love as deep; the more I give to thee,
The more I have, for both are infinite. (*Nurse calls within.*)
I hear some noise within. Dear love, adieu!
Anon, good nurse! Sweet Montague, be true.
Stay but a little, I will come again. (*Exit.*)

---

### SCENE FOR ONE MAN, ONE WOMAN
### FROM ACT III, SCENE 1 OF *HAMLET*
### (c. 1601)

*By William Shakespeare*

CHARACTERS: Hamlet, prince of Denmark
                Ophelia, daughter to Polonius, the lord chamberlain

SETTING: A room in the castle at Elsinore in Denmark.

TIME: Day; Middle Ages.

SITUATIONS: King Claudius and Polonius have sent for Hamlet so that they might overhear a conversation between Hamlet and Ophelia. They hope, thereby, to determine if Hamlet's peculiar behavior is caused by his love for Ophelia. Polonius has instructed his daughter to read a book as she walks nearby, and the men have withdrawn to a place where they can hear the conversation but not be seen. Hamlet at first does not see Ophelia; and during the famous "To be, or not to be" soliloquy, in which he contemplates suicide, he does not realize that Ophelia, Claudius, and Polonius are listening.

60

COMMENTS: Ophelia is an exquisitely delicate young lady, an obedient daughter, a lovely innocent girl. Hamlet is a disturbed young man because his uncle, Claudius, killed Hamlet's father, married Hamlet's mother, and seized the crown. Opinions differ as to whether this tragedy has made Hamlet mad or has made him pretend to be so, but in this scene it is possible that Hamlet suspects that Claudius and Polonius are listening and is acting irrationally to make them think he is insane.

**Hamlet:** To be, or not to be—that is the question:
Whether 'tis nobler in the mind to suffer
The slings and arrows of outrageous fortune
Or to take arms against a sea of troubles,
And by opposing end them. To die—to sleep—
No more; and by a sleep to say we end
The heartache, and the thousand natural shocks
That flesh is heir to. 'Tis a consummation
Devoutly to be wish'd. To die—to sleep.
To sleep—perchance to dream: ay, there's the rub!
For in that sleep of death what dreams may come
When we have shuffled off this mortal coil,
Must give us pause. There's the respect
That makes calamity of so long life.
For who would bear the whips and scorns of time,
The oppressor's wrong, the proud man's contumely,
The pangs of despis'd love, the law's delay,
The insolence of office, and the spurns
That patient merit of the unworthy takes
When he himself might his quietus make
With a bare bodkin? Who would these fardels bear,
To grunt and sweat under a weary life,
But that the dread of something after death—
The undiscover'd country, from whose bourn
No traveller returns—puzzles the will,
And makes us rather bear those ills we have
Than fly to others that we know not of?
Thus conscience does make cowards of us all,
And thus the native hue of resolution
Is sicklied o'er with the pale cast of thought,
And enterprises of great pith and moment
With this regard their currents turn awry
And lose the name of action—Soft you now!
The fair Ophelia!—Nymph, in thy orisons
Be all my sins rememb'red.
**Ophelia:** Good, my lord,
How does your honour for this many a day?
**Hamlet:** I humbly thank you: well, well, well.
**Ophelia:** My lord, I have remembrances of yours
That I have longed long to re-deliver.
I pray you, now receive them.

**Hamlet:** No, not I!
I never gave you aught.
**Ophelia:** My honour'd lord, you know right well you did,
And with them words of so sweet breath compos'd
As made the things more rich. Their perfume lost,
Take these again; for the noble mind
Rich gifts wax poor when givers prove unkind.
There, my lord.
**Hamlet:** Ha, ha! Are you honest?
**Ophelia:** My lord?
**Hamlet:** Are you fair?
**Ophelia:** What means your lordship?
**Hamlet:** That if you be honest and fair, your honesty should
admit no discourse to your beauty.
**Ophelia:** Could beauty, my lord, have better commerce than
with honesty?
**Hamlet:** Ay, truly; for the power of beauty will sooner transform
honesty from what it is to a bawd than the force of honesty
can translate beauty into his likeness. This was sometime a
paradox, but now the time gives it proof. I did love you once.
**Ophelia:** Indeed, my lord, you made me believe so.
**Hamlet:** You should not have believ'd me; for virtue cannot so
inoculate our old stock but we shall relish of it. I loved you
not.
**Ophelia:** I was the more deceived.
**Hamlet:** Get thee to a nunnery! Why wouldst thou be a breeder
of sinners? I am myself indifferent honest, but yet I could
accuse me of such things that it were better my mother had not
borne me. I am very proud, revengeful, ambitious; with more
offences at my beck than I have thoughts to put them in,
imagination to give them shape, or time to act them in. What
should such fellows as I do, crawling between earth and
heaven? We are arrant knaves all; believe none of us. Go thy
ways to a nunnery. Where's your father?
**Ophelia:** At home, my lord.
**Hamlet:** Let the doors be shut upon him, that he may play the
fool nowhere but in's own house. Farewell.
**Ophelia:** O, help him, you sweet heavens!
**Hamlet:** If thou dost marry, I'll give thee this plague for thy
dowry: be thou as chaste as ice, as pure as snow, thou shalt not
escape calumny. Get thee to a nunnery. Go, farewell. Or if
thou wilt needs marry, marry a fool; for wise men know well
enough what monsters you make of them. To a nunnery, go;
and quickly too. Farewell.
**Ophelia:** O heavenly powers, restore him!
**Hamlet:** I have heard of your paintings too, well enough. God
hath given you one face, and you make yourselves another.
You jig, you amble, and you lisp; you nickname God's creatures
and make your wantonness your ignorance. Go to, I'll no more

on't! It hath made me mad. I say, we will have no more
marriages. Those that are married already—all but one—shall
live; the rest shall keep as they are. To a nunnery, go. (*Exit.*)
**Ophelia:** O, what a noble mind is here o'er-thrown!
The courtier's, scholar's, soldier's eye, tongue, sword,
The expectancy and rose of the fair state,
The glass of fashion and the mould of form,
The observ'd of all observers—quite, quite down!
And I, of ladies most deject and wretched,
That suck'd the honey of his music vows,
Now see that noble and most sovereign reason,
Like sweet bells jangled, out of tune and harsh;
That unmatch'd form and feature of blown youth
Blasted with ecstasy. O, woe is me
To have seen what I have seen, see what I see!

---

## SCENE FOR ONE MAN, ONE WOMAN
## FROM ACT V, SCENE 2 OF *OTHELLO*
### (c. 1604)

### By *William Shakespeare*

CHARACTERS: Othello, a noble Moor in the service of the Venetian state
          Desdemona, wife to Othello

SETTING: A bedchamber in the castle on Cyprus.

TIME: Night; sixteenth century.

SITUATION: Convinced by Iago that Desdemona has been unfaithful to him
with Cassio, Othello has decided to kill her and has given Iago the task of mur-
dering Cassio.

COMMENTS: Desdemona is innocent and guiltless and does not understand
why her husband has become distraught. She is devoted to Othello, who, enraged by jealousy, is determined that Desdemona must die to preserve his honor.

**Othello:** She wakes.
**Desdemona:** Who's there? Othello?
**Othello:** Ay, Desdemona.
**Desdemona:** Will you come to bed, my lord?
**Othello:** Have you pray'd tonight, Desdemona?
**Desdemona:** Ay, my lord.
**Othello:** If you bethink yourself of any crime
   Unreconciled as yet to heaven and grace,
   Solicit for it straight.
**Desdemona:** Alas, my lord, what do you mean by that?
**Othello:** Well, do it, and be brief; I will walk by:
   I would not kill thy unprepar̀ed spirit;
   No; heaven forfend! I would not kill thy soul.

**Desdemona:** Talk you of killing?

**Othello:** Ay, I do.

**Desdemora:** Then heaven
Have mercy on me!

**Othello:** Amen, with all my heart!

**Desdemona:** If you say so, I hope you will not kill me.

**Othello:** Hum!

**Desdemona:** And yet I fear you; for you are fatal then
When your eyes roll so: why I should fear I know not,
Since guiltiness I know not; but yet I feel I fear.

**Othello:** Think on thy sins.

**Desdemona:** They are loves I bear to you.

**Othello:** Ay, and for that thou diest.

**Desdemona:** That death's unnatural that kills for loving.
Alas, why gnaw you so your nether lip?
Some bloody passion shakes your very frame:
These are portents; but yet I hope, I hope,
They do not point on me.

**Othello:** Peace, and be still!

**Desdemona:** I will so. What's the matter?

**Othello:** That handkerchief which I so loved and gave thee
Thou gavest to Cassio.

**Desdemona:** No, by my life and soul!
Send for the man, and ask him.

**Othello:** Sweet soul, take heed,
Take heed of perjury; thou art on thy deathbed.

**Desdemona:** Ay, but not yet to die.

**Othello:** Yes, presently:
Therefore confess thee freely of thy sin;
For to deny each article with oath
Cannot remove nor choke the strong conception
That I do groan withal. Thou art to die.

**Desdemona:** Then Lord have mercy on me!

**Othello:** I say, amen.

**Desdemona:** And have you mercy too! I never did
Offend you in my life; never loved Cassio
But with such general warranty of heaven
As I might love; I never gave him token.

**Othello:** By heaven, I saw my handkerchief in 's hand.
O perjured woman! thou dost stone my heart,
And makest me call what I intend to do
A murder, which I thought a sacrifice:
I saw the handkerchief.

**Desdemona:** He found it then;
I never gave it him: send for him hither;
Let him confess a truth.

**Othello:** He hath confess'd.

Desdemona: What, my lord?

Othello: That he hath used thee.

Desdemona: How? unlawfully?

Othello: Ay.

Desdemona: He will not say so.

Othello: No, his mouth is stopp'd;
  Honest Iago hath ta'en order for 't.

Desdemona: O! my fear interprets: what, is he dead?

Othello: Had all his hairs been lives, my great revenge
  Had stomach for them all.

Desdemona: Alas! he is betray'd and I undone.

Othello: Out, strumpet! weep'st thou for him to my face?

Desdemona: O, banish me, my lord, but kill me not!

Othello: Down, strumpet!

Desdemona: Kill me tomorrow: let me live tonight!

Othello: Nay, if you strive—

Desdemona: But half an hour!

Othello: Being done, there is no pause.

Desdemona: But while I say one prayer!

Othello: It is too late. (He stifles her.)

---

## SCENE FOR THREE MEN
## FROM ACT I, SCENES 4 AND 5 OF *VOLPONE*
### (1606)

*By Ben Jonson*

CHARACTERS: Volpone, a magnifico
  Mosca, his parasite
  Corvino, a merchant

SETTING: A room in Volpone's house in Venice.

TIME: Day.

SITUATION: Volpone is a cagey old miser who desires to be wealthier through tricking some rich people into believing that he is dying and that he will give his estate to them in exchange for favors. Assisted by the energetic Mosca, he has just seen Signiors Voltore and Corbaccio, who have given him gifts, and the latter has just exited.

COMMENTS: *Volpone* means fox; *Mosca*, fly; and *Corvino*, raven.

Volpone: (*Leaping from his couch*) Oh, I shall burst!
  Let out my sides—

Mosca: Contain
  Your flux of laughter, sir; you know this hope
  Is such a bait, it covers any hook.

Volpone: O, but thy working, and thy placing it!

I cannot hold; good rascal, let me kiss thee:
I never knew thee in so rare a humor.

Mosca: Alas, sir, I but do as I am taught;
Follow your grave instructions, give 'em words,
Pour oil into their ears, and send them hence.

Volpone: 'T is true, 't is true. What a rare punishment
Is avarice to itself!

Mosca: Ay, with our help, sir.

Volpone: So many cares, so many maladies
So many fears attending on old age.
Yea, death so often call'd on, as no wish
Can be more frequent with 'em, their limbs faint,
Their senses dull, their seeing, hearing, going,
All dead before them; yea, their very teeth,
Their instruments of eating, failing them:
Yet this is reckon'd life! Nay, here was one,
Is now gone home, that wishes to live longer!
Feels not his gout, nor palsy; feigns himself
Younger by scores of years, flatters his age
With confident belying it, hopes he may
With charms like Aeson have his youth restor'd;
And with these thoughts so battens, as if fate
Would be as easily cheated on as he;
And all turns air! (*Another knocks.*) Who's that there, now? a third?

Mosca: Close; to your couch again; I hear his voice.
It is Corvino, our spruce merchant.

Volpone: (*Lying down*) Dead.

Mosca: Another bout, sir, with your eyes. (*Anointing them*) Who's there?
(*Corvino enters.*) Signior Corvino! come most wish'd for! Oh,
How happy were you, if you knew it, now!

Corvino: Why? what? wherein?

Mosca: The tardy hour is come, sir.

Corvino: He is not dead?

Mosca: Not dead, sir, but as good;
He knows no man.

Corvino: How shall I do then?

Mosca: Why, sir?

Corvino: I have brought him here a pearl.

Mosca: Perhaps he has
So much remembrance left as to know you, sir:
He still calls on you; nothing but your name
Is in his mouth. Is your pearl orient, sir?

Corvino: Venice was never owner of the like.

Volpone: Signior Corvino!

Mosca: Hark!

Volpone: Signior Corvino.

**Mosca:** He calls you; step and give it him. H' is here, sir.
And he has brought you a rich pearl.

**Corvino:** How do you, sir?
Tell him it doubles the twelfth carat.

**Mosca:** Sir,
He cannot understand: his hearing's gone;
And yet it comforts him to see you—

**Corvino:** Say
I have a diamond for him, too.

**Mosca:** Best show't, sir;
Put it into his hand; 't is only there
He apprehends; he has his feeling yet.
See, how he grasps it!

**Corvino:** 'Las, good gentleman!
How pitiful the sight is!

**Mosca:** Tut, forget, sir.
The weeping of an heir should still be laughter
Under a visor.

**Corvino:** Why, am I his heir?

**Mosca:** Sir, I am sworn, I may not show the will
Till he be dead. But here has been Corbaccio,
Here has been Voltore, here were others too—
I cannot number 'em, they were so many—
All gaping here for legacies; but I,
Taking the vantage of his naming you,
"Signior Corvino, Signior Corvino," took
Paper, and pen, and ink, and there I ask'd him
Whom he would have his heir! "Corvino." Who
Should be executor? "Corvino." And
To any question he was silent to,
I still interpreted the nods he made,
Through weakness, for consent; and sent home th'others,
Nothing bequeath'd them, but to cry and curse.

**Corvino:** Oh, my dear Mosca. (*They embrace.*) Does he not perceive us?

**Mosca:** No more than a blind harper. He knows no man,
No face of friend, nor name of any servant,
Who't was that fed him last, or gave him drink;
Not those he hath begotten, or brought up,
Can he remember.

**Corvino:** Has he children?

**Mosca:** Bastards,
Some dozen, or more, that he begot on beggars . . .
Knew you not that, sir? 'T is the common fable.
The dwarf, the fool, the eunuch, are all his;
H' is the true father of his family,
In all save me. But he has giv'n 'em nothing.

**Corvino:** That's well, that's well. Art sure he does not hear us?

**Mosca:** Sure, sir! Why, look you, credit your own sense.
*(Shouts in Volpone's ear.)*
The pox approach, and add to your diseases,
If it would send you hence the sooner, sir;
For your incontinence it hath deserv'd it
Throughly and throughly, and the plague to boot!—
You may come near, sir.—Would you would once close
Those filthy eyes of yours, that flow with slime
Like two frog-pits; and those same hanging cheeks,
Cover'd with hide instead of skin—Nay, help, sir—
That look like frozen dishclouts set on end.

**Corvino:** Or like an old smok'd wall, on which the rain
Ran down in streaks.

**Mosca:** Excellent, sir! speak out;
You may be louder yet; a culverin
Discharged in his ear would hardly bore it.

**Corvino:** His nose is like a common sewer, still running.

**Mosca:** 'T is good! And what his mouth?

**Corvino:** A very draught.

**Mosca:** O, stop it up—

**Corvino:** By no means.

**Mosca:** Pray you, let me;
Faith, I could stifle him rarely with a pillow
As well as any woman that should keep him.

**Corvino:** Do as you will; but I'll be gone.

**Mosca:** Be so;
It is your presence makes him last so long.

**Corvino:** I pray you use no violence.

**Mosca:** No, sir? why?
Why should you be thus scrupulous, 'pray you, sir?

**Corvino:** Nay, at your discretion.

**Mosca:** Well, good sir, begone.

**Corvino:** I will not trouble him now to take my pearl?

**Mosca:** Pooh, nor your diamond. What a needless care
Is this afflicts you? Is not all here yours?
Am not I here, whom you have made, your creature,
That owe my being to you?

**Corvino:** Grateful Mosca!
Thou art my friend, my fellow, my companion,
My partner, and shalt share in all my fortunes.

**Mosca:** Excepting one.

**Corvino:** What's that?

**Mosca:** Your gallant wife, sir. *(Exit Corvino)* Now is he gone; we had no other
means

To shoot him hence but this.

**Volpone:**   My divine Mosca!
Thou hast today outgone thyself. *(Another knocks.)* Who's there?
I will be troubled with no more. Prepare
Me music, dances, banquets, all delights;
The Turk is not more sensual in his pleasures
Than will Volpone. *(Exit Mosca.)*

---

# Chapter Six

# French Neoclassicism

Around 1630, Cardinal Richelieu and other important Frenchmen began to look to Italy for guidance in the theatre; and, as a result, neoclassicism became the dominant style for the French theatre for about two hundred years.

## PLAYS

The French Academy, formed in 1635, became the watchdog of all literary works. After studying the ancient Greeks and Romans, the Academy insisted that plays have the three unities of time, place, and action and a strict separation of tragedy and comedy. Tragedies should deal only with the nobility, while comedies should be about the middle and lower classes, and all plays should teach a lesson in an enjoyable way. Plays were to have decorum, formal beauty, and verisimilitude (the appearance of truth). Violence was to be avoided, as reason and restraint were the goals. Playwrights were also encouraged to write in alexandrine couplets (rhymed iambic hexameters).

Jean Racine (1639–1699) is noted as the finest of the writers of French neoclassical tragedy. His *Andromaque* (1667), *Britannicus* (1669), *Bérénice* (1670), *Phèdre* (*Phaedra*, 1677), *Esther* (1689), and *Athalie* (1691) have little physical action but demonstrate great inner conflict for the protagonist.

Jean-Baptiste Poquelin, who took the name of Molière (1622–1673), is known as one of the world's greatest writers of comedy. Borrowing liberally from the *commedia dell'arte*, Roman comedy, and French, Spanish, and Italian stories and plays, he produced neoclassic comedies that ranged from farcical to serious comedies with important messages. He wrote farce comedies of intrigue, such as *Le Médecin malgré lui* (*The Doctor in Spite of Himself*, 1666), *L'Avare* (*The Miser*, 1668), and *Les Fourberies de Scapin* (*The Cheats of Scapin*, 1671); comedy–ballets like *Le Bourgeois Gentilhomme* (*The Would-Be Gentleman*, 1670), and comedies of manners such as *L'École des maris* (*The School for Husbands*, 1661), *L'École des femmes* (*The School for Wives*, 1662), *Le Misanthrope* (1666), *Tartuffe* (1669), and *Le Malade imaginaire* (*The Imaginary Invalid*, 1673). Thirty-three plays, ten of which are one-act plays, are in existence today.

Molière's great contribution to world literature is that he refined and improved previous comedy techniques, adding his special wit and satiric touches, tightening plot lines, and creating some remarkable characterizations.

## PRODUCTIONS THEN

**Theatres and Scenery.** The medieval practice of using simultaneous sets was prevalent in France until about 1641, when Cardinal Richelieu had a theatre constructed in Paris with a proscenium arch. A unified Italian set of wings, drops, and borders was used at this new court theatre, and shortly thereafter others adopted the Italian system for theatres and scenery.

By the middle of the seventeenth century, spectators were regularly seated on benches or chairs at the sides of the stage, except for special plays that had unusual scenic effects. This arrangement narrowed the space for acting so, consequently, writers called for little physical action, scenery, or properties.

**Costumes.** Actors provided their own costumes, usually contemporary clothing and as elaborate as they could afford. Many actors wore wigs; and if they were playing a *commedia* character, they might use a mask. Accessories included fans, handkerchiefs, jewelry, and parasols for the ladies, and staffs, canes, snuffboxes, rings, and handkerchiefs for the men.

**Acting.** At the time of Molière, Parisian acting troupes usually had ten to fifteen shareholders plus others whom they hired. Women had acted on French stages since the early seventeenth century and were allowed to be shareholders.

Acting in seventeeth-century tragedies was usually formal, oratorical, and presentational. For the most part, actors came to the front of the stage and stood in an erect posture while using a full, resonant voice and graceful arm movements as they declaimed or chanted their lines. Movements were stately and unhurried since they believed that tragic acting, while passionate, should have grandeur, dignity, and grace.

Acting in Molière's company was probably different, however. Molière opposed the oratorical style of acting; and in *L'Impromptu de Versailles* (1663), he made fun of the large, bloated men who played kings in tragedies while using broad gestures and thundering out the last line of a speech to get an audience response. He also poked fun at a trage-dienne who always smiled through her supposed sufferings. From this play we may infer that Molière urged the actors in his company to be-come their characters, to look thoughtful, to speak naturally, and to ges-ture realistically.

Molière, who was an accomplished actor as well as a playwright, trained with Italian *commedia dell'arte* actors and learned much from ob-serving the Italian troupes who played in France during his lifetime. Some of the characters, situations, jokes, and business in Molière's com-edies derive from the *commedia*, and undoubtedly his company used as much skillful movement, pantomime, and comic buffoonery as the Italians.


## PRODUCTIONS NOW

**Acting.**  Playing a Racine tragedy today is similar to acting a Greek or Roman classical tragedy, except that the French characters generally have more internal, psychological struggling. For example, in Euripides' tragedy *Hippolytus*, Aphrodite causes Phaedra to fall in love with her stepson, Hippolytus, to punish him. In Racine's version of the same leg-end, while Phaedra blames Venus for her stress, the play concentrates on her agonizing guilt; and the actress playing Phaedra must be able to ex-press a wide range of intense, emotional reactions that eventually lead to Phaedra's death.

To play a Racine tragedy today, we must study the play and charac-ters thoroughly, analyzing their objectives, motives, conflicts, and moods; understand the characters and why they do what they do; work so that our voices and bodies respond to the subtle changes of emotions; and totally absorb ourselves into our characterizations, concentrating on projecting honestly the actions of the tragedy.

Today, more properties and furniture will probably be onstage than were used in the seventeenth century, so directors may block more realis-tic actions, such as sitting and eating. We must remember, however, that in trying to be more realistic for our audiences we cannot sacrifice the stateliness, the elegance, and the dramatic intensity of these tragic roles.

When playing a Molière comedy, we must realize that his characters are not ordinary, everyday people. Even when this playwright was using a type of character found in the *commedia dell'arte*, such as Harpagon in *The Miser*, he gave the part unique qualities. Your work is to discover the peculiarities and obsessions in your role and magnify them to amuse your audience. Invent comic business; pay particular attention to the melody of your voice, which is likely to need a wide pitch range with great variety of loudness, rate, and pitch; be sure your enunciation is distinct; and generally use presentational acting with asides directly to the audience. Directors often choose to interpolate appropriate music and dancing into the comedies and to use an overall fast tempo for the play.

For appropriate bows, curtsies, music, and some customs of this time period, see Chapter 7.

**Costumes.**    Costuming may be suggestive of the period and place depicted; it may be in the elaborate clothing and wigs of the seventeenth century; or it may be a simpler, modified version of this fashion. Some comedies may use overexaggerated costumes, perhaps with *commedia*-like masks for some characters. These plays, like other masterpieces, have also been costumed in modern dress or in fashions of other periods or countries.

**Scenery.**    Scene designers often use wing–drop–border sets, such as those used originally, an exaggerated version of this type, or realistic or selective realistic settings. *Scapino!*, a modern adaptation by Frank Dunlop and Jim Dale of Molière's *Les Fourberies de Scapin*, used in its Broadway production a pop art set based on Italian advertisements.

## SUGGESTED READING

Barzun, Jacques. *Classic, Romantic, and Modern.* Garden City, N.Y.: Anchor Books, 1961.

Hubert, Judd D. *Molière and the Comedy of Intellect.* Berkeley: University of California Press, 1962.

Fernandez, Ramon. *Molière, the Man Seen Through the Plays.* New York: Hill & Wang, 1958.

Moore, Will G. *Molière: A New Criticism.* New York: Doubleday, 1962.

Saint-Denis, Michel. *Theatre: The Rediscovery of Style.* New York: Theatre Arts Books, 1960.

Do the following improvisations to help you prepare to perform in French neoclassical plays:

1. Look at a portrait of King Louis XIV of France and pictures of rooms at Versailles. Imagine what it would have been like to attend a court function in this time period. Improvise a scene in which the king enters a room and greets the courtiers.

2. Improvise a comic scene in which an old, miserly father discovers that the daughter he wants to wed to an elderly, wealthy gentleman is in love with his own steward. (See Molière's *The Miser*.)

3. Improvise a comic scene in which Orgon, a foolish middle-aged man, is put under a table by his young wife so that Orgon can hear Tartuffe make advances to her. Until this scene, Orgon has refused to believe anything bad about Tartuffe, a con man who is trying to trick Orgon out of his estate and wife. (See Molière's *Tartuffe*.)

4. Imagine a comic scene in which a rich bourgeois in France in 1670 tries to imitate the aristocracy. Improvise his taking lessons from different instructors in music, dancing, and fencing. (See Molière's *The Would-Be Gentleman*.)

5. Improvise a serious scene with Theseus, king of Athens, and his son, Hippolytus. Theseus has been told a lie by Phaedra's nurse that Hippolytus made advances to his stepmother, Phaedra, during the king's absence. The truth is that Hippolytus does not want Phaedra because he is in love with Aricia. In your improvisation, Theseus should angrily confront Hippolytus, who tries to defend himself. (See Racine's *Phaedra*.)

---

### SCENE FOR ONE MAN, ONE WOMAN
### FROM ACT II, SCENE 5 OF *THE SCHOOL FOR WIVES*
#### (1662)

*By Molière*

Translated by Richard Wilbur

CHARACTERS: Arnolphe, also known as Monsieur de la Souche
Agnès, Arnolphe's ward

SETTING: A square in front of Arnolphe's house in a provincial French town.

TIME: Morning; seventeenth century.

SITUATION: Arnolphe, a middle-aged provincial bourgeois, has remained a bachelor because of his fear of being a cuckold. He decided thirteen years ago to become the guardian of four-year-old Agnès and to raise her to be docile and ignorant so that she might become his perfect bride. Arnolphe has been away for ten days and has decided that he will wed Agnès tomorrow. He has met Horace, the son of a friend, who (not knowing of Arnolphe's relationship to Agnès) had confided that he loves Agnès and that she has encouraged him. Shortly thereafter, Arnolphe has called Agnès to take a morning stroll, and she has told him how she met a young man who swore that he loved her.

COMMENTS: Arnolphe is forty-two and very insecure. Agnès is seventeen, sweet, uneducated, and innocent.

**Arnolphe** Besides these compliments, these sweet addresses,
Were there not also kisses, and caresses?
**Agnès** Oh, yes! He took my hands, and kissed and kissed
Them both, as if he never would desist.
**Arnolphe** And did he not take—something else as well?
*(He notes that she is taken aback.)*
Agh!
**Agnès** Well, he—
**Arnolphe** Yes?
**Agnès** Took—
**Arnolphe** What?
**Agnès** I dare not tell.
I fear that you'll be furious with me.
**Arnolphe** No.
**Agnès** Yes.
**Arnolphe** No, no.
**Agnès** Then promise not to be.
**Arnolphe** I promise.
**Agnès** He took my—oh, you'll have a fit.
**Arnolphe** No.
**Agnès** Yes.
**Arnolphe** No, no. The devil! Out with it!
What did he take from you?
**Agnès** He took—
**Arnolphe,** *aside* God save me!
**Agnès** He took the pretty ribbon that you gave me.
Indeed, he begged so that I couldn't resist.
**Arnolphe,** *taking a deep breath*
Forget the ribbon. Tell me: once he'd kissed
Your hands, what else did he do, as you recall?
**Agnès** Does one do other things?
**Arnolphe** No, not at all;
But didn't he ask some further medicine
For the sad state of health that he was in?
**Agnès** Why, no. But had he asked, you may be sure
I'd have done anything to speed his cure.
**Arnolphe,** *aside*
I've got off cheap this once, thanks be to God;
If I slip again, let all men call me clod.
*(To Agnès:)*
Agnès, my dear, your innocence is vast;
I shan't reproach you; what is past is past.

But all that trifler wants to do—don't doubt it—
Is to deceive you, and then boast about it.
**Agnès** Oh, no. He's often assured me otherwise.
**Arnolphe** Ah, you don't know how that sort cheats and lies.
But do grasp this: to accept a jewel-case,
And let some coxcomb praise your pretty face,
And be complaisant when he takes a notion
To kiss your hands and fill you with "commotion"
Is a great sin, for which your soul could die.
**Agnès** A sin, you say! But please, Sir, tell me why.
**Arnolphe** Why? Why? Because, as all authority states,
It's just such deeds that Heaven abominates.
**Agnès** Abominates! But why should Heaven feel so?
It's all so charming and so sweet, you know!
I never knew about this sort of thing
Till now, or guessed what raptures it could bring.
**Arnolphe** Yes, all these promises of love undying,
These sighs, these kisses, are most gratifying,
But they must be enjoyed in the proper way;
One must be married first, that is to say.
**Agnès** And once you're married, there's no evil in it?
**Arnolphe** That's right.
**Agnès** Oh, let me marry, then, this minute!
**Arnolphe** If that's what you desire, I feel the same;
It was to plan your marriage that I came.
**Agnès** What! Truly?
**Arnolphe** Yes.
**Agnès** How happy I shall be!
**Arnolphe** Yes, wedded life will please you, I foresee.
**Agnès** You really intend that we two—
**Arnolphe** Yes, I do.
**Agnès** Oh, how I'll kiss you if that dream comes true!
**Arnolphe** And I'll return your kisses, every one.
**Agnès** I'm never sure when people are making fun.
Are you quite serious?
**Arnolphe** Yes, I'm serious. Quite.
**Agnès** We're to be married?
**Arnolphe** Yes.
**Agnès** But when?
**Arnolphe** Tonight.
**Agnès**, *laughing* Tonight?
**Arnolphe** Tonight. It seems you're moved to laughter.
**Agnès** Yes.
**Arnolphe** Well, to see you happy is what I'm after.
**Agnès** Oh, Sir, I owe you more than I can express!
With him, my life will be pure happiness!
**Arnolphe** With whom?
**Agnès** With . . . him.
**Arnolphe** With *him!* Well, think again.

You're rather hasty in your choice of men.
It's quite another husband I have in mind;
And as for "him," as you call him, be so kind,
Regardless of his pitiable disease,
As never again to see him, if you please.
When next he calls, girl, put him in his place
By slamming the door directly in his face;
Then, if he knocks, go up and drop a brick
From the second-floor window. That should do the trick.
Do you understand, Agnès? I shall be hidden
Nearby, to see that you do as you are bidden.
**Agnès** Oh, dear, he's so good-looking, so—
**Arnolphe** Be still!
**Agnès** I just won't have the heart—
**Arnolphe** Enough; you will.
Now go upstairs.
**Agnès** How can you—
**Arnolphe** Do as I say.
I'm master here; I've spoken; go, obey.

---

### SCENE FOR ONE MAN, TWO WOMEN
### FROM ACT II, SCENE 4 OF *TARTUFFE*
### (1669)

*By Molière*

Translated by Richard Wilbur

CHARACTERS: Valère, in love with Mariane
                Mariane, Orgon's daughter, in love with Valère
                Dorine, her maid

SETTING: Orgon's house in Paris.

TIME: Day; seventeenth century.

SITUATION: Tartuffe, a swindler, has maneuvered his way into the affections of Orgon, a rich bourgeois, who has just informed his daughter, Mariane, that she must marry Tartuffe. An unhappy Mariane has just told the man she loves, Valère, of her father's decision.

COMMENTS: Valère and Mariane are handsome young lovers. Dorine is a clever, saucy maid who is trying to get them married.

**Valère** Am I to yield you to a rival's arms
And not console myself with other charms?
**Mariane** Go then: console yourself; don't hesitate.
I wish you to; indeed, I cannot wait.
**Valère** You wish me to?
**Mariane** Yes.

**Valère** That's the final straw.
Madam, farewell. Your wish shall be my law.
(*He starts to leave, and then returns: this repeatedly:*)
**Mariane** Splendid.
**Valère** (*Coming back again:*)
This breach, remember, is of your making;
It's you who've driven me to the step I'm taking.
**Mariane** Of course.
**Valère** (*Coming back again:*)
Remember, too, that I am merely
Following your example.
**Mariane** I see that clearly.
**Valère** Enough. I'll go and do your bidding, then.
**Mariane** Good.
**Valère** (*Coming back again:*)
You shall never see my face again.
**Mariane** Excellent.
**Valère** (*Walking to the door, then turning about:*)
Yes?
**Mariane** What?
**Valère** What's that? What did you say?
**Mariane** Nothing. You're dreaming.
**Valère** Ah. Well, I'm on my way.
Farewell, *Madame.*
(*He moves slowly away.*)
**Mariane** Farewell.
**Dorine** (*To Mariane:*)
If you ask me,
Both of you are as mad as mad can be.
Do stop this nonsense, now. I've only let you
Squabble so long to see where it would get you.
Whoa there, Monsieur Valère!
(*She goes and seizes Valère by the arm; he makes a
great show of resistance.*)
**Valère** What's this, Dorine?
**Dorine** Come here.
**Valère** No, no, my heart's too full of spleen.
Don't hold me back; her wish must be obeyed.
**Dorine** Stop!
**Valère** It's too late now; my decision's made.
**Dorine** Oh, pooh!
**Mariane** (*Aside:*)
He hates the sight of me, that's plain.
I'll go, and so deliver him from pain.
**Dorine** (*Leaving Valère, running after Mariane:*)
And now *you* run away! Come back.
**Mariane** No, no.
Nothing you say will keep me here. Let go!
**Valère** (*Aside:*)
She cannot bear my presence, I perceive.

To spare her further torment, I shall leave.
**Dorine** (*Leaving Mariane, running after Valère:*)
Again! You'll not escape, Sir; don't you try it.
Come here, you two. Stop fussing, and be quiet.
(*She takes Valère by the hand, then Mariane, and draws them together.*)
**Valère** (*To Dorine:*)
What do you want of me?
**Mariane** (*To Dorine:*)
What is the point of this?
**Dorine** We're going to have a little armistice.
(*To Valère:*)
Now, weren't you silly to get so overheated?
**Valère** Didn't you see how badly I was treated?
**Dorine** (*To Mariane:*)
Aren't you a simpleton, to have lost your head?
**Mariane** Didn't you hear all the hateful things he said?
**Dorine** (*To Valère:*)
You're both great fools. Her sole desire, Valère.
Is to be yours in marriage. To that I'll swear.
(*To Mariane:*)
He loves you only, and he wants no wife
But you, Mariane. On that I'll stake my life.
**Mariane** (*To Valère:*)
Then why you advised me so, I cannot see.
**Valère** (*To Mariane:*)
On such a question, why ask advice of *me?*
**Dorine** Oh, you're impossible. Give me your hands, you two.
(*To Valère:*)
Yours first.
**Valère** (*Giving Dorine his hand:*)
But why?
**Dorine** (*To Mariane:*)
And now a hand from you.
**Mariane** (*Also giving Dorine her hand:*)
What are you doing?
**Dorine** There: a perfect fit.
You suit each other better than you'll admit.
(*Valère and Mariane hold hands for some time without looking at each other.*)
**Valère** (*Turning toward Mariane:*)
Ah, come, don't be so haughty. Give a man
A look of kindness, won't you, Mariane?
(*Mariane turns toward Valère and smiles.*)
**Dorine** I tell you, lovers are completely mad!
**Valère** (*To Mariane:*)
Now come, confess that you were very bad
To hurt my feelings as you did just now
I have a just complaint, you must allow.
**Mariane** *You* must allow that you were most unpleasant . . .

**Dorine** Let's table that discussion for the present;
Your father has a plan which must be stopped.
**Mariane** Advise us, then; what means must we adopt?
**Dorine** We'll use all manner of means, and all at once.
(*To Mariane:*)
Your father's addled; he's acting like a dunce.
Therefore you'd better humor the old fossil.
Pretend to yield to him, be sweet and docile,
And then postpone, as often as necessary,
The day on which you have agreed to marry.
You'll thus gain time, and time will turn the trick.
Sometimes, for instance, you'll be taken sick,
And that will seem good reason for delay;
Or some bad omen will make you change the day—
You'll dream of muddy water, or you'll pass
A dead man's hearse, or break a looking-glass.
If all else fails, no man can marry you
Unless you take his ring and say "I do."
But now, let's separate. If they should find
Us talking here, our plot might be divined.
(*To Valère:*)
Go to your friends, and tell them what's occurred,
And have them urge her father to keep his word.
Meanwhile, we'll stir her brother into action,
And get Elmire, as well, to join our faction.
Good-bye.
**Valère** (*To Mariane:*)
Though each of us will do his best,
It's your true heart on which my hopes shall rest.
**Mariane** (*To Valère:*)
Regardless of what Father may decide,
None but Valère shall claim me as his bride.
**Valère** Oh, how those words content me! Come what will . . .
**Dorine** Oh, lovers, lovers! Their tongues are never still.
Be off, now.
**Valère** (*Turning to go, then turning back:*)
One last word . . .
**Dorine** No time to chat:
*You* leave by this door; and *you* leave by that.
(*Dorine pushes them, by the shoulders, toward opposing doors.*)

---

### SCENE FOR TWO WOMEN
### FROM ACT III, SCENES 2 AND 3 OF *PHAEDRA*
### (1677)

*By Jean Racine*

Translated by John Cairncross

CHARACTERS: Phaedra, wife of King Theseus
Oenone, Phaedra's nurse and confidante

SETTING: At the palace in Troezen, a town in the Peloponnesus.

TIME: In the days of the Greek legends.

SITUATION: Thinking, as everyone did, that her husband Theseus was dead, Phaedra has allowed herself to be persuaded by Oenone to declare her love for her stepson, Hippolytus; but he, who is in love with Aricia, is too amazed and disgusted to answer her. Later, Phaedra has sent Oenone to Hippolytus to offer him the crown and Phaedra as his wife. She is waiting for Oenone to return.

COMMENTS: Phaedra is in such distress from her obsessive love that she is weak and near death. Oenone, an older woman who has been with Phaedra since her birth, loves Phaedra and is trying to save her from death. Compare this version of this famous story with Seneca's *Phaedra* and Euripides' *Hippolytus*. The three playwrights told the same story, but there are significant differences in the three plays.

**Phaedra:** O you who see the depths of this my shame,
Relentless Venus, is my fall complete?
Your cruelty could go no further. Now
You triumph. All your arrows have struck home.
O cruel goddess! if you seek new fame,
Attack a more rebellious enemy.
Frigid Hippolytus, flouting your wrath,
Has at your altars never bowed the knee.
Your name seems to offend his haughty ear.
Goddess, avenge yourself. Our cause is one.
Make him love . . . but Oenone, you are back.
Did he not listen? Does he loathe me still?

**Oenone:** Your love is vain and you must stifle it,
O Queen, and summon up your former strength.
The King we thought was dead will soon be here;
Theseus is come; Theseus is on his way.
Headlong, the crowd rushes to welcome him.
I had gone out to seek Hippolytus
When, swelling to the heavens, a thousand cries . . .

**Phaedra:** My husband lives. Oenone, say no more.
I have confessed a love that soils his name.
He is alive, and more I will not know.

**Oenone:** What?

**Phaedra:** I foretold it but you would not hear.
Your tears prevailed over my keen remorse.
I died this morning worthy to be mourned;
I took your counsel and dishonored die.

**Oenone:** You mean to die?

**Phaedra:** Great God, what have I done?
My husband and his son are on their way.
I will behold the witness of my guilt
Observe me as I dare approach the King,

My heart heavy with sighs he heard unmoved,
My eyes wet with the tears the wretch disdained.
Mindful of Theseus' honor, as he is,
Will he conceal from him my fierce desires?
Will he be false to father and to king,
Restrain the horror that he feels for me?
His silence would be vain, Oenone, for
I know my baseness, and do not belong
To those bold wretches who with brazen front
Can revel in their crimes unblushingly.
I know my transports and recall them all.
Even now I feel these very walls, these vaults,
Will soon give tongue and, with accusing voice,
Await my husband to reveal the truth.
Then, death, come free me from so many woes.
Is it so terrible to cease to live?
Death holds no terrors for the wretched. No.
I fear only the name I leave behind,
For my poor children what a heritage.
The blood of Jove should make their spirit swell;
But, whatsoever pride that blood inspires,
A mother's crime lies heavy on her sons.
I tremble lest reports, alas, too true,
One day upbraid them with a mother's guilt.
I tremble lest, crushed by this odious weight,
Neither will ever dare hold up his head.
**Oenone:** Ah! do not doubt it. Pity both of them.
Never was fear more justified than yours.
But why expose them to such base affronts?
And why bear witness now against yourself?
That way lies ruin. Phaedra, they will say,
Fled from the dreaded aspect of her lord.
Hippolytus is fortunate indeed.
By laying down your life, you prove him right.
How can I answer your accuser's charge?
I will be all too easy to confound.
I will behold his hideous triumph as
He tells your shame to all who care to hear.
Ah! sooner let the flames of heaven fall.
But tell me truly do you love him still?
What do you feel for this audacious prince?
**Phaedra:** He is a fearful monster in my eyes.
**Oenone:** Then why concede him such a victory?
You fear him. Dare then to accuse him first
Of the offense he soon may charge you with.
Nothing is in his favor; all is yours—
His sword, left by good fortune in your hands,
Your present agitation, your past grief,

His father, turned against him by your cries,
And, last, his exile you yourself obtained.

**Phaedra:** Should I oppress and blacken innocence?

**Oenone:** All I need is your silence to succeed.
Like you I tremble and I feel remorse.
Sooner would I affront a thousand deaths
But, since without this remedy you die,
For me your life must come before all else.
Therefore I'll speak. Despite his wrath, the King
Will do naught to his son but banish him.
A father when he punishes is still
A father, and his judgment will be mild.
But, even if guiltless blood must still be shed,
What does your threatened honor not demand?
It is too precious to be compromised.
Its dictates, all of them, must be obeyed.
And, to safeguard your honor, everything,
Yes, even virtue, must be sacrificed.
But who comes here? Theseus!

**Phaedra:** Hippolytus!
In his bold gaze my ruin is writ large.
Do as you will.
My fate is in your hands.
My whirling mind has left me powerless.

# Chapter Seven

# Restoration and Eighteenth-Century English Theatre

The theatres in England were officially closed by the Puritans from 1642 to 1660. When the monarchy was restored in 1660 with Charles II as king, theatre activity began anew but with a different kind of playwriting, audiences, theatres, and acting than before 1642.

## PLAYS

Playwrights were now more influenced by the neoclassicism prevalent in France and Italy. Some writers felt compelled to adhere to classical rules, such as John Dryden (1631–1700), who defended the writing of heroic drama with its superhuman protagonist, virtuous heroine, and emphasis on love and valor.

Other innovations were imported from the continent, such as putting actresses in female parts instead of boys and using the French and Italian styles of scenery and theatres. These also affected the playwriting of the period.

While other types of plays were written, the Restoration period (which is often considered to be from 1660 to about 1707) is best known today for the sparkling comedies of manners that were written to appeal to the aristocratic audiences that attended the theatres. Elizabethan plays had been produced for all classes of people, but only the upper classes, including royalty, came to the Restoration theatres.

Gay and full of action, these high comedies, which are written mostly in prose, have artificial characters whose names often reveal the type of people they are—names like Sir Fopling Flutter, Mrs. Loveit, Sir Novelty Fashion, Sir Tunbelly Clumsey, and Lady Wishfort. Most characters are witty, wealthy, sophisticated, and heartless, with a few coarse bumpkins thrown in so that the elite can be shocked and amused at their bad manners. Some frequent characters are the fop, the rake, the wit, the coquette, the gossip, the elderly roué, the cuckold, and the aging beauty.

Sir George Etherege (c. 1635–1691), a member of the court, is best known today for *The Man of Mode* (1676). William Wycherley (c. 1640–1716), also a member of the court, wrote *The Country Wife* (1675) and *The Plain Dealer* (1676), both of which were based in part on Molière's plays. William Congreve (1670–1729) produced *The Way of the World* in 1700. Sir John Vanbrugh (1664–1726) is remembered for *The Relapse* (1696) and *The Provoked Wife* (1697), and George Farquhar (1678–1707) is best known for *The Recruiting Officer* (1706) and *The Beaux Stratagem* (1707).

Because a lack of ethical values was evident in these plays, some people began to protest their immorality, with the result that in the eighteenth century a period of sentimentality became dominant in the English theatre. "Laughing" comedy of the Restoration type did not return to the English stage until Oliver Goldsmith (1728–1774) wrote *She Stoops to Conquer* (1773) and Richard Brinsley Sheridan (1751–1816) produced *The Rivals* (1775) and *The School for Scandal* (1777). These three comedies of manners are generally considered to be three of the finest plays in English literature.

## PRODUCTIONS THEN

**Theatres and Scenery.** Soon after the Restoration, new indoor theatres were built in London that had a proscenium arch with two or three doors and windows or balconies on each side. There was a large forestage; scenes painted in perspective on wings, borders, and shutters or backdrops; traps; and flying machinery. The curtain was raised after the prologue and fell at the end of the play; scene changes of the wings and shutters or drops were made in view of the audience. Chandeliers of candles hung over the stage, and footlights of candles were at the edge of the apron. Daylight came in through a skylight in the auditorium because performances started at 3:00 or 3:30 P.M. Young men sat in the pit on backless benches; the highest-ranking bought seats in boxes on the sides, in the rear where the masked ladies were, or on the stage; the gallery above was for less fashionable spectators with the top gallery for servants.

In the eighteenth century, the apron of the stage became smaller, and there was usually only one proscenium door on each side. Theatres became larger to accommodate more people, and performances started later, at about 6:00 P.M. David Garrick (1717–1779), a manager, playwright, and the finest English actor of his century, is credited with successfully banning spectators from the stage and using more realistic acting, scenery, and lighting.

Performances lasted about three hours and customarily opened with music, followed by the prologue and a full-length play with the intervals between acts filled with singing and dancing. After the play, a short afterpiece was performed and, finally, a song and dance.

**Costumes.** Costumes were as elaborate as the actor or the company could provide. For the most part they wore contemporary dress with little attempt at historical accuracy; however, there were a few standard costumes, such as the black velvet gowns of the tragic actresses and plumes worn on the head by both heroic men and women. A page often attended the train of the tragic heroine's dress to see that it draped properly.

**Acting.** Actors in heroic dramas stood in stately posture and declaimed their lines in an oratorical manner, often intoning or chanting their big speeches. Using big, formal gestures, they acted most of the time on the forestage because the light was better there. Great emphasis was placed on having a striking, expressive voice; and from the number of songs found in these plays, it is probable that most actors could sing. The comedies, however, demanded more realistic acting because they purported to imitate the behavior of contemporary society.

## PRODUCTIONS NOW

Because the dramas and tragedies of this period are rarely performed today, this section will be devoted to acting the high style comedies of manners from the Restoration writers and Goldsmith and Sheridan. Since these comedies reflect the life of a particular society and period, they are usually produced with costumes, props, and sets as close to those used originally as the budget will permit.

**Acting.** To act high comedy well, the actor must understand the type of character he is playing, what the author is satirizing, where the humor lies, and what the witty lines mean. The actor must analyze the character and the play to find out what aspect of the person can be exaggerated. Is the character a fop like Lord Foppington? Does she habitually say the wrong words like Mrs. Malaprop? The actor should emphasize the main idiosyncracy of the character's personality so that the author's satire will amuse an audience.

As for vocal characterizations, there is an elegance and artificial brilliance about many of these characters that demands great pointing of lines, a wide pitch range, and precise articulation. Movements, such as bowing, curtsying, and using properties like canes and fans, should be designed to help the audience understand the life style of the time period and the types of people in the play. Voice and movement must be integrated smoothly so that the sophistication and grace of most of these roles will be evident.

The tempo in these comedies is usually fast and lively. The style of acting needed is highly presentational with many asides and speeches going directly to the audience.

**Costumes.**    Both the ladies and gentlemen of the Restoration and eighteenth century were elaborately dressed, and modern actors may need many rehearsals to handle these clothes skillfully. Fashions changed from year to year, as they do today, and actors should find pictures of the appropriate year when studying a part to determine authentic costumes, wigs, shoes, and accessories.

In general, gentlemen dressed in knee-length coats and waistcoats, breeches, and shirts with lace, ruffles, ribbons, and wide cuffs. They wore periwigs, large plumed hats, and shoes with medium-high heels and buckles. As accessories, they used handkerchiefs, muffs, canes, snuffboxes, swords, and watches.

The ladies wore full, wide bell-skirts with small waists and low necklines. Outside the house, a lady wore a hooded cloak and often a muff and half-mask. A fan, jewelry, handkerchief, pomander, parasol, lace headdress, and high heels may add to the costume. Both ladies and some gentlemen wore makeup.

**Customs.**    Restoration men often stood with feet turned out at a comfortable distance apart or in ballet's third position (heel of the front foot near the arch of the back foot) with the weight on the rear foot. When walking and sitting, they maintained an upright posture. Men customarily sat with the feet turned out, one foot farther front than the other. Hands of both men and women were usually above the waist, moving so that others could see and admire their rings, lace cuffs, and handkerchiefs.

Men sometimes smoked tobacco in long pipes or used snuff. The latter involved taking a small box from his coat pocket and tapping the top to loosen snuff adhering to the lid. A pinch of snuff was then brought directly to each nostril with a thumb and finger, or it was placed on the back of his hand and raised to the nose for sniffing. It was not polite to sneeze, but he could bring forth a lace-trimmed handkerchief to brush away any snuff on his clothing. In the eighteenth century, the more daring women also took snuff on occasion.

Gentlemen rose when a lady entered a room, bowed, and kissed her hand; ladies curtsied. When a lady and gentleman walked together, she rested her hand on his sleeve. On meeting, two male friends might clasp hands, but shaking hands was not popular among the upper classes in England until the nineteenth century.

While all men's movements of this period may seem rather affected today, most men in these comedies are masculine and will fight a duel quickly to avenge a slight. The fop is an exception. He is a comic eccentric who may walk or move rather effeminately. His flexible wrists and fingers may wave a handkerchief or cane, caress his periwig, show off rings and lace cuffs, or play with a muff or flower. He sees himself as the epitome of fashion, grace, and sparkling wit, but everything he does is overdone.

Actresses playing ladies of this period should walk with small steps to appear to glide across the stage. When sitting, they should keep both feet on the floor and never cross their legs. Those playing wenches and peasant women may use bigger steps, cross their legs while sitting, and have freer movements because their costumes are not as restrictive.

A lady's fan is a particularly useful device because, among other things, it can be used for coyly flirting by moving it to just below her eyes, asking for a kiss by placing the handle on her lips, saying "I love you" by drawing the fan across her cheek, dismissing an uninteresting man by flipping the fan towards him, or indicating displeasure by snapping it altogether.

**Bows and Curtsies.**   With both feet turned out, the man may step back with bent knee and transfer his weight to the rear foot. After bending from the waist, the forward foot may be brought back to the rear or the back foot moved up to the front. When bowing, the right hand or hat may be placed over his heart, the hat may be swept back low, or his hand may be extended forward and then down to the floor.

Through the years there were slight differences in ladies' curtsies, but for stage purposes, the two types described in Chapter 5 will suffice for this period also.

Male servants put their heels together and, with arms at their sides, bowed when entering and leaving a room. Maids still did "bob" curtsies.

**Scenery.**   Scene designers may select a wing-drop-border set for these plays with a minimum amount of furniture, which is similar to the original productions. Other possibilities are a realistic, selective realistic, or exaggerated representation of Restoration or eighteenth-century rooms.

**Music.** Songs and dances are often used within these plays and as entertainment at the entr'actes. Harpsichords, violins, violas, cellos, flutes, trumpets, oboes, drums, and organs are appropriate instruments.

## SUGGESTED READING

Brown, J. R., and B. Harris. *Restoration Theatre.* New York: Putnam, 1967.

Dobrèe, Bonamy. *Restoration Comedy, 1660–1720.* Oxford: Clarendon Press, 1924.

————. *Restoration Tragedy, 1660–1720.* Oxford: Clarendon Press, 1929.

Fujimura, Thomas H. *Restoration Comedy of Wit.* Princeton, N.J.: Princeton University Press, 1952.

Krutch, Joseph W. *Comedy and Conscience after the Restoration.* New York: Columbia University Press, 1949.

Perry, Henry T. *Comic Spirit in Restoration Drama.* New York: Russell, 1962.

Summers, Montague. *The Restoration Theatre.* London: Paul, Trench, Trubner & Co., 1934.

## EXERCISES

To increase your ability to act in Restoration and eighteenth-century English plays, work on the following:

1. Practice the movements for taking snuff, as described in this chapter.
2. Practice walking as couples with the lady's hand resting on the gentleman's arm, which is held at a comfortable height for her. As you pass another couple, greet each other by doing the *en passant,* which was a way to bow and keep on walking. Bend the left leg; move the pointed right toe in an arc from behind the left foot to in front of it as you bow slightly to the right. Then step on the right foot and continue walking. To bow to the left, reverse the above.
3. Improvise a scene in which Mrs. Malaprop meets Lord Foppington. (See the scenes from *The Rivals* and *The Relapse* in this chapter.)
4. Take the characters described in the following three scenes from the *The Relapse, The Country Wife,* and *The Rivals* and do an improvisation in which these people arrive at a threatre to see a play and to talk with each other.
5. English plays of this period customarily had both a prologue and epilogue, which were sometimes written by guest writers. Study the following eight lines, which begin a forty-one-line prologue that was composed by David Garrick for Sheridan's *The School for Scandal.* Imagine how the actor who played Sir Peter Teazle in the play might have spoken the following to gain and hold the attention of the audience.

A School for Scandal! tell me, I beseech you,
Needs there a school this modish art to teach you?
No need of lessons now, the knowing think—
We might as well be taught to eat and drink.
Caused by a dearth of scandal, should the vapors
Distress our fair ones—let 'em read the papers;
Their pow'rful mixtures such disorders hit;
Crave what they will, there's *quantum sufficit*.

6. The minuet was a popular dance in England from about 1650 to 1800. Find suitable recorded music for a minuet, consult books on period dances, and choreograph a dance that could be used in a Restoration or eighteenth-century comedy.

7. Practice the asides used by Mrs. Malaprop or Captain Absolute in the scene in this chapter from *The Rivals*.

---

### SCENE FOR ONE MAN, ONE WOMAN
### FROM ACT IV, SCENE 2 OF *THE COUNTRY WIFE*
#### (1675)

*By William Wycherley*

CHARACTERS: Mr. Pinchwife
                    Mrs. Margery Pinchwife, his wife

SETTING: A bedchamber in London.

TIME: Day; 1675.

SITUATION: During a long stay in the country, Pinchwife has married a naive country girl, Margery, and brought her to London. His biggest fear is that he will be made a cuckold by Horner or some other gallant of the city. Margery begins the scene by relating to her husband an experience she has had with a man the evening before when she was disguised as her brother. She has reported how this gentleman kissed her and talked about his love for Margery. Pinchwife is irate and has demanded that she write a letter to the man.

COMMENTS: Margery, the pretty country wife, takes great delight in the pleasures of the city in contrast with the cynical pretenses of the city folks. At forty-nine, her husband is considerably older than she and extremely jealous. This comedy is in the tradition of Molière; for example, compare this scene with the one from Molière's *The School for Wives* in Chapter 6.

**Pinchwife:** Come, begin *(Dictates)* —"Sir"—

**Mrs. P.:** Shan't I say, "Dear Sir"? You know one says always something more than bare "Sir."

**Pinchwife:** Write as I bid you, or I will write whore with this penknife in your face.

**Mrs. P.:** Nay, good bud *(She writes)* —"Sir"—

**Pinchwife:** "Though I suffered last night your nauseous, loathed kisses and embraces"—Write!

**Mrs. P.:** Nay, why should I say so? You know I told you he had a sweet breath.

**Pinchwife:** Write!

**Mrs. P.:** Let me but put out "loathed."

**Pinchwife:** Write, I say!

**Mrs. P.:** Well then. *(Writes)*

**Pinchwife:** Let's see, what have you writ?— *(Takes the paper and reads)* "Though I suffered last night your kisses and embraces"—Thou impudent creature! where is "nauseous" and "loathed"?

**Mrs. P.:** I can't abide to write such filthy words.

**Pinchwife:** Once more write as I'd have you, and question it not, or I will spoil thy writing with this. I will stab out those eyes that cause my mischief. *(Holds up penknife)*

**Mrs. P.:** O Lord! I will.

**Pinchwife:** So—so—let's see now. *(Reads)* "Though I suffered last night your nauseous, loathed kisses and embraces"—go on—"yet I would not have you presume that you shall ever repeat them"—so— *(She writes)*

**Mrs. P.:** I have writ it.

**Pinchwife:** On then—"I then concealed myself from your knowledge, to avoid your insolencies." *(She writes)*

**Mrs. P.:** So—

**Pinchwife:** "The same reason, now I am out of your hands"— *(She writes)*

**Mrs. P.:** So—

**Pinchwife:** "Makes me own to you my unfortunate, though innocent frolic, of being in man's clothes"— *(She writes)*

**Mrs. P.:** So—

**Pinchwife:** "That you may for evermore cease to pursue her, who hates and detests you"— *(She writes)*

**Mrs. P.:** So-h— *(Sighs)*

**Pinchwife:** What, do you sigh?—"detests you—as much as she loves her husband and her honor."

**Mrs. P.:** I vow, husband, he'll ne'er believe I should write such a letter.

**Pinchwife:** What, he'd expect a kinder from you? Come, now your name only.

**Mrs. P.:** What, shan't I say "Your most faithful humble servant till death"?

**Pinchwife:** No, tormenting fiend! *(Aside)* Her style, I find, would be very soft.—Come, wrap it up now, whilst I go fetch wax and a candle; and write on the backside, "For Mr. Horner." *(Exit Pinchwife)*

**Mrs. P.:** "For Mr. Horner."—So, I am glad he has told me his name. Dear Mr. Horner! But why should I send thee such a letter that will vex thee, and make thee angry with me? Well, I will not send it. Ay, but then my husband will kill me—for I see plainly he won't let me love Mr. Horner—but what care I for my husband? I won't, so I won't send poor Mr. Horner such a letter. But then my husband—but oh, what if I writ at bottom my husband made me write it? Ay, but then my husband would see't. Can one have no shift? Ah, a London woman would have had a hundred presently. Stay—what if I should write a letter, and wrap it up like this, and write upon't too? Ay, but then my husband would see't—I don't know what to do. But yet evade I'll try, so I will—for I will not send this letter to poor Mr. Horner, come what will on't. *(She writes)* "Dear, sweet Mr. Horner"—so—"my husband would have me send you a base, rude, unmannerly letter; but I won't"—so—"and would have me forbid you loving me; but I won't"—so—"and would have me say to you, I hate you, poor Mr. Horner; but I won't tell a lie for him"—there—"for I'm sure if you and I were in the country at cards together"—so—"I could not help treading on your toe under the table"—so—"or rubbing knees with you, and staring in your face, till you saw me"—very well—"and then looking down, and blushing for an hour together"—so—"but I must make haste before my husband come; and now he has taught me to write letters, you shall have longer ones from me, who am, dear, dear, poor, dear Mr. Horner, your most humble friend, and servant to command till death.—Margery Pinchwife." Stay, I must give him a hint at bottom—so—now wrap it up just like t'other—so—now write "for Mr. Horner"—but oh now, what shall I do with it? for here comes my husband.

*(Enter Pinchwife)*

**Pinchwife:** *(Aside)* I have been detained by a sparkish coxcomb, who pretended a visit to me; but I fear 'twas to my wife.—What, have you done?

**Mrs. P.:** Ay, ay, bud, just now.

**Pinchwife:** Let's see't; what d'ye tremble for? what, you would not have it go?

**Mrs. P.:** Here.— *(Aside)* No, I must not give him that; so I had been served if I had given him this. *(He opens and reads the first letter)*

**Pinchwife:** Come, where's the wax and seal?

**Mrs. P:** *(Aside)* Lord, what shall I do now? Nay, then I have it.—Pray let me see't. Lord, you think me so arrant a fool I cannot seal a letter; I will do't, so I will.

*(Snatches the letter from him, changes it for the other, seals it, and delivers it to him)*

**Pinchwife:** Nay, I believe you will learn that, and other things too, which I would not have you.

**Mrs. P.:** So, han't I done it curiously?— *(Aside)* I think I have; there's my letter going to Mr. Horner, since he'll needs have me send letters to folks.

**Pinchwife:** 'Tis very well; but I warrant you would not have it go now?

**Mrs. P.:** Yes, indeed, but I would, bud, now.

**Pinchwife:** Well, you are a good girl then. Come, let me lock you up in your chamber till I come back; and be sure you come not within three strides of the window when I am gone, for I have a spy in the street. *(Exit Mrs . Pinchwife; Pinchwife locks the door)* At least, 'tis fit she think so. If we do not cheat women, they'll cheat us, and fraud may be justly used with secret enemies, of which a wife is the most dangerous; and he that has a handsome one to keep, and a frontier town, must provide against treachery, rather than open force. Now I have secured all within, I'll deal with the foe without, with false intelligence. *(Holds up the letter and exits)*

# SCENE FOR TWO MEN
## FROM ACT III, SCENE 1 OF *THE RELAPSE*
### (1696)

*By John Vanbrugh*

CHARACTERS: Sir Novelty Fashion, newly created Lord Foppington
                 Young Thomas Fashion, his brother

SETTING: Lord Foppington's lodgings in London.

TIME: Afternoon; 1696.

SITUATION: Lord Foppington has wounded himself slightly in a fight with Loveless, husband of Amanda, the woman he covets. He has been recuperating in his house but has just put on his cloak to go out to a play. Young Fashion, who needs money, has come to ask his older brother for some.

COMMENTS: Lord Foppington is a typical fop character. He is an egocentric snob who bought his title; he is constantly trying to impress others but only manages to appear absurd. His speech sounds affected because he changes his *o*'s to *a*'s, as indicated in the script. Young Fashion, an attractive young man, is desperately in need of money; and his poverty has made him cunning.

*(Enter Young Fashion.)*

**Y. Fashion:** Brother, your servant: how do you find yourself today?

**L. Foppington:** So well, that I have ardered my coach to the door: so there's no great danger of death this baut, Tam.

**Y. Fashion:** I'm very glad of it.

**L. Foppington:** *(Aside)* That I believe's a lie.—Prithee, Tam, t ell me one thing: did nat your heart cut a caper up to your mauth, when you heard I was run through the bady?

**Y. Fashion:** Why do you think it should?

**L. Foppington:** Because I remember mine did so, when I heard my father was shat through the head.

**Y. Fashion:** It then did very ill.

**L. Foppington:** Prithee, why so?

**Y. Fashion:** Because he used you very well.

**L. Foppington:** Well?—naw strike me dumb, he starved me. He has let me want a thausand women for want of a thausand paund.

**Y. Fashion:** Then he hindered you from making a great many ill bargains, for I think no woman is worth money, that will take money.

**L. Foppington:** If I were a younger brother, I should think so too.

**Y. Fashion:** Why, is it possible you can value a woman that's to be bought?

**L. Foppington:** Prithee, why not as well as a pad-nag?

**Y. Fashion:** Because a woman has a heart to dispose of; a horse has none.

**L. Foppington:** Look you, Tam, of all things that belang to a woman, I have an aversion to her heart; far when once a woman has given you her heart—you can never get rid of the rest of her bady.

**Y. Fashion:** This is strange doctrine. But pray, in your amours how is it with your own heart?

**L. Foppington:** Why, my heart in my amours—is like my heart aut of my amours: *à la glace.* My bady, Tam, is a watch, and my heart is the pendulum to it; whilst the finger runs raund to every hour in the circle, that still beats the same time.

**Y. Fashion:** Then you are seldom much in love?

**L. Foppington:** Never, stap my vitals.

**Y. Fashion:** Why then did you make all this bustle about Amanda?

**L. Foppington:** Because she was a woman of an insolent virtue, and I t hought myself piqued in honor to debauch her.

**Y. Fashion:** Very well. *(Aside)* Here's a rare fellow for you, to have the spending of five thousand pounds a year. But now for my business with him. *(To Lord Foppington)* Brother, though I know to talk to you of business (especially of money) is a theme not quite so entertaining to you as that of the ladies, my necessities are such, I hope you'll have patience to hear me.

**L. Foppington:** The greatness of your necessities, Tam, is the worst argument in the world far your being patiently heard. I do believe you are going to make me a very good speech, but, strike me dumb, it has the worst beginning of any speech I have heard this twelvemonth.

**Y. Fashion:** I'm very sorry you think so.

**L. Foppington:** I do believe thau art. But come, let's know thy affair quickly; far 'tis a new play, and I shall be so rumpled and squeezed with pressing through the crawd to get to my servant, the women will think I have lain all night in my clothes.

**Y. Fashion:** Why then (that I may not be the author of so great a misfortune) my case in a word is this: the necessary expenses of my travels have so much exceeded the wretched income of my annuity that I have been forced to mortgage it for five hundred pounds, which is spent; so that unless you are so kind to assist me in redeeming it, I know no remedy but to go take a purse.

**L. Foppington:** Why, faith, Tam—to give you my sense of the thing, I do think taking a purse the best remedy in the world; for if you succeed, you are relieved that way; if you are taken—you are relieved t'other.

**Y. Fashion:** I'm glad to see you are in so pleasant a humor; I hope I shall find the effects on't.

**L. Foppington:** Why, do you then really think it a reasonable thing I should give you five hundred paunds?

**Y. Fashion:** I do not ask it as a due, brother; I am willing to receive it as a favor.

**L. Foppington:** Thau art willing to receive it any how, strike me speechless. But these are damned times to give money in: taxes are so great, repairs so exorbitant, tenants such rogues, and periwigs so dear, that the devil take me, I am reduced to that extremity in my cash, I have been forced to retrench in that one article of sweet pawder, till I have braught it dawn to five guineas a manth. Naw judge, Tam, whether I can spare you five hundred paunds?

**Y. Fashion:** If you can't, I must starve, that's all. *(Aside)* Damn him!

**L. Foppington:** All I can say is, you should have been a better husband.

**Y. Fashion:** 'Oons, if you can't live upon five thousand a year, how do you think I should do't upon two hundred?

**L. Foppington:** Don't be in a passion, Tam, far passion is the most unbecoming thing in the world—to the face. Look you, I don't love to say anything to you to make you melancholy; but upon this occasion I must take leave to put you in mind that a running horse does require more attendance than a coach-horse. Nature has made some difference 'twixt you and I.

**Y. Fashion:** Yes, she has made you older. *(Aside)* Pox take her!

**L. Foppington:** That is nat all, Tam.

**Y. Fashion:** Why, what is there else?

**L. Foppington:** *(Looking first upon himself, then upon his brother)* Ask the ladies.

**Y. Fashion:** Why, thou essence bottle, thou muskcat, dost thou then think thou hast any advantage over me but what fortune has given thee?

**L. Foppington:** I do—stap my vitals.

**Y. Fashion:** Now, by all that's great and powerful, thou art the prince of coxcombs.

**L. Foppington:** Sir—I am praud of being at the head of so prevailing a party.

**Y. Fashion:** Will nothing then provoke thee?—Draw, coward!

**L. Foppington:** Look you, Tam, you know I have always taken you for a mighty dull fellow, and here is one of the foolishest plats broke out that I have seen a long time. Your paverty makes your life so burthensome to you, you would provoke me to a quarrel, in hopes either to slip through my lungs into my estate, or to get yourself run through the guts, to put an end to your pain. But I will disappoint you in both your designs; far with the temper of a philasapher and the discretion of a statesman—I will go to the play with my sword in my scabbard *(Exit Lord Foppington.)*

**Y. Fashion:** So! Farewell, snuff-box.

---

### SCENE FOR ONE MAN, TWO WOMEN
### FROM ACT III, SCENE 3 OF *THE RIVALS*
### (1775)

*By Richard Brinsley Sheridan*

CHARACTERS: Mrs. Malaprop
                Captain Jack Absolute, son of Sir Anthony Absolute
                Lydia Languish, niece of Mrs. Malaprop

SETTING: Mrs. Malaprop's lodgings in Bath, England.

TIME: Day; 1775.

SITUATION: Mrs. Malaprop and Sir Anthony Absolute want her niece, Lydia Languish, and his son, Captain Jack Absolute, to marry. Accordingly, Mrs. Malaprop has asked Lydia to give up Ensign Beverley, who is actually Jack in disguise, but Lydia has refused to do this. Mrs. Malaprop has just read to Jack a letter he wrote to Lydia as Beverley, telling her that he has a scheme to see her shortly with her aunt's consent.

COMMENTS: Mrs. Malaprop is one of the most delightful characters in all of dramatic literature. Her humor lies in confusing words that are similar in sound, which we have come to call a malapropism; for example, she says "pineapple of politeness" when she means "pinnacle." She is a pretentious, affected, older woman—vain and foolish—who thinks she is still attractive to men. Captain Jack Absolute is a handsome young man, whom Sheridan may have modelled after himself, since the author was only twenty-three when he wrote this play. Lydia, a rich girl of seventeen, thinks she is in love with Beverley, who is really Jack.

**Mrs. Malaprop:** Did you ever hear anything like it? He'll elude my vigilance, will he? Yes, yes! ha! ha! He's very likely to enter these doors! We'll try who can plot best!

**Absolute:** So we will, Ma'am—so we will. Ha! ha! ha! A conceited puppy, ha! ha! ha! Well, but Mrs. Malaprop, as the girl seems so infatuated by this fellow, suppose you were to wink at her corresponding with him for a little time—let her even plot an elopement with him—then do you connive at her escape—while I, just in the nick, will have the fellow laid by the heels, and fairly contrive to carry her off in his stead.

**Mrs. Malaprop:** I am delighted with the scheme; never was anything better perpetrated!

**Absolute:** But, pray, could not I see the lady for a few minutes now? I should like to try her temper a little.

**Mrs. Malaprop:** Why, I don't know—I doubt she is not prepared for a visit of this kind. There is a decorum in these matters.

**Absolute:** O Lord! She won't mind *me*—only tell her Beverley—

**Mrs. Malaprop:** Sir!—

**Absolute:** *(Aside)* Gently, good tongue.

**Mrs. Malaprop:** What did you say of Beverley?

**Absolute:** Oh, I was going to propose that you should tell her, by way of jest, that it was Beverley who was below—she'd come down fast enough then—ha! ha! ha!

**Mrs. Malaprop:** 'Twould be a trick she well deserves. Besides, you know the fellow tells her he'll get my consent to see her—ha! ha! Let him if he can, I say again. *(Calling)* Lydia, come down here!—He'll make me a "go-between in their interviews!"—ha! ha! ha!—Come down, I say, Lydia!—I don't wonder at your laughing, ha! ha! ha!—his impudence is truly ridiculous.

**Absolute:** 'Tis very ridiculous, upon my soul, Ma'am, ha! ha! ha!

**Mrs. Malaprop:** The little hussy won't hear. Well, I'll go and tell her at once who it is. She shall know that Captain Absolute is come to wait on her. And I'll make her behave as becomes a young woman.

**Absolute:** As you please, Ma'am.

**Mrs. Malaprop:** For the present, Captain, your servant. Ah! you've not done laughing yet, I see—"elude my vigilance!"— yes, yes, ha! ha! ha! *(Exit.)*

**Absolute:** Ha! ha! ha! one would think now that I might throw off all disguise at once, and seize my prize with security—but such is Lydia's caprice that to undeceive were probably to lose her. I'll see whether she knows me.

*(Walks aside, and seems engaged in looking at the pictures. Enter Lydia.)*

**Lydia:** What a scene am I now to go through! Surely nothing can be more dreadful than to be obliged to listen to the loathsome addresses of a stranger to one's heart. I have heard of girls persecuted as I am, who have appealed in behalf of their favoured lover to the generosity of his rival: suppose I were to try it. There stands the hated rival—an officer, too!—but oh, how unlike my Beverley! I wonder he don't begin. Truly he seems a very negligent wooer! Quite at his ease, upon my word! I'll speak first. *(Aloud)* Mr. Absolute.

**Absolute:** Madam. *(Turns around.)*

**Lydia:** O heavens! Beverley!

**Absolute:** Hush—hush, my life! Softly! Be not surprised.

**Lydia:** I am so astonished! and so terrified! and so overjoyed! For heaven's sake! how came you here?

**Absolute:** Briefly—I have deceived your aunt. I was informed that my new rival was to visit here this evening, and contriving to have him kept away, have passed myself on her for Captain Absolute.

**Lydia:** Oh, charming! And she really takes you for young Absolute?

**Absolute:** Oh, she's convinced of it.

**Lydia:** Ha! ha! ha! I can't forbear laughing to think how her sagacity is overreached!

**Absolute:** But we trifle with our precious moments. Such another opportunity may not occur. Then let me now conjure my kind, my condescending angel, to fix the time when I may rescue her from undeserved persecution, and with a licensed warmth plead for my reward.

**Lydia:** Will you then, Beverley, consent to forfeit that portion of my paltry wealth? that burden on the wings of love?

**Absolute:** Oh, come to me—rich only thus—in loveliness. Bring no portion to me but thy love—'twill be generous in you, Lydia—for well you know, it is the only dower your poor Beverley can repay.

**Lydia:** How persuasive are his words! How charming will poverty be with him!

**Absolute:** Ah! my soul, what a life will we then live! Love shall be our idol and support! We will worship him with a monastic strictness; abjuring all worldly toys, to center every thought and action there. Proud of calamity, we will enjoy the wreck of wealth; while the surrounding gloom of adversity shall make the flame of our pure love show doubly bright. By heavens! I would fling all goods of fortune from me with a prodigal hand to enjoy the scene where I might clasp my Lydia to my bosom, and say, the world affords no smile to me—but here. *(Embracing her.)* — *(Aside)* If she holds out now the devil is in it!

**Lydia:** *(Aside)* Now could I fly with him to the Antipodes! but my persecution is not yet come to a crisis.

*(Enter Mrs. Malaprop, listening.)*

**Mrs. Malaprop:** *(Aside)* I am impatient to know how the little hussy deports herself.

**Absolute:** So pensive, Lydia!—is then your warmth abated?

**Mrs. Malaprop:** *(Aside)* *Warmth abated!* So! she has been in a passion, I suppose.

**Lydia:** No—nor ever can while I have life.

**Mrs. Malaprop:** *(Aside)* An ill-tempered little devil! She'll be *in a passion all her life*—will she?

**Lydia:** Think not the idle threats of my ridiculous aunt can ever have any weight with me.

**Mrs. Malaprop:** *(Aside)* Very dutiful, upon my word!

**Lydia:** Let her choice be Captain Absolute, but Beverley is mine.

**Mrs. Malaprop:** *(Aside)* I am astonished at her assurance!—to his face—this is to his face!

**Absolute:** Thus then let me enforce my suit. *(Kneeling)*

**Mrs. Malaprop:** *(Aside)* Aye—poor young man! down on his knees entreating for pity! I can contain no longer.— *(Aloud)* Why, thou vixen! I have overheard you.

**Absolute:** *(Aside)* Oh, confound her vigilance!

**Mrs. Malaprop:** Captain Absolute—I know not how to apologize for her shocking rudeness.

**Absolute:** *(Aside)* So—all's safe, I find. *(Aloud)* I have hopes, Madam, that time will bring the young lady—

**Mrs. Malaprop:** Oh, there's nothing to be hoped for from her! She's as headstrong as an allegory on the banks of Nile.

**Lydia:** Nay, Madam, what do you charge me with now?

**Mrs. Malaprop:** Why, thou unblushing rebel—didn't you tell this gentleman to his face that you loved another better?—didn't you say you never would be his?

**Lydia:** No, Madam—I did not.

**Mrs. Malaprop:** Good heavens! what assurance! Lydia, Lydia, you ought to know that lying don't become a young woman! Didn't you boast that Beverley—that stroller Beverley—possessed your heart? Tell me that, I say.

**Lydia:** 'Tis true, Ma'am, and none but Beverley—

**Mrs. Malaprop:** Hold—hold, Assurance! You shall not be so rude.

**Absolute:** Nay, pray Mrs. Malaprop, don't stop the young lady's speech: she's very welcome to talk thus—it does not hurt *me* in the least, I assure you.

**Mrs. Malaprop:** You are *too* good, Captain—*too* amiably patient—but come with me, Miss. Let us see you again soon, Captain. Remember what we have fixed.

**Absolute:** I shall, Ma'am.

**Mrs. Malaprop:** Come, take a graceful leave of the gentleman.

**Lydia:** May every blessing wait on my Beverley, my loved Bev—

**Mrs. Malaprop:** Hussy! I'll choke the word in your throat!—come along—come along.

*(Exeunt severally, Absolute kissing his hand to Lydia—Mrs. Malaprop stopping her from speaking.)*

# Chapter Eight

# Romanticism

In the theatre, the term *romanticism* is usually reserved for a type of play written in the first half of the nineteenth century, for some similar ones written later, and for the style of acting and scenery used in their productions; however, many elements of romanticism can be found in the earlier plays of Shakespeare and other Elizabethans, some Spanish writers of the sixteenth and seventeenth centuries, the German *Sturm und Drang* (Storm and Stress) movement of the late eighteenth century, and others.

The main impetus for the romantic development in the latter part of the 1700s and the first half of the 1800s in art, music, architecture, literature, and drama came as a reaction to neoclassicism and the Age of Reason. In this period, there were political, social, and economic changes, as evidenced by the American and French Revolutions, which emphasized individual rights and freedoms. Poets, artists, philosophers, and playwrights proposed to shake off the neoclassical restrictions and to create a new, freer style.

## PLAYS

In drama, neoclassicism had, more or less, guaranteed that if a writer followed the rules for playwriting, he could produce a good play. Romanticism placed more emphasis on man's natural instincts to understand and reveal the complexities of the world. Genius must not be restricted by regulations but must be free to write as desired, as Shakespeare had been free. Writers, therefore, worked with stories other than those of Greco-Roman mythology; they rediscovered the Middle Ages and their own history; they learned about exotic, faraway places; they preserved legends, folk tales, and music; they wrote about the world of dreams, fantasy, and the supernatural; and they sought an atmosphere of idealism and sentimentality.

Gotthold Ephraim Lessing (1729–1781), Johann Wolfgang von Goethe (1749–1832), and Friedrich von Schiller (1759–1805) were some of the Germans who led the way toward romanticism, although they spurned this label.

While Goethe wrote in other styles, three of his plays show traits of romanticism: *Götz von Berlichingen* (1773), *Egmont* (1788), and his masterpiece, *Faust*, which he worked on almost his entire life. Schiller is best known today for his trilogy, *Wallenstein* (1799), *Maria Stuart* (*Mary Stuart*, 1800), *Die Jungfrau von Orleans* (*The Maid of Orleans*, 1801), and *Wilhelm Tell* (1804).

In 1827 in France, Victor Hugo (1802–1885) called for a new style of drama, free of classical rules. The romantic plays that resulted are characterized by loosely constructed plots that ignore the classical unities of time and place; a noble romantic hero and an ideal heroine who become involved in a tragic love affair; emotional and poetic language; a mixture of the tragic and the comic; large casts and numerous scenes. To summarize romantic tragedy, Prosper Mérimée (1803–1870) wrote: "Curtain rises. Smile, suffer, weep, kill. He is killed, she is dead. Finis."

With the production of Hugo's *Hernani* in 1830 in Paris, romantic drama was accepted in France. In 1838 Hugo produced his finest play, *Ruy Blas*, but by 1843, when Hugo's *Les Burgraves* (*The Governors*) failed, the romantic era was finished in France.

Romantic plays have much in common with melodrama, which also developed in the nineteenth century. They both use spectacular effects, intrigue, disguises, mistaken identity, sudden disclosures, and a love story; but the romantic plays are considered to be of a higher literary quality in that they have finer characterizations, are written in poetry, and end tragically. A melodrama usually has stock characters of hero, heroine, villain, and comedian, is in prose, and has a happy ending as the hero triumphs and the villain is defeated.

While melodramas were a popular type of play with nineteenth-century audiences, most melodramas of this period are considered to be worthless and are produced today only to be laughed at. Since the time of Hugo, there have been a few successful romantic plays. The most popular one of all, *Cyrano de Bergerac*, by Edmond Rostand (1868–1918), was produced in Paris in 1897. Others include Henrik Ibsen's (1828–1906)

*Brand* (1866) and *Peer Gynt* (1867) and Maxwell Anderson's (1888–1959) *Elizabeth the Queen* (1930), *Mary of Scotland* (1933), *Joan of Lorraine* (1946), and *Anne of the Thousand Days* (1948).

## PRODUCTIONS THEN

**Theatres.**   By the nineteenth century all classes of people were again attending the theatre to see programs that lasted five hours or so. More theatres were built, some seating as many as three thousand. A good number were elaborately decorated with new comforts for the patrons like foyers, salons, and carpet. The usual auditorium was still in a horse-shoe shape with pit, boxes, and galleries.

**Scenery.**   The trend in stage productions in the nineteenth century was to more illusion and historical accuracy in the theatre. In stage settings the romantic era was a painter's stage. While still of wing-drop-border construction, the wings were pushed to the extreme limits of either side so that the painted backdrop dominated the stage. Stages became shallower and wider as the apron became smaller, and stage machinery and traps increased to handle the spectacular effects.

In the early nineteenth century, designers began to use the box set for rooms, but the walls continued to have a painted canvas quality and part of the furniture was often painted on them.

**Costumes.**   In costuming, Goethe was one of the first to insist on historically accurate clothing. Stars in this period usually wore authentic costumes, but the rest of the company wore contemporary dress. Throughout this century, however, there was a trend toward more accurate costumes for everyone in the cast.

**Lighting.**   One of the best innovations of the first half of the nineteenth century was the introduction of gas, lime, and carbon arc light to theatres. The development of spectacular effects onstage was greatly aided by these inventions; and magnificent painted scenes, when adequately lighted, could produce a great reaction in the audience.

**Acting.**   In England, the classical acting of John Philip Kemble (1757–1823) and his sister, Mrs. Sarah Siddons (1755–1831), was challenged by the great romantic actor, Edmund Kean (1787–1833). It was Kean's fiery, emotional acting that prompted Coleridge to write that to see Kean play is "like reading Shakespeare by flashes of lightning."

In France, while playwrights were urged to try romanticism, the acting was still mainly classical. François Joseph Talma (1763–1826) and

Rachel (1820–1858), the greatest French actors of their times, were primarily classical actors. In fact, French actors, trained as they were in the formal elegance of traditional classical acting, found it difficult to adjust to romantic writing.

In the United States, English actors were touring the country, acting with resident companies; and some, like Junius Brutus Booth (1796–1852), father of Edwin and John Wilkes Booth, stayed. The leading American actor in the first half of the nineteenth century was Edwin Forrest (1806–1872), who ranted, bellowed, and roared his lines.

## PRODUCTIONS NOW

Since the plot structure, tone, and poetic language of a romantic play are similar to those described in Chapter 5, the suggestions given there should now be reviewed.

**Acting.** In acting romantic plays, the actor is challenged to make intensely emotional scenes believable. One difficulty to conquer may be the poetry, which often has many figures of speech. The meaning of the words must be communicated without losing the beauty of the lines. For this, actors' voices should have distinct articulation and appropriate flexibility.

There may be movement and action in these plays that call for agility, grace, and flowing gestures from many characters. The superhuman hero must be, above all, dashing, graceful, poised, and energetic. The heroine, of course, is sweet, beautiful, and feminine.

**Costumes.** Today we usually select costumes that are historically accurate for the time of the drama. Because these plays are often set in an earlier century than the one they were written in, reference books should be consulted to learn the costumes, manners, and customs of the period of the play. Nineteenth-century costumes and movements will be reviewed briefly in Chapter 9.

**Scenery.** Because most of these plays contain many locales with large casts, the painted wings and drops on a wide stage, as used in the nineteenth century, seem appropriate today because they can be changed quickly. Other possibilities might be a formalistic design with simple props and area lighting, selective realistic, or impressionistic sets. Whatever the selection, the show must progress quickly from one locale to the next.

102

# SUGGESTED READING

Barzun, Jacques. *Classic, Romantic, and Modern*. Garden City, N.Y.: Anchor Books, 1961.

Carlson, Marvin A. *The French Stage in the Nineteenth Century*. Metuchen, N.J.: Scarecrow Press, Inc., 1972.

Furst, Lilian R. *Romanticism in Perspective*. New York: Humanities Press, 1969.

George, A. J. *The Development of French Romanticism*. Syracuse: University Press, 1955.

Prudhoe, John. *The Theatre of Goethe and Schiller*. Oxford: Basil Blackwell & Mott, Ltd., 1973.

# EXERCISES

Get ready for acting in romantic plays by first doing the following exercises:

1. After reading the scene from Schiller's *Mary Stuart* in this chapter, improvise another meeting between Mary and Elizabeth I in another location. (For an idea, look at Act III of *Mary of Scotland* by Maxwell Anderson.)
2. Two of the most popular protagonists of all times are Cyrano de Bergerac (see the scene from Edmund Rostand's romantic play in this chapter) and Hamlet (see the scene from this Shakespearean play in Chapter 5.) Improvise a scene in which Cyrano and Hamlet meet and talk about their problems.
3. Listen to music from composers of the romantic period, such as Franz Schubert, Felix Mendelssohn, or Robert Schumann. Improvise movement to fit the music.
4. Study the famous "nose" speech from Act I of *Cyrano de Bergerac* in which Cyrano answers Valvert, who has said, "Your nose . . . is very large!" The time is 1640; the place, a French theatre. The following is a brief excerpt from this speech for practicing variety of rate, pitch, volume, and quality.

CYRANO:
Ah, no, young man, that is not enough! You might
have said, dear me, there are a thousand things . . .
varying the tone . . . For instance . . . here you are:
AGGRESSIVE: "I, monsieur, if I had such a nose,
nothing would serve but I must cut it off!"
AMICABLE: "It must be in your way while drinking;
you ought to have a special beaker made!"

DESCRIPTIVE: "It is a crag! . . . a peak! . . . a promontory!
A promontory, did I say? It is a peninsula!"
INQUISITIVE: "What may the office be of that oblong receptacle?
Is it an inkhorn or a scissor-case?"

---

## SCENE FOR TWO WOMEN
## FROM ACT III, SCENE 4 OF *MARY STUART*
### (1800)

*By Friedrich von Schiller*

Translated by Joseph Mellish; Adapted by Eric Bentley

CHARACTERS: Elizabeth, Queen of England
     Mary Stuart, Queen of Scots, a prisoner in England
     Robert Dudley, Earl of Leicester (1 line)
     George Talbot, Earl of Shrewsbury (3 lines)

SETTING: Outside the castle of Fotheringay.

TIME: February 7, 1587, the day before Mary was executed.

SITUATION: Obliged to flee from Scotland, Mary sought sanctuary in England but was imprisoned by Elizabeth. She is now confined to the castle of Fotheringay. Mary has been declared guilty by a court, but Elizabeth must authorize the execution. Leicester has arranged it so that, while Elizabeth is on a hunt near Fotheringay, Mary should be allowed to be outside so that the two can meet.

COMMENTS: Schiller deliberately took many liberties with history. Although 1587 would make Elizabeth fifty-four and Mary forty-four, Schiller stated that in this play Mary is about twenty-five and Elizabeth is at most thirty. Historians say that Elizabeth and Mary never met, but Schiller, Maxwell Anderson, and other authors have had them meet in plays.

**Mary:** Now stand we face to face; now, sister, speak;
 Name but my crime, I'll fully satisfy you.
 Alas, had you vouchsafed to hear me then,
 When I, so earnest, sought to meet your eye,
 It never would have come to this, my sister—
 This so distressful, this so mournful meeting!

**Elizabeth:** Accuse not fate. Your own deceitful heart
 It was, the wild ambition of your house.
 As yet no emnities had passed between us
 When your imperious uncle, the proud priest,
 Whose shameless hand grasps at all crowns, attacked me
 With unprovoked hostility and taught
 You, but too docile, to assume my arms
 And meet me in the lists in mortal strife.
 What means employed he not to storm my throne?
 The curses of the priests, the people's sword,

The dreadful weapons of religious frenzy——
Even here in my own kingdom's peaceful haunts
He fanned the flames of civil insurrection.
But God is with me, and the haughty priest
Has not maintained the field. The blow was aimed
Full at my head. But yours it is that falls!

**Mary:** I'm in the hand of Heaven. You never will
Exert so cruelly the power it gives you.

**Elizabeth:** Who shall prevent me? Ha? Did not your uncle
Set all the kings of Europe the example—
How to conclude a peace with those they hate?
Be mine the school of Saint Bartholomew:
The church can break the bonds of every duty,
It consecrates the regicide, the traitor.
I only practise what your priests have taught.
Say, then, what surety can be offered me,
Should I magnanimously loose your chains?

**Mary:** Had you declared me heir to your dominions,
As is my right, then gratitude and love
In me had fixed, for you, a faithful friend
And kinswoman.

**Elizabeth:** Your friendship is abroad,
Your house is popery, the monk your brother.
Name *you* my successor! Oh, treacherous snare!
That in my life you might seduce my people,
And when I——

**Mary:** Sister, rule your realm in peace:
I give up every claim to these domains.
Alas, the pinions of my soul are lamed;
Greatness entices me no more; your point
Is gained. I am but Mary's shadow now.
You have destroyed me in my bloom. Now speak
The word which to pronounce has brought you hither.
Pronounce this word. Say: "Mary you are free.
You have already felt my power, learn now
To honour too my generosity."

**Elizabeth:** So: you confess at last that you are conquered?
Are all your schemes run out? No more assassins
Now on the road? Will no adventurer
Attempt again, for you, the sad achievement?
Yes, madam, it is over. You'll seduce
No mortal more. The world has other cares.
None is ambitious of the dangerous honour
Of being your fourth husband!

**Mary:** *starting angrily.* Sister, sister!
Grant me forbearance, all ye powers of heaven!

**Elizabeth:** *regards her long, with a look of proud contempt.* Those then, my Lord of
Leicester, are the charms

**105**

Which no man with impunity can view,
Near which no woman dare attempt to stand?
In sooth, this honour has been cheaply gained.
She who to all is common may with ease
Become the common object of applause!

**Mary:** This is too much!

**Elizabeth:** *laughing insultingly.* You show us now, indeed,
Your real face! Till now, 'twas but the mask!

**Mary:** *burning with rage, yet dignified and noble.*
My sins were human and the faults of youth.
Superior force misled me. I have never
Denied or sought to hide it. I despised
All false appearance as became a queen.
The worst of me is known, and I can say
That I am better than the fame I bear.
Woe to you when in time to come the world
Shall strip the robe of honour from your deeds!
Virtue was not your portion from your mother:
Well know we what it was that brought the head
Of Anne Boleyn down on the fatal block!

**Shrewsbury:** *stepping between both Queens.*
Is this the moderation, the submission,
My lady?——

**Mary:** Moderation! I've supported
What human nature can support. Farewell,
Lamb-hearted resignation, passive patience,
Fly to your native heaven! Burst at length
In all your fury, long-suppressèd rancour!

**Shrewsbury:** She is distracted. My liege, forgive her.
*Elizabeth, speechless with anger, casts enraged looks at Mary.*

**Leicester:** *in the most violent agitation. He seeks to lead Elizabeth away.* Away from this
disastrous place!

**Mary:** *raising her voice.* A bastard
Profanes the English throne! The generous Britons
Are cheated by a juggler! Her whole person
Is false and painted—heart as well as face!
*Into Elizabeth's face.*
If right prevailed, you'd be lying in the dust
Before me! For I am your rightful queen!
*Elizabeth hastily quits the stage; the Lords follow her in consternation.*

---

### SCENE FOR ONE MAN, ONE WOMAN
### FROM ACT V OF *CYRANO DE BERGERAC*
#### (1897)

*By Edmond Rostand*

Translated by Gertrude Hall

CHARACTERS: Cyrano de Bergerac
Roxane

SETTING: The park belonging to the convent of the Sisters of the Cross in Paris. A chair and a large tapestry frame for Roxane and a large armchair for Cyrano are under the trees.

TIME: An evening in autumn, 1655.

SITUATION: For fourteen years, since shortly after the death of her husband, Christian, Roxane has lived in mourning at this convent. Her good friend and cousin, Cyrano, who has always loved Roxane, has visited her every Saturday to bring her news. He has never spoken to her of his love and the fact that he helped Christian woo Roxane by speaking and writing letters for him. Today, an enemy has thrown a block of wood from a window at Cyrano, and his head is bandaged under his plumed hat. Roxane, working at the tapestry, at first speaks to him without looking at him.

COMMENTS: Cyrano is a courageous, intelligent, idealistic hero, but he is extremely sensitive about his large nose. Roxane, who is in her middle thirties, is dressed in mourning. Cyrano is a little older and is wearing a worn black coat, sword, cane, and plumed hat.

Cyrano: The leaves!

Roxane: [looking up from her work and gazing off toward the avenues]. They are the russet gold of a Venetian beauty's hair . . . Watch them fall!

Cyrano: How [well] they do it! In that brief fluttering from bough to ground, how they contrive still to put on beauty! And though foredoomed to moulder upon the earth that draws them, they wish their fall invested with the grace of a free bird's flight!

Roxane: Serious, you?

Cyrano: [remembering himself]. Not at all, Roxane!

Roxane: Come, never mind the falling leaves! Tell me the news, instead . . . Where is my [gazette]?

Cyrano: Here it is!

Roxane: Ah!

Cyrano: [growing paler and paler, and struggling with pain]. Saturday, the nineteenth: the king having filled his dish eight times with Cette preserves, and emptied it, was taken with a fever; his distemper, for high treason, was condemned to be let blood, and now the royal pulse is [normal]! On Sunday: at the Queen's great ball, were burned seven hundred and sixty-three wax candles; our troops, it is said, defeated Austrian John; four sorcerers were hanged; Madame Athis's little dog had a distressing turn, the case called for a . . .

Roxane: Monsieur de Bergerac, leave out the little dog!

Cyrano: Monday, . . .nothing, or next to it: Lygdamire took a fresh lover.

Roxane: Oh!

Cyrano: [over whose face is coming a change more and more marked] Tuesday: the whole Court assembled at Fontainebleau. Wednesday, the fair Monglat said to Count Fiesco "No!" Thursday, Mancini [was the] Queen of France, . . .or little less. Twenty-fifth, the fair Monglat said to Court Fiesco "Yes!" And Saturday, the twenty-sixth . . .

*[He closes his eyes. His head drops on his breast. Silence]*

Roxane: *[surprised at hearing nothing further, turns, looks at him and starts to her feet in alarm.]* Has he fainted? *[She runs to him, calling]* Cyrano!

Cyrano: *[opening his eyes, in a faint voice].* What is it? . . .What is the matter! *[He sees Roxane bending over him, hurriedly readjusts his hat, pulling it more closely over his head, and shrinks back in his armchair in terror]* No! no! I assure you, it is nothing! . . .Do not mind me!

Roxane: But surely . . .

Cyrano: It is merely the wound I received at Arras . . .Sometimes . . .you know . . .even now . . .

Roxane: Poor friend!

Cyrano: But it is nothing . . .It will pass . . . *[He smiles with effort]* It has passed.

Roxane: Each one of us has his wound. I too have mine. It is here, never to heal, that ancient wound . . . *[She places her hand on her breast]* It is here, beneath the yellowing letter on which are still faintly visible tear-drops and drops of blood!

*[The light is beginning to grow less]*

Cyrano: His letter? . . .Did you not once say that some day . . .you might show it to me?

Roxane: Ah! . . .Do you wish? . . .His letter?

Cyrano: Yes . . .today . . .I wish to . . .

Roxane: *[handing him the little bag from her neck].* Here!

Cyrano: I may open it?

Roxane: Open it . . .read!

*[She goes back to her embroidery frame, folds it up, orders her wools]*

Cyrano: "Good-bye, Roxane! I am going to die!"

Roxane: *[stopping in astonishment].* You are reading it aloud?

Cyrano: *[reading].* "It is fated to come this evening, beloved, I believe! My soul is heavy, oppressed with love it had not time to utter . . .and now Time is at end! Never again, never again shall my worshipping eyes . . ."

Roxane: How strangely you read his letter!

Cyrano: *[continuing].* " . . .whose passionate revel it was, kiss in its fleeting grace your every gesture. One, usual to you, of tucking back a little curl, comes to my mind . . .and I cannot refrain from crying out . . ."

Roxane: How strangely you read his letter! . . . *[The darkness gradually increases]*

Cyrano: "and I cry out: Good-bye!"

Roxane: You read it . . .

Cyrano: "my dearest, my darling, . . .my treasure . . ."

Roxane: . . .in a voice . . .

Cyrano: " . . .my love! . . ."

Roxane: . . .in a voice . . .a voice which I am not hearing for the first time!

*[Roxane comes quietly nearer to him, without his seeing it; she steps behind his armchair, bends noiselessly over his shoulder, looks at the letter. The darkness deepens]*

Cyrano: " . . .My heart never desisted for a second from your side . . .and I am and shall be in the world that has no end, the one who loved you without measure, the one . . ."

**Roxane:** *[laying her hand on his shoulder]* How can you go on reading? It is dark. *[Cyrano starts, and turns round; sees her close to him, makes a gesture of dismay and hangs his head. Then, in the darkness which has completely closed round them, she says slowly, clasping her hands]* And he, for fourteen years, has played the part of the comical old friend who came to cheer me!

**Cyrano:** Roxane!

**Roxane:** So it was you.

**Cyrano:** No, no, Roxane!

**Roxane:** I ought to have [quessed] it, if only by the way in which he speaks my name!

**Cyrano:** No, it was not I!

**Roxane:** So it was you!

**Cyrano:** I swear to you . . .

**Roxane:** Ah, I detect at last the whole generous [deception]. The letters . . .were yours!

**Cyrano:** No!

**Roxane:** The tender fancy, the dear folly, . . . yours!

**Cyrano:** No!

**Roxane:** The voice in the night, was yours!

**Cyrano:** I swear to you that it was not!

**Roxane:** The soul . . .was yours!

**Cyrano:** I did not love you, no!

**Roxane:** And you loved me!

**Cyrano:** Not I . . .it was the other!

**Roxane:** You loved me!

**Cyrano:** No!

**Roxane:** Already your denial comes more faintly!

**Cyrano:** No, no, my darling love, I did not love you!

**Roxane:** Ah, how many things within the hour have died . . .how many have been born! Why, why have you been silent these long years, when on this letter, in which he had no part, the tears were yours?

**Cyrano:** *[handing her the letter]*. Because . . .the blood was his.

---

# Chapter Nine

# Early Realism
# and Naturalism

During the nineteenth century, there was a trend toward more realism in the theatre that paralleled similar developments in art and literature. This was abetted by political and social changes, discoveries in science, and a growing interest in sociology and psychology. Romanticism's idealistic outlook on the world soon seemed to be old-fashioned as writers began to look at people and their environment realistically.

## PLAYS

The plot construction for realistic drama was aided by the work of a Frenchman, Eugène Scribe (1791–1861), who brought attention to the well-made play (*pièce bien faite*). Consisting of exposition with the introduction of the situation, mounting action and suspense, complications, unexpected reversals, a big climax, and dénouement, this was plot construction reduced to a simple formula. While Scribe's plays are belittled for inadequate thought and characterizations, his tightly knit plots influenced other dramatists.

Some early realists were Russia's Nikolai Gogol (1809–1852), Ivan Turgenev (1818–1883), and Alexander Ostrovsky (1823–1886); Germany's Georg Büchner (1818–1837) and Friedrich Hebbel (1813–1863); and France's Alexandre Dumas *fils* (1824–1895). It was, however,

Norway's Henrik Ibsen (1828–1906) who popularized realism with *A Doll's House* in 1879; *Ghosts* in 1881; *An Enemy of the People* in 1882; *The Wild Duck* in 1884; *Rosmersholm* in 1886; and in 1890 his greatest realistic play, *Hedda Gabler.*

By now, certain characteristics of realism were evident: plays were tightly constructed, building to a major climax and dénouement; asides, soliloquies, and poetry were abandoned; dialogue was close to actual speech, yet each line contributed to the development of the plot; each action was motivated; all scenes were causally related; each character was shown to be the result of heredity and environment; and, above all, the author attempted to give a truthful picture of life.

In Russia, Anton Chekhov (1860–1904) wrote four of the finest examples of realistic plays in *The Sea Gull* (1896), *Uncle Vanya* (1899), *The Three Sisters* (1901), and *The Cherry Orchard* (1904).

In England, Irish-born George Bernard Shaw (1856–1950), whose witty approach to serious problems made him the top British playwright of his era, produced the popular *Arms and the Man* (1894), *Candida* (1895), *The Devil's Disciple* (1897), *Caesar and Cleopatra* (1899), *Man and Superman* (1903), *Major Barbara* (1905), *Pygmalion* (1913), *Saint Joan* (1923), and others.

In 1904, the Irish National Theatre Society obtained the famous Abbey Theatre in Dublin, where the works of such great playwrights as William Butler Yeats (1865–1939), John Millington Synge (1871–1909), and Sean O'Casey (1880–1964) were produced. Synge's best-known plays are a lyrical one-act tragedy, *Riders to the Sea* (1904), and the comic, ironic *The Playboy of the Western World* (1907). While O'Casey later turned to nonrealistic styles, he started playwriting with three realistic tragicomedies, *The Shadow of a Gunman* (1923), *Juno and the Paycock* (1924), and *The Plough and the Stars* (1926).

The difference between realism and naturalism, which are both called representational or illusionistic styles, is mainly one of degree. The realistic writer is more selective in choosing the details to be used in the play. In writing naturalism, which was fathered by Émile Zola (1840–1902) in his preface to *Thérèse Raquin* in 1873, the playwright ignores the importance of a tightly knit plot and tries to present a slice of life (*tranche de vie*) onstage. Naturalistic writers were urged to concentrate on data objectively and to take a scientific approach to drama, to reproduce everything onstage and not select, distort, or interpret the material to make it interesting to an audience. The result was that they produced loosely organized plots that ignored theatrical contrivances, climaxes, and the unities of time, place, and action. They also tended to concentrate on the sordid, ugly lives of lower-class people, who were shown to be the products and victims of heredity and environment.

Some of the great naturalistic writers were France's Henri Becque (1837–1899), who wrote *The Vultures* (1882) and *The Woman of Paris*

(1885); Sweden's August Strindberg (1849–1912), who finished *The Father* in 1887 and *Miss Julie* a year later; Germany's Gerhart Hauptmann (1862–1946), who produced *The Weavers* in 1892; and Russia's Maxim Gorki (1868–1936), whose best play is *The Lower Depths* (1902).

By the early years of the twentieth century, however, naturalism was no longer an important movement; and realism was left as the dominant style in our theatre.

## PRODUCTIONS THEN

**Theatres.** In the last half of the nineteenth century, theatres began to specialize in a particular kind of entertainment, so that plays were separated from the variety acts that prolonged performances to five hours. By 1900 a play lasted about two and one-half to three hours. Now, once again plays were being done for the more sophisticated elements of society, and playhouses were becoming smaller with better sightlines and acoustics. Comfortable seats were put in the pit, now called the orchestra; and in some new theatres a mezzanine and balcony replaced boxes.

**Scenery.** Scenery became more realistic, with box sets on almost-level stage floors becoming common. The revolving stage, elevator stage, and rolling platforms were introduced to change scenery quickly. In the late 1870s in some theatres, the front curtain was lowered at the ends of scenes and acts so that the audience could no longer see the set changes.

**Lighting.** By 1880 some play and opera houses had electricity, and now for the first time realistic lighting effects could be achieved easily without the great danger of fire that gas light had presented. Another innovation, credited to Sir Henry Irving, was turning off the lights in the auditorium during the performance.

**Directing.** In the last half of the nineteenth century, pioneering directors, such as Duke Georg II of Saxe-Meiningen (1826–1914), demanded more realistic scenery and acting. He carefully integrated costumes, scenery, properties, and actors to obtain the desired effect. He held long, painstaking rehearsals in which actors were taught to ignore the audience and play to other actors. There were no stars in Saxe-Meiningen's company; instead, ensemble acting was stressed.

**Acting.** The great actors of this period were primarily of the classical or romantic style. They were England's Sir Henry Irving (1838–1905) and Ellen Terry (1847–1928); Italy's Tommaso Salvini (1829–1916) and Eleanora Duse (1859–1924); Germany's Fanny Janauschek (1830–1904); France's Constant Coquelin (1841–1909) and Sarah Bernhardt

(1844–1923); Poland's Helena Modjeska (1840–1909); and America's Charlotte Cushman (1816–1876) and Edwin Booth (1833–1893). While most of these actors would not be considered realistic today, some of them, like Edwin Booth, led the way to more realistic acting.

**Experimental Theatres.**   Since in the nineteenth century the large commercial theatres and the reigning stars seldom performed the new realistic and naturalistic plays, experimental theatre organizations were started to produce them, often with amateur actors. In Paris, André Antoine (1858–1943) established the Théâtre Libre in 1887. In Berlin in 1889, Otto Brahm (1856–1912) founded the Freie Bühne. In London in 1891, J. T. Grein (1862–1935) opened the Independent Theatre; and in 1898, Constantin Stanislavski (1863–1938) and Vladimir Nemirovich-Danchenko (1859–1943) started the Moscow Art Theatre.

In these experimental theatres, costumes, sets, lighting, acting, and playwriting had to give the impression of real life on the stage. Every effort was made to disguise the fact that the stage is a platform for players and to create the illusion that it is a true environment. The people in the audience were to look at the onstage action through the invisible "fourth wall," and the goal was to have them forget that they were seated in an auditorium watching actors and to empathize completely with the characters onstage.

To do this, the directors of realistic plays saw that the elegant, formal acting of the past was no longer suitable. Realistic writers did not write poetry that needed beautiful, outstanding voices. The realists and naturalists wrote ordinary speech in dialects, and the plays were not about superhuman heroes and heroines but common men and women. To speak realistic lines believably, actors must talk to each other as in ordinary conversation, use simple gestures, and ignore the audience.

**The Stanislavski System.**   In the late nineteenth and early twentieth centuries, Stanislavski evolved a system of acting that called for an inner as well as an outer truth. (In the United States a version of this system fostered by the Group Theatre, Actors Studio, and others is commonly referred to as "the Method".) Based on a thorough analysis of the play and a psychological examination of the character, Stanislavski's procedure advocated that actors work on both their voices and bodies so that they can convey the subtle nuances of the inner life of the character. Stanislavski hoped to prepare actors so that they might enjoy a creative state in which to act truthfully the events of a play. To achieve this, actors must concentrate completely upon imagining, feeling, and projecting the truth of the situation.

While this plan was created for realistic and naturalistic plays, many who advocate the Stanislavski System contend that it can be used for all styles and all types of plays. Others state that this representational

113

method is useful for only realistic and naturalistic plays and that other styles of playwriting need technical or presentational acting.

**Technical Acting.** The technical approach grew out of the heroic presentational acting of the eighteenth century. Denis Diderot (1713–1784), a French philosopher, playwright, and critic, wrote *The Paradox of Acting*, which, when it was published in 1830, made a great impression on actors of that time. His main idea was that actors should not feel their roles but should carefully think out their parts and rely on their technique to sustain a performance day after day. This approach to acting was detailed by François Delsarte (1811–1871) in 1839. According to him, an actor could portray any emotion if he knew the right posture, gesture, position of the head, and facial expressions for that emotion because he believed that feelings are always expressed by everyone in the same ways. Actors today who pay more attention to the outer manifestations of feelings than trying to feel the emotion inside are called technical, presentational, or mechanical actors. Those who work on feeling the inner emotions and who care little for the outer appearance of the body are called emotional, representational, psychological, intuitive, or Method actors. Of course, many actors are in the middle—somewhere between the two extremes—using the best ideas from both approaches.

## PRODUCTIONS NOW

When these early realistic and naturalistic plays are performed today, the usual choice for scenery, costumes, lighting, and acting is realistic or selective realistic, but other styles have been used.

**Acting.** Because the Stanislavski System was developed to act the realistic and naturalistic dramas of Chekhov, Gorki, and others, it is an excellent approach to use for plays in these styles. Surely, all actors today, whether they choose to use the Method or not, should be familiar with Stanislavski's ideas as presented in his popular books, *An Actor Prepares, Creating a Role, Building a Character*, and *My Life in Art*.

Briefly, Stanislavski's System encourages you to work on your voice and body so that you may play all types of parts. To prepare a role, you should study the entire play thoroughly, deciding on the theme, analyzing the characters and their relationships, and understanding the subtext (the underlying meaning). Determine what Stanislavski called the "given circumstances": the time and place, the plot, the director's interpretation of the play, the needed properties, lighting, and sound effects. Discover your character's "super-objective" or major goal for the entire play and objectives, motivations, and actions for each scene. To build your characterization, research your character's past and use observations of similar people, your imagination, and remembrances of your past emotional and sensory experiences that have been similar to your character's. Decide on the best tempo-rhythms and changes of moods. While acting onstage, concentrate as your character would and have communion with your fellow actors in ensemble playing.

Whatever approach is selected to preparing a realistic part—emotional, technical, or somewhere in between—actors must give the illusion of living their parts onstage. They should appear to ignore the audience and play to the other actors onstage with ensemble acting as the goal. They should listen to the others, think about what is said, react, and speak. All gestures and movements must appear to be motivated by thoughts and emotions; and voice, articulation, and dialect or accent must sound natural.

Realistic comedies may demand more technical skills than dramas, because in comedy—even realistic comedy—actors often exaggerate a character trait, voice, movement, or costume to arouse laughter. Actors in comedies cannot live their parts to the extent that they ignore audiences because they are involved with such techniques as pointing, timing, and topping lines; pausing for effect; and holding for laughs.

**Costumes.** If historically accurate clothes are wanted, costume reference books must be consulted because fashions changed drastically during the nineteenth century. In 1800 in France and England, ladies wore a thin, narrow, décolleté dress known as the "Empire" gown, usually with a shawl. By 1850 they had numerous petticoats under full, wide skirts. By 1870 they used bustles, and by 1900 skirts were narrow again.

Men's clothes became progressively more practical during this century. Trousers replaced breeches and hose; and the feathers, ruffs, and heavy ornamented coats of previous days were eliminated in favor of simpler clothing.

**Customs.** Most nineteenth-century ladies were feminine and helpless. Girls were educated to be "ladylike," to lower their eyes, to blush at an off-color remark, to faint at an unpleasant sight, and to rely on men to assist them.

Gentlemen were masculine and protective, with a stolid posture and walk. They, of course, never sat if a lady was standing; and when they did sit, they did not cross their legs or smoke in the presence of a lady, only with men. During this century, the cigar and cigarette became increasingly popular.

**Bows and Curtsies.** In formal situations, curtsies and bows were used throughout this century. If the lady's dress were full enough, she might curtsy by placing the ball of one foot in back of the other and bending both knees. If her dress were narrow, she might step back while bending the knee and putting all of her weight on the back foot. She pointed the other foot in front as she bent forward from the waist. When the bustle came in, ladies did not curtsy as much as formerly, except to royalty.

In the first half of the nineteenth century in England, shaking hands, which had been done by the lower classes for some time, became more fashionable among well-to-do men; however, on formal occasions a man might bow by placing the ball of one foot in front of the other and bending forward from the waist. Hands might be brought to the heart. During the last half of this century, gentlemen put their heels together and bowed with hands at the sides.

Butlers bowed and maids did "bob" curtsies both when entering and leaving a room. A butler's bow required that the backs of his hands show at his sides as he put his heels together and bent forward from the waist.

**Music.** Appropriate musical instruments to use for a play set in the nineteenth century might include the spinet, piano, violin, cello, bass, banjo, guitar, horns, reeds, and percussion.

## SUGGESTED READING

Barzun, Jacques. *Classic, Romantic, and Modern.* Garden City, N.Y.: Anchor Books, 1961.

Boleslavsky, Richard. *Acting: The First Six Lessons.* New York: Theatre Arts Books, 1933.

Brockett, Oscar G., and Robert R. Findley. *Century of Innovation.* Englewood Cliffs, N.J.: Prentice-Hall, Inc., 1973.

Diderot, Denis. *The Paradox of Acting.* New York: Hill and Wang, 1957.

Moore, Sonia. *The Stanislavski System.* New York: Viking Press, 1960.

Stanislavski, Constantin. *An Actor Prepares.* Tr. by Elizabeth Reynolds Hapgood. New York: Theatre Arts Books, 1936.

————. *Building a Character.* Tr. by Elizabeth Reynolds Hapgood. New York: Theatre Arts Books, 1949.

————. *Creating a Role.* Tr. by Elizabeth Reynolds Hapgood. New York: Theatre Arts Books, 1961.

————. *My Life in Art.* Tr. by J. J. Robbins. New York: Theatre Arts Books, 1924.

Wilson, Garff B. *Three Hundred Years of American Drama and Theatre.* Englewood Cliffs, N.J.: Prentice-Hall, Inc., 1973.

# EXERCISES

To practice some of the teachings of Stanislavski, try the following:

1. As an exercise in observation, observe three people of different ages: a child, a middle-aged person, and an old person. Practice walking and talking like these people.

2. As an exercise in sense memory, recreate an experience you had in which you tasted, smelled, touched, heard, or saw something unusual.

3. As an exercise in emotional memory, recreate a time in your life when you were afraid, sad, or happy.

4. Standing or sitting before other people, tell them about a recent true personal experience. Next assume a characterization that is very different from you in age, dialect, personality, or physical structure, and tell the same story to the group as this character would do it.

5. To practice thinking as a character would think, assume a characterization that is not like you and vocalize the thoughts, called by Stanislavski the "inner monologue," as you do the following actions:
   a. Scratch an insect bite on your leg.
   b. Step on a nail.
   c. Brush away a fly that is annoying you.
   d. Look at a beautiful sunset.
   e. Wait in a busy doctor's office to be examined for an ailment.

6. Stanislavski wrote about the "magic if." He encouraged actors to ask themselves, "What would I do *if* I were the character in this situation?" As an exercise, select a character from Column A and do one of the actions indicated in Column B. Vocalize the "inner monologue."

| A | B |
|---|---|
| Child of 12 | Find a $100 bill on the street. |
| Rock star | Eat dinner. |
| College professor | Walk your dog. |
| Professional athlete | Use a computer. |
| Retired person | Receive a bill that you don't owe. |
| Model | Decide to ask someone for a date. |
| Homeless person | Decide how to eliminate an enemy. |
| Foreign diplomat | Read a newspaper article that mentions your name. |

7. For the following exercise in ensemble playing, you and another actor should assume characterizations that are different from your own personalities. Improvise the following:
   a. One of you receives a letter that affects both of your lives.
   b. One of you is an employer who must fire the other from a job.
   c. You are both trapped in an elevator when the electricity goes off.

d. You both discover a ticking device that you believe to be a bomb.

e. One of you is a lawyer; the other is a client who has been sentenced to death.

f. You are close relatives waiting in a hospital for news of a dear friend who is dying.

g. One of you is trying to sell the other a used car.

h. One of you is trying to persuade the other that you should live together.

8. Stanislavski said that spectators come to the theatre to hear the subtext, since they can read the text at home. As an exercise in discovering the subtext, or underlying meaning, of a scene and projecting it to an audience, look at Act IV of *The Cherry Orchard* by Anton Chekhov. Lopakhin, a merchant, wants to ask Varya, a young lady of twenty-four, to marry him, and she wants him to do this. The two are left alone briefly so that he may propose. They talk about various things but not about what is foremost in their thoughts before he is called and quickly leaves the room. Disregarding the actual lines of the text, improvise this scene concentrating on staying in character and thinking the thoughts that are in the minds of Lopakhin and Varya as they talk.

---

SCENE FOR ONE MAN, ONE WOMAN
FROM ACT III OF *A DOLL'S HOUSE*
(1879)

*By Henrik Ibsen*

Translated by William Archer

CHARACTERS: Torvald Helmer
Nora Helmer, his wife

SETTING: A room furnished comfortably and tastefully, but not extravagantly, in the Helmers' apartment.

TIME: Night, after a party; winter; 1879.

SITUATION: Earlier, when her husband had been ill and needed money, Nora had borrowed money from Krogstad and signed her dying father's name to the note. Shortly before the following excerpt, Torvald has received a letter from Krogstad revealing the forgery and threatening to expose Nora unless Torvald reinstated him in a position from which he had been dismissed. Torvald has upbraided his wife unmercifully until a second letter from Krogstad has arrived stating he had changed his mind. Now, Torvald has been ready to forgive Nora and forget the incident; but she has been so shocked by her husband's attitude that she has demanded that he sit down and talk with her. She has then said that she is leaving him.

COMMENTS: Nora is an attractive, doll-like, charming wife and mother. Torvald is the stolid, stuffy, master of the house. Because of this play's influence on women's rights, Nora's last exit has been called "the door slam heard around the world."

118

Helmer: Nora, you are ill, you are feverish. I almost think you are out of your senses.

Nora: I never felt so much clearness and certainty as to-night.

Helmer: You are clear and certain enough to forsake husband and children?

Nora: Yes, I am.

Helmer: Then there is only one explanation possible.

Nora: What is that?

Helmer: You no longer love me.

Nora: No, that is just it.

Helmer: Nora! Can you say so?

Nora: Oh, I'm so sorry, Torvald; for you've always been so kind to me. But I can't help it. I do not love you any longer.

Helmer: [keeping his composure with difficulty]. Are you clear and certain on this point too?

Nora: Yes, quite. That is why I won't stay here any longer.

Helmer: And can you also make clear to me, how I have forfeited your love?

Nora: Yes, I can. It was this evening when the miracle did not happen. For then I saw you were not the man I had taken you for.

Helmer: Explain youself more clearly; I don't understand.

Nora: I have waited so patiently all these eight years; for, of course, I saw clearly enough that miracles do not happen every day. When this crushing blow threatened me, I said to myself, confidently, "Now comes the miracle!" When Krogstad's letter lay in the box, it never occurred to me that you would think of submitting to that man's conditions. I was convinced that you would say to him, "Make it known to all the world," and that then——

Helmer: Well? When I had given my own wife's name up to disgrace and shame——?

Nora: Then I firmly believed that you would come forward, take everything upon yourself, and say, "I am the guilty one."

Helmer: Nora!

Nora: You mean I would never have accepted such a sacrifice? No, certainly not. But what would my assertions have been worth in opposition to yours? That was the miracle that I hoped for and dreaded. And it was to hinder that that I wanted to die.

Helmer: I would gladly work for you day and night, Nora—bear sorrow and want for your sake—but no man sacrifices his honor, even for one he loves.

Nora: Millions of women have done so.

Helmer: Oh, you think and talk like a silly child.

Nora: Very likely. But you neither think nor talk like the man I can share my life with. When your terror was over—not for me, but for yourself—when there was nothing more to fear,—then it was to you as though nothing had happened. I was your lark again, your doll—whom you would take twice as much care of in the future, because she was so weak and fragile. [Stands up.] Torvald, in that moment it burst upon me, that I had been living here these eight years with a strange man, and had borne him three children—Oh! I can't bear to think of it—I could tear myself to pieces!

Helmer: [sadly]. I see it, I see it; an abyss has opened between us—But, Nora, can it never be filled up?

**Nora:** As I now am, I am no wife for you.

**Helmer:** I have strength to become another man.

**Nora:** Perhaps—when your doll is taken away from you.

**Helmer:** To part—to part from you! No, Nora, no; I can't grasp the thought.

**Nora** *[going into room, right].* The more reason for the thing to happen. *[She comes back with out-door things and a small travelling bag, which she puts on a chair.]*

**Helmer:** Nora, Nora, not now! Wait till to-morrow.

**Nora:** *[putting on cloak].* I can't spend the night in a strange man's house.

**Helmer:** But can't we live here as brother and sister?

**Nora:** *[fastening her hat].* You know very well that would not last long. Good-by, Torvald. No, I won't go to the children. I know they are in better hands than mine. As I now am, I can be nothing to them.

**Helmer:** But some time, Nora—some time——

**Nora:** How can I tell? I have no idea what will become of me.

**Helmer:** But you are my wife, now and always?

**Nora:** Listen, Torvald—when a wife leaves her husband's house, as I am doing, I have heard that in the eyes of the law he is free from all the duties toward her. At any rate I release you from all duties. You must not feel yourself bound any more than I shall. There must be perfect freedom on both sides. There, there is your ring back. Give me mine.

**Helmer:** That too?

**Nora:** That too.

**Helmer:** Here it is.

**Nora:** Very well. Now it is all over. Here are the keys. The servants know about everything in the house, better than I do. To-morrow, when I have started, Christina will come to pack up my things. I will have them sent after me.

**Helmer:** All over! All over! Nora, will you never think of me again?

**Nora:** Oh, I shall often think of you, and the children—and this house.

**Helmer:** May I write to you, Nora?

**Nora:** No, never. You must not.

**Helmer:** But I must send you——

**Nora:** Nothing, nothing.

**Helmer:** I must help you if you need it.

**Nora:** No, I say. I take nothing from strangers.

**Helmer:** Nora, can I never be more than a stranger to you?

**Nora:** *[taking her travelling bag].* Oh, Torvald, then the miracle of miracles would have to happen.

**Helmer:** What is the miracle of miracles?

**Nora:** Both of us would have to change so that——Oh, Torvald, I no longer believe in miracles.

**Helmer:** But I will believe. We must so change that——

**Nora:** That communion between us shall be a marriage. Good-by. *[She goes out.]*

**Helmer:** *[sinks in a chair by the door with his face in his hands].* Nora! Nora! *[He looks around and stands up.]* Empty. She's gone! *[A hope inspires him.]* Ah! The miracle of miracles——?! *[From below is heard the reverberation of a heavy door closing.]*

## SCENE FOR TWO MEN, ONE WOMAN
## FROM ACT III OF *CANDIDA*
### (1895)

*By George Bernard Shaw*

CHARACTERS: The Reverend James Marvor Morell, a clergyman of the
                 Church of England
                 Candida Morell, his wife
                 Eugene Marchbanks, a young poet

SETTING: The Morells' drawing room in St. Dominic's parsonage.

TIME: After 10:00 P.M. on a night in October 1894.

SITUATION: Eugene has fallen in love with Candida; and in this excerpt, the
last part of the play, James asks Candida to choose between them.

COMMENTS: Morell is a vigorous, genial, popular clergyman of forty, robust
and good–looking, with pleasant, considerate manners and the voice of a prac-
ticed orator. Candida is a pretty, well-built woman of thirty-three with great
charm. Eugene is a shy youth of eighteen, slight, boyish, sensitive, and poetic.

**Candida:** Oh! I am to choose, am I? I suppose it is quite settled that I must
belong to one or the other.

**Morell:** *[firmly]* Quite. You must choose definitely.

**Marchbanks:** *[anxiously]* Morell: you dont understand. She means that she belongs to herself.

**Candida:** *[turning on him]* I mean that, and a good deal more, Master Eugene, as
you will both find out presently. And pray, my lords and masters, what have
you to offer for my choice? I am up for auction, it seems. What do you bid,
James?

**Morell:** *[reproachfully]* Cand— *[He breaks down: his eyes and throat fill with tears: the
orator becomes a wounded animal].* I cant speak—

**Candida:** *[impulsively going to him]* Ah, dearest—

**Marchbanks:** *[in wild alarm]* Stop: it's not fair. You musnt shew her that you
suffer, Morell. I am on the rack too; but I am not crying.

**Morell:** *[rallying all his forces]* Yes: you are right. It is not for pity that I am bidding. *[He disengages himself from Candida].*

**Candida:** *[retreating, chilled]* I beg your pardon, James: I did not mean to touch
you. I am waiting to hear your bid.

**Morell:** *[with proud humility]* I have nothing to offer you but my strength for your
defence, my honesty for your surety, my ability and industry for your
livelihood, and my authority and position for your dignity. That is all it becomes a man to offer to a woman.

**Candida:** *[quite quietly]* And you, Eugene? What do you offer?

**Marchbanks:** My weakness. My desolation. My heart's need.

**Candida:** *[impressed]* Thats a good bid, Eugene. Now I know how to make my
choice.

    *She pauses and looks curiously from one to the other, as if weighing them. Morell, whose lofty
      confidence has changed into heartbreaking dread at Eugene's bid, loses all power of con-
      cealing his anxiety. Eugene, strung to the highest tension, does not move a muscle.*

**Morell:** [in a suffocated voice: the appeal bursting from the depths of his anguish] Candida!

**Marchbanks:** [aside, in a flash of contempt] Coward!

**Candida:** [significantly] I give myself to the weaker of the two.

*Eugene divines her meaning at once: his face whitens like steel in a furnace.*

**Morell:** [bowing his head with the calm of collapse] I accept your sentence, Candida.

**Candida:** Do you understand, Eugene?

**Marchbanks:** Oh, I feel I'm lost. He cannot bear the burden.

**Morell:** [incredulously, raising his head and voice with comic abruptness] Do you mean me, Candida?

**Candida:** [smiling a little] Let us sit and talk comfortably over it like three friends. [To Morell] Sit down, dear. [Morell, quite lost, takes the chair from the fireside: the children's chair]. Bring me that chair, Eugene. [She indicates the easy chair. He fetches it silently, even with something like cold strength, and places it next Morell, a little behind him. She sits down. He takes the visitor's chair himself, and sits, inscrutable. When they are all settled she begins, throwing a spell of quietness on them by her calm, sane, tender tone]. You remember what you told me about yourself, Eugene: how nobody has cared for you since your old nurse died: how those clever fashionable sisters and successful brothers of yours were your mother's and father's pets: how miserable you were at Eton: how your father is trying to starve you into returning to Oxford: how you have had to live without comfort or welcome or refuge: always lonely, and nearly always disliked and misunderstood, poor boy!

**Marchbanks:** [faithful to the nobility of his lot] I had my books. I had Nature. And at last I met you.

**Candida:** Never mind that just at present. Now I want you to look at this other boy here: my boy! spoiled from his cradle. We go once a fortnight to see his parents. You should come with us, Eugene, to see the pictures of the hero of that household. James as a baby! the most wonderful of all babies. James holding his first school prize, won at the ripe age of eight! James as the captain of his eleven! James in his first frock coat! James under all sorts of glorious circumstances! You know how strong he is (I hope he didnt hurt you): how clever he is: how happy. [With deepening gravity] Ask James's mother and his three sisters what it cost to save James the trouble of doing anything but be strong and clever and happy. Ask me what it costs to be James's mother and three sisters and wife and mother to his children all in one. Ask Prossy and Maria how troublesome the house is even when we have no visitors to help us to slice the onions. Ask the tradesmen who want to worry James and spoil his beautiful sermons who it is that puts them off. When there is money to give, he gives it: when there is money to refuse, I refuse it. I build a castle of comfort and indulgence and love for him, and stand sentinel always to keep little vulgar cares out. I make him master here, though he does not know it, and could not tell you a moment ago how it came to be so. [With sweet irony] And when he thought I might go away with you, his only anxiety was—what should become of me! And to tempt me to stay he offered me [leaning forward to stroke his hair caressingly at each phrase] his strength for my defence! his industry for my livelihood! his dignity for my position! his— [relenting] ah, I am mixing up your beautiful cadences and spoiling them, am I not, darling? [She lays her cheek fondly against his].

**Morell:** *[quite overcome, kneeling beside her chair and embracing her with boyish ingenuousness]* It's all true, every word. What I am you have made me with the labor of your hands and the love of your heart. You are my wife, my mother, my sisters: you are the sum of all loving care to me.

**Candida:** *[in his arms, smiling, to Eugene]* Am I your mother and sisters to you, Eugene?

**Marchbanks:** *[rising with a fierce gesture of disgust]* Ah, never. Out, then, into the night with me!

**Candida:** *[rising quickly]* You are not going like that, Eugene?

**Marchbanks:** *[with the ring of a man's voice—no longer a boy's—in the words]* I know the hour when it strikes. I am impatient to do what must be done.

**Morell:** *[who has also risen]* Candida: don't let him do anything rash.

**Candida:** *[confident, smiling at Eugene]* Oh, there is no fear. He has learned to live without happiness.

**Marchbanks:** I no longer desire happiness: life is nobler than that. Parson James: I give you my happiness with both hands: I love you because you have filled the heart of the woman I loved. Goodbye. *[He goes towards the door]*.

**Candida:** One last word. *[He stops, but without turning to her. She goes to him]*. How old are you, Eugene?

**Marchbanks:** As old as the world now. This morning I was eighteen.

**Candida:** Eighteen! Will you, for my sake, make a little poem out of the two sentences I am going to say to you? And will you promise to repeat it to yourself whenever you think of me?

**Marchbanks:** *[without moving]* Say the sentences.

**Candida:** When I am thirty, she will be forty-five. When I am sixty, she will be seventy-five.

**Marchbanks:** *[turning to her]* In a hundred years, we shall be the same age. But I have a better secret than that in my heart. Let me go now. The night outside grows impatient.

**Candida:** Goodbye *[She takes his face in her hands; and as he divines her intention and falls on his knees, she kisses his forehead. Then he flies out into the night. She turns to Morell, holding out her arms to him]*. Ah, James!

*They embrace. But they do not know the secret in the poet's heart.*

---

### SCENE FOR THREE WOMEN
### FROM ACT III OF *THE THREE SISTERS*
(1901)

*By Anton Chekhov*

Translated by Eugene K. Bristow

CHARACTERS: Olga ⎫
             Masha ⎬ sisters of Andrey
             Irina ⎭
             Natasha, wife of Andrey (no lines)

SETTING: The bedroom of Olga and Irina. There are two beds, screens, and a sofa.

TIME: About 3:00 A.M.

SITUATION: A fire has burned a block of nearby houses, including the residence of the Vershinin family; and in the background a fire alarm bell is still striking. Under the leadership of Olga, they have tried to help the homeless. As they are resting from their efforts, Masha has stated how bored she is and angry at their brother for mortgaging their home. Masha's husband has just left the room to sit outside while Masha rests for half an hour. The Protopopov mentioned by Irina is the lover of Natasha.

COMMENTS: The youngest sister, Irina, who works for the City Council, is almost twenty-four. The baby of the family, she grows more dispirited during the play; and in this scene, she confides to her sisters just how miserable she is. Masha, the beautiful middle sister who is about a year older, married Kulygin as a young girl, thinking that he was a brilliant scholar rather than the boring schoolteacher he turned out to be. Olga, a schoolteacher of about thirty-one, runs the household, but Natasha is trying to take over control. Olga is thin, weary, and unhappy with her life as a spinster.

**Irina:** If the truth were said, our Andrey has been cut to pieces, lost whatever depth he had. Look how he's used up, how he's aged beyond his years living around that woman! At one time he was working to be a professor, but yesterday he was boasting how at last he's become a member of the District Council. Oh, yes, he's a member of the Council, but Protopopov is the chairman . . . The whole town is talking about it, laughing at him, and he's the only one who knows nothing and sees nothing . . . And at this very moment while everyone is running off to the fire, he sits in his room and pays no attention, none. Only sits playing his violin. *[Nervously.]* Oh, it's terrible, terrible, terrible! *[Weeps.]* I can't, I can't stand it any longer! . . . I can't, I can't! *[Olga enters, clears up around her little table. Irina sobs loudly.]* Throw me out, throw me out, I can't stand it any longer! . .

**Olga:** *[frightened]* What is it, what? My dearest!

**Irina:** *[sobbing]* Where? Where has it all gone? Where is it? Oh, dear God, dear God in Heaven! I've forgotten everything, forgotten . . . My head is all muddled up . . . I don't even remember the Italian for window or ceiling . . . I'm forgetting everything, every day I keep forgetting, and life is slipping away and will never come back, never, ever. And we shall never go to Moscow . . . I see that we won't go . . .

**Olga:** Dearest, dearest . . .

**Irina:** *[restraining herself]* Oh, I'm so unhappy. . . . I can't work, I won't work. Enough of working, enough! I was a telegraph clerk, now I work in the City Council. And I hate and despise everything they give me to do . . . I'm already twenty-three, I've been working for a long time, and my brain's drying up. I've grown thin, old, ugly, and nothing, nothing, nothing at all satisfies me. And time is slipping away, and you feel as if you're always moving away from a beautiful, genuine life, you're always moving further and further away into some kind of abyss. I've lost heart, why I'm still alive, why I haven't killed myself before now I don't understand . . .

**Olga:** Don't cry, dear little one, don't cry . . . It hurts me too.

**Irina:** I'm not crying, I'm not . . . Enough . . . Well, there, I've stopped crying. Enough . . . Enough!

**Olga:** Dearest, I'm going to talk to you as a sister, as a friend, if you want my advice, marry the Baron! [*Irina weeps quietly.*] You know you respect him, you think well of him, even highly . . . He's not good-looking, it's true, but he's so honest, pure . . . You know, don't you, a person doesn't marry for love, but only to do one's duty. At least, that's what I think, and I'd marry without love. If someone made me a proposal, so long as he were an honest person, it doesn't matter who, I'd marry him. I'd even marry an old man . . .

**Irina:** All the time I expected that we'd move to Moscow, there I'd meet the right man for me, the one I've dreamed about, the one I've come to love . . . But it's all turned out as nonsense, all, all nonsense . . .

**Olga:** [*embraces her sister*] My dear beautiful sister, I understand you, I do. When Baron Nikolay Lvovich resigned from the army and came to see us dressed in civilian clothes, he seemed so ugly to me I even started to cry . . . "Why are you crying?" he asked me. As if I could ever tell him! But if it's God's will for him to marry you, then I'd feel happy. You see that's a different matter, altogether different.

*Natasha, with a candle, enters through the right door, walks across the stage, and goes out through the left door. She does not speak.*

**Masha:** [*sitting up*] She keeps walking around, just as if she'd started the fire herself.

**Olga:** Masha, you are silly and stupid. The most stupid in our family—it's you. Forgive me, please. [*Pause.*]

**Masha:** My dear sisters, I've something I want to confess. It's tearing me apart inside, so I shall tell you two and then say nothing more to anyone, ever . . . I'll tell you now. [*Quietly.*] It's my secret, but you must know everything . . . I can keep silent no longer . . . [*Pause.*] I love, I love . . . I love that person . . . You saw him just now . . . Oh, why go on this way. To come to the point, I love Vershinin . . .

**Olga:** [*goes behind her screen*] Stop it. It doesn't matter, I'm not listening.

**Masha:** What can I do! [*Clutches her head.*] At the very beginning he seemed strange to me, then I felt sorry for him . . . then I fell in love . . . I fell in love with his voice, with his words, his misfortunes, his two little girls . . .

**Olga:** [*behind the screen*] It doesn't matter, I'm not listening. Whatever stupid things you say, it doesn't matter, I'm not listening.

**Masha:** Oh, you amaze me, Olga. I am in love, that's all there is to it. It's my fate. There's no other choice . . . And he loves me . . . It's all so frightening. Yes? It's not right, is it? [*Pulls Irina by the hand, draws her to her.*] Oh, my dear . . . how is it we shall live through the rest of our lives, what shall become of us . . . When you read a novel this sort of thing seems old and everything in it—so, so clear. But when you fall in love yourself, then you see for yourself that no one really and truly understands, and each person must come to a decision by himself . . . My dear, dear sisters . . . I've confessed everything to you, now I shall keep silent . . . I shall be like Gogol's madman now . . . silence . . . silence . . .

## SCENE FOR ONE MAN, ONE WOMAN
## FROM ACT II OF *THE LOWER DEPTHS*
### (1902)

### By Maxim Gorki

### Translated by Jenny Covan

CHARACTERS: Vassilisa Karpovna, wife of Kostilyoff
Vaska Pepel, a young thief
Anna, wife of Kleshtch (no lines)
Luka, an old hobo (no lines)
Milhail Ivanoff Kostilyoff, keeper of a flophouse (no lines)

SETTING: A dark Russian cellar, used as a flophouse for derelicts. The room has a Russian stove, bed, bunks, table, and benches, all of which are dirty and unpainted. A thin partition turns one corner of the stage into a room for Pepel.

TIME: A night in early spring.

SITUATION: Kostilyoff's wife, Vassilisa, is having an affair with Vaska Pepel, but the latter is in love with her younger sister, Natasha. Shortly before this excerpt, Vaska has entered slightly drunk, disheveled, and sullen. Two other people are onstage during this scene: Anna, who is dying, is lying in the bed, and Luka is in a bunk over the stove.

COMMENTS: Vassilisa, who is twenty-six, is unhappily married to a brutal older man, Kostilyoff. She takes out her frustrations by beating her younger sister. Vaska, twenty-eight, steals for Kostilyoff and Vassilisa, who act as his fence.


**Vassilisa:** [*calling from Pepel's room*]. Vaska—come here!

**Pepel:** I won't come—I don't want to . . .

**Vassilisa:** Why? What are you angry about?

**Pepel:** I'm sick of the whole thing . . .

**Vassilisa:** Sick of me, too?

**Pepel:** Yes! of you, too!

[*Vassilisa draws her shawl about her, pressing her hands over her breast. Crosses to Anna, looks carefully through the bed curtains, and returns to Pepel*]

Well—out with it!

**Vassilisa:** What do you want me to say? I can't force you to be loving, and I'm not the sort to beg for kindness. Thank you for telling me the truth.

**Pepel:** What truth?

**Vassilisa:** That you're sick of me—or isn't it the truth? [*Pepel looks at her silently. She turns to him*] What are you staring at? Don't you recognize me?

**Pepel:** [*sighing*]. You're beautiful, Vassilisa! [*She puts her arm about his neck, but he shakes it off*] But I never gave my heart to you. . . . I've lived with you and all that—but I never really liked you . . .

**Vassilisa:** [*quietly*]. That so? Well—?

**Pepel:** What is there to talk about? Nothing. Go away from me!

**Vassilisa:** Taken a fancy to some one else?

**Pepel:** None of your business! Suppose I have—I wouldn't ask you to be my match-maker!

**Vassilisa:** [significantly]. That's too bad . . . perhaps I might arrange a match . . .

**Pepel:** [suspiciously]. Who with?

**Vassilisa:** You know—why do you pretend? Vassily—let me be frank. [With lower voice] I won't deny it—you've offended me . . . it was like a bolt from the blue . . . you said you loved me—and then all of a sudden . . .

**Pepel:** It wasn't sudden at all. It's been a long time since I . . . woman, you've no soul! A woman must have a soul . . . we men are beasts—we must be taught—and you, what have you taught me—?

**Vassilisa:** Never mind the past! I know—no man owns his own heart—you don't love me any longer . . . well and good, it can't be helped!

**Pepel:** So that's over. We part peaceably, without a row—as it should be!

**Vassilisa:** Just a moment! All the same, when I lived with you, I hoped you'd help me out of this swamp—I thought you'd free me from my husband and my uncle—from all this life—and perhaps, Vassya, it wasn't you whom I loved—but my hope—do you understand? I waited for you to drag me out of this mire . . .

**Pepel:** You aren't a nail—and I'm not a pair of pincers! I thought you had brains—you are so clever—so crafty . . .

**Vassilisa:** [leaning closely towards him]. Vassa—let's help each other!

**Pepel:** How?

**Vassilisa:** [low and forcibly]. My sister—I know you've fallen for her . . .

**Pepel:** And that's why you beat her up, like the beast you are! Look out, Vassilisa! Don't you touch her!

**Vassilisa:** Wait. Don't get excited. We can do everything quietly and pleasantly. You want to marry her. I'll give you money . . . three hundred rubles—even more than that . . .

**Pepel:** [moving away from her]. Stop! What do you mean?

**Vassilisa:** Rid me of my husband! Take that noose from around my neck . . .

**Pepel:** [whistling softly]. So that's the way the land lies! You certainly planned it cleverly . . . in other words, the grave for the husband, the gallows for the lover, and as for yourself . . .

**Vassilisa:** Vassya! Why the gallows? It doesn't have to be yourself—but one of your pals! And supposing it were yourself—who'd know? Natalia—just think—and you'll have money—you go away somewhere . . . you free me forever—and it'll be very good for my sister to be away from me—the sight of her enrages me. . . . I get furious with her on account of you, and I can't control myself. I tortured the girl—I beat her up—beat her up so that I myself cried with pity for her—but I'll beat her—and I'll go on beating her!

**Pepel:** Beast! Bragging about your beastliness?

**Vassilisa:** I'm not bragging—I speak the truth. Think now, Vassa. You've been to prison twice because of my husband—through his greed. He clings to me like a bedbug—he's been sucking the life out of me for the last four years—and what sort of a husband is he to me? He's forever abusing Natasha—calls her a beggar—he's just poison, plain poison, to every one . . .

**Pepel:** You spin your yarn cleverly . . .

**Vassilisa:** Everything I say is true. Only a fool could be as blind as you . . .

    *[Kostilyoff enters stealthily and comes forward noisily]*

**Pepel:** *[to Vassilisa].* Oh—go away!

**Vassilisa:** Think it over!

# Chapter Ten

# Departures
# from Realism

Realism has continued to be the dominant style in our theatre since the nineteenth century, but other styles have been conceived by artists and writers to challenge realism's supremacy. In this chapter, we shall consider symbolism, expressionism, epic theatre, and theatre of the absurd.

## PLAYS

**Symbolism.** This style came into the theatre about 1880 in France as a reaction against naturalism. Naturalists had banished the poetic and the spiritual from the stage and had substituted the sordid, crude, and ugly. Some playwrights and designers felt that mere verisimilitude was not enough, that the theatre should concern itself with the deeper meaning of life rather than superficial exteriors, and that poetry and beauty should once again be on the stage. Through the use of symbols, they hoped to suggest ideas and feelings that are difficult to express in words.

Henrik Ibsen (1828–1906), who brought realism to prominence, used symbolism in *The Wild Duck* (1884), *The Lady from the Sea* (1889), *The Master Builder* (1892), *Little Eyolf* (1894), *John Gabriel Borkman* (1896), and *When We Dead Awaken* (1899).

Others joined the symbolistic movement: Belgium's Maurice Maeterlinck (1862–1949), Austria's Hugo von Hofmannsthal (1874–

1929), Ireland's William Butler Yeats (1865–1939), Spain's Federico García Lorca (1899–1936), and others.

Symbolistic plays are often poetic and beautiful, but the meaning of the plots is sometimes vague and obscure so that audiences may be mystified by the symbolism. Generally, these dramas do not adhere to the unities of time, place, and action; they use type characters who are controlled by fate; and the mood and atmosphere are designed to give feelings of unreality.

As a conscious theatrical movement, symbolism was, more or less, over by the early years of the twentieth century; but its influence has affected later playwriting.

**Expressionism.**   A later development of symbolism was expressionism, an angry revolt against realism and the mechanized, dehumanized life of man.

While a writer's expression may take different forms, often the protagonist, representing the playwright, is searching for a better life; and as the protagonist becomes more disturbed and tortured by events and society, the acting, scenery, lighting, costumes, and sound get more distorted or exaggerated to represent how the protagonist sees the world.

Since most of these writers wanted social changes, the themes are strongly presented so that the audience will get the message. The authors used such theatrical devices as a chorus, a narrator, music, dancing, soliloquies, and unusual sounds and technical effects. Typically there are many symbols and episodes, some dreamlike in quality, which build to a major climax. The dialogue may vary from long, passionate speeches to short, choppy lines. Often the hero is the only psychologically motivated character, with others seen as automatons or abstractions that represent elements of society.

The term *expressionism* had first been used in art, but it was not until about 1910 in Germany that the label was applied to playwriting. The best-known German expressionists are Ernst Toller (1893–1939) and Georg Kaiser (1878–1945). In Ireland, Sean O'Casey (1880–1964) changed from realism to expressionism for *The Silver Tassie* (1928), *Within the Gates* (1934), *Red Roses for Me* (1943), and *Purple Dust* (1945). Writers from the United States who tried this genre include Elmer Rice (1892–1967) in *The Adding Machine* (1923); Eugene O'Neill (1888–1953) in *The Emperor Jones* (1920), *The Hairy Ape* (1922), *Lazarus Laughed* (1927), and *Days Without End* (1934); and Marc Connelly (1890–1980) and George S. Kaufman (1889–1961) in *Beggar on Horseback* (1924).

By the end of the 1920s, the expressionistic movement in the theatre was over, but it, too, had great influence on later writers.

**Epic Theatre.**   A form of expressionistic drama that is highly didactic is epic theatre, which was developed by Bertolt Brecht (1898–1956) and

Erwin Piscator (1893–1966) in the 1920s in Germany. It was, in part, inspired by the Oriental theatre.

The aim of epic theatre is to present a demonstration of some aspect of society that is epic in scope. The plot structure consists of a series of episodes, interspersed with narration and songs, that make no attempt to achieve suspense or a climax.

Brecht advocated alienation or detachment (deliberately reminding spectators that they are in a theatre so that they will not empathize with the actors), historification (placing the events of the play in the past or distant places to make them strange to the audience), and theatrical devices (songs, narration, films, signs, and the like) to remind spectators that it is a play so that they will think objectively about the theme and be moved to action outside the theatre.

Brecht wrote many shows, but his biggest successes in the United States have been *The Threepenny Opera* (1928), which has music by Kurt Weill, *Mother Courage and Her Children* (1939), *The Good Woman of Setzuan* (1940), *The Caucasian Chalk Circle* (1945), and *Galileo* (final version in 1947).

In the United States, Thornton Wilder (1897–1975) produced *Our Town* in 1938 and *The Skin of Our Teeth* in 1942, both of which are similar in style to epic theatre. In Germany and Switzerland, Brecht had great influence on later writers like Peter Weiss (1916–    ), Max Frisch (1911–    ), and Friedrich Duerrenmatt (1921–    ), on documentary drama, and the theatre of fact.

**Theatre of the Absurd.**   Martin Esslin, who gave this style its name, traced the theatre of the absurd back to the ancient mimes, the *commedia dell'arte*, the Keystone Kops, and the Marx brothers, among others. But three men living in Paris after World War II are called the prime exponents of this style: they are Beckett, Ionesco, and Genet.

Samuel Beckett (1906–    ) from Ireland was the first to attract attention to this style in 1953, when *Waiting for Godot* was produced at a small Parisian theatre. Other plays by Beckett include *Endgame* (1957), *Krapp's Last Tape* (1958), *Happy Days* (1961), *Play* (1963), *Come and Go* (1966), *Not I* (1972), and *That Time* (1976).

Eugène Ionesco (1912–    ), Rumanian-born French playwright, who calls his comedies "anti-plays," "pseudo-dramas," or "tragic farces," created *The Bald Soprano* and *The Lesson* in 1950, *The Chairs* in 1951, *Victims of Duty, The New Tenant,* and *Amédée* in 1953, *Rhinoceros* in 1960, *Exit the King* in 1962, *Macbett* in 1972, and *The Man with the Suitcase* in 1975.

Jean Genet (1910–    ) from France wrote *The Maids* (1947), *Deathwatch* (1948), *The Balcony* (1956), *The Blacks* (1958), and *The Screens* (1961).

These are strange and puzzling plays, devoid of traditional plot structure, characters, and realistic dialogue and actions, that offer a grotesque, symbolical, satirical comment on life. The authors do not wish to expound a thesis or tell a story but to communicate poetic images of a disintegrating world that has lost its meaning, its purpose. They hope to immerse the audience in a total dramatic situation in which man's fears, shames, obsessions, and hopes are acted out in an atmosphere as absorbing as a dream or a carnival or a mass.

Characters are mere types, devoid of personality, frequently without names, who act illogically and irrationally. The language often disagrees with the action, is meaningless, and shows the characters' inability to communicate. Absurdist writers devalue language, and usually more meaning is obtained from the action than the dialogue.

Among writers whose plays show some absurdist influence is Harold Pinter (1930–    ) from England. His works *The Room* (1957), *The Dumb Waiter* (1957), *The Birthday Party* (1958), *The Caretaker* (1960), *The Homecoming* (1965), *Old Times* (1970), *No Man's Land* (1975), *Betrayal* (1978), and *The Hothouse* (1980) are sometimes called comedies of menace, but Pinter has said that he does not like to have any definitive label applied to his plays.

Another major English playwright is Tom Stoppard (1937–    ), who in 1967 finished *Rosencrantz and Guildenstern are Dead*, which has been called a cross between Shakespeare's *Hamlet* and Beckett's *Waiting for Godot*. Other Stoppard plays are *The Real Inspector Hound* (1968), *Jumpers* (1972), *Travesties* (1974), *Dirty Linen* (1976), *Night and Day* (1979), and *The Real Thing* (1983).

In the United States, Edward Albee (1928–    ) wrote *The Zoo Story* (1959), *The Sandbox* (1960), *Tiny Alice* (1964), *A Delicate Balance* (1966), *Seascape* (1974), and *The Lady from Dubuque* (1979), which show some influence from the theatre of the absurd; however, his biggest success has been *Who's Afraid of Virginia Woolf?* (1962), which is more realistic in style than the others.

## PRODUCTIONS THEN

**Symbolism.** The symbolists wanted simplicity of setting and costumes that were unrealistic and of no particular time or country, so they could apply to any period and place. The object of a symbolistic design was to create atmosphere, mood, and dramatic intensity, not naturalistic details. The aim was to make spectators lose themselves in an imaginary world or in a mystical experience.

Three major designers contributed ideas as to how the symbolists' aims could be achieved: Adolphe Appia (1862–1928) from Switzerland; Gordon Craig (1872–1966) from England; and Robert Edmond Jones (1887–1954) from the United States. In general, they wanted simplification; a proper relationship between actor and background; suggestion, as when one prop may be used in place of a large realistic set; and the complete fusion of set, lights, actors, and play. With lighting effects that enhanced the mood, the result was great visual beauty on the stage.

**Expressionism.** Whereas symbolism brought beauty to the stage, expressionistic designers featured the striking, explosive, macabre, and often spectacular. When the protagonist met frustration and troubles, certain changes in set, lighting, sound, costumes, and acting might take place to show how the central character perceived the environment. The scenery might acquire exaggerated shapes, abnormal colorings, tilting walls, or unusual sizes; and actors might change to bizarre costumes and makeup or grotesque masks. As examples, in a scene from *From Morn till Midnight* (1912) by Georg Kaiser, a tree changes into a skeleton as the protagonist makes a long, impassioned speech. In Elmer Rice's *The Adding Machine* (1923), when the protagonist is fired from a job he has held for twenty-five years, the playwright calls for the platform to revolve rapidly, for music and all sorts of sound effects to swell to a deafening roar that changes to a loud clap of thunder, a flash of red, and then a blackout.

Rhythm was a dominant element, found in the repetition of the same sound or movement or choral chant. The actors might move in nonrealistic, unpredictable ways that were frankly theatrical and presentational; and unnatural speech, such as "telegraphic," might be used to give the impression of a mechanized, chaotic world.

**Epic Theatre.** In 1935 in Moscow, Brecht saw the Chinese actor Mei-Lan-Fang perform, and Brecht admired this actor who seemed to stand aside from his part and make it clear that he knew he was being observed. In writing about detachment, Brecht described the Chinese actor's methods and said that he wanted performers to show both themselves and the characters to the audience; to think of their parts in the third person; to present the behavior of the characters to the audience in a kind of demonstration that comments upon the actions and the characters. Brecht hoped that, if the actor remained detached from the character, the audience would not empathize and, thus, would view the action objectively and think about the ideas of the play. To aid detachment, Brecht wrote the scripts so that characters leave a scene periodically to address the audience or sing a song.

However, despite this aim of detachment, audiences have been affected emotionally by good performances of a moving play like *Mother Courage and Her Children;* and when members of Brecht's own company were questioned about how they prepared their parts, they stated that they did not approach roles in his plays differently from those by other writers.

To Brecht, a stage set should help explain the theme of the play, not create a mood. It should be unrealistic, theatrical, and mobile, and should present the environment of the play in a way that the audience will find strange and unfamiliar. Only those items that are needed by the action should be onstage. Then, to change locale quickly, designers should use revolving stages, wagons, treadmills, escalators, elevators, projections of films and slides, fragmentary sets, and signs. Furthermore, musicians, lighting equipment, and machinery for changing sets should be completely visible to the audience, so that spectators are reminded continually that they are in a theatre.

Lighting should only be used to illuminate, never to develop a mood; and costumes should only vaguely suggest the locale and type of person. In some scripts, he calls for masks to be worn.

Epic theatre's staging methods have been tried throughout the world, and its influence is easily seen in the current multimedia productions and other forms.

**Theatre of the Absurd.** In the 1950s, the first plays of the French absurdists were introduced in small Parisian theatres that could present them cheaply. Later, when this style became popular in France, larger theatres produced them. It is difficult to generalize about past productions of these plays because each play is unique and demands an individual approach. Also, subsequent directors and designers have found different aspects to emphasize, with the result that these plays have been presented in many ways.

## PRODUCTIONS NOW

**Symbolism.** When a symbolistic play is done today, the type of staging depends on the amount of symbolism in the play. When the play is basically realistic with just a few symbols, such as Ibsen's *The Wild Duck,* the style of production may be realistic or selective realistic. However, when symbolism pervades the entire script, as in Maeterlinck's *Pelléas and Mélisande,* the set designer will probably want the style of impressionism, in which the mood of the scene is heightened in an atmospheric but unrealistic way, or symbolism, in which a fragment of a set or prop may stand for the entire locale. In any event, the choice will probably be beautiful settings, in which lighting will be of great importance to create the right mood.

For costumes, the designer will probably select historically accurate clothing for *The Wild Duck,* but the costumes for *Pelléas and Mélisande* may be of such a general design that they do not indicate any particular country or period.

The acting for *The Wild Duck* should be realistic. The acting in *Pelléas and Mélisande* should probably be realistic today; but when it was first acted in 1893, the actors chanted their lines and used unnatural gestures to make the play as unrealistic as possible. Today, the option should be the director's as to how unrealistic the production should appear.

**Expressionism.** Expressionistic plays demand exciting, imaginative sets, costumes, lighting, and props. To communicate to an audience the author's intent, the visual and aural elements must reinforce the condition of the protagonist. Fragmentary sets can be used, as they often were originally, but they and the costumes and makeup should become more fantastic as the protagonist gets more disturbed. Unrealistic, strange lighting and sound may also emphasize the protagonist's confusion.

The actor may be challenged to move and speak in nonrealistic ways, such as being part of a machine, a robot, or a puppet. While the protagonist may have realistic qualities, others may be dehumanized stereotypes; yet they must be appealing enough to interest an audience. Above all, actors should be certain that the meaning of the play is communicated.

**Epic Theatre.** Plays in this style profit from unrealistic, theatrical staging similar to that used originally since there are many scenes and it is necessary to move easily from one locale to another. Costumes may have some authentic elements, but for the most part, they need only suggest the period or place. Masks or unusual makeups may be used.

As for acting, Brecht said there are three devices that can contribute to the alienation of the words and actions for the actor: in early rehearsals, the actor should: first, change the dialogue from first to third person; second, change the dialogue from present to past tense; and third, read all stage directions aloud. In later rehearsals, the actor should keep these feelings of detachment as he or she begins to use the lines as written in the script. Brecht wanted the actor to observe the character; be surprised at what the character does; demonstrate the character's actions; but not identify with the role. He thought that the actor should stand between the audience and the part. Note how different this is from Stanislavski's System of acting.

Actually, the director is the one who must decide whether actors should empathize with or remain detached from their characters; but it is important that actors understand Brecht's alienation or detachment concept whether or not they are ever called upon to use it.

**Theatre of the Absurd.** To find your approach to an absurdist play, study the entire script carefully to determine the author's theme and viewpoint. Decide whether the purpose is to get laughs, arouse horror, show despair, appear grotesque, or whatever it may be. Examine any stage directions in detail.

In some plays the set may at first appear to be realistic; but as the show progresses it may become strange and unrealistic, where the scenery and objects may move and seemingly come to life. In *The New Tenant*, Ionesco stipulates that everything should be realistic at the beginning, but later the rhythm should accelerate and there should be a dreamlike state. Then, near the end, the style should become realistic again.

Many of these plays have dreamlike qualities; for example, in *Deathwatch* Genet says that the entire play should unfold as in a dream. He also states that the set and costumes should be in violent colors and that the movements of actors should be either heavy or else extremely and incomprehensibly rapid, like flashes of lightning. He asked actors, if they could, to deaden the timbre of their voices.

The acting in many of these works may appear realistic, although the actors may be asked to do strange things, such as in *The New Tenant* when the furniture movers handle heavy furniture with ease but strain to carry a small vase. Ionesco did not like what Brecht and Piscator had done to the actor in epic theatre. Ionesco thought that they had squashed the actor's initiative. He did not want the actor to be dehumanized, but he said that actors must not be afraid of not being natural.

In many of these plays, actors cannot be natural. For example, in *Interview*, the first of three short plays in *America Hurrah!* (1966) by Jean-Claude van Itallie, four interviewers at the beginning, wearing masks and speaking quickly without expression, should appear dehumanized. Later, both the interviewers and four applicants change instantaneously from one character to another (this is called a "transformation") and from one locale to the next without actual change of costumes or set. At the end, all eight characters speak and move like mechanical dolls. In the third play, entitled *Motel*, actors are inside large dolls.

To present an absurdist play, remember that the avowed aim of these dramatists is to bring theatricality into the theatre. In this enchanted place of the stage anything can happen—reality can flow into dreams and back to reality—and the unexpected, the grotesque, the illogical may occur.

## SUGGESTED READING

Bablet, Denis. *Edward Gordon Craig.* New York: Theatre Arts Books, 1967.

Barzun, Jacques. *Classic, Romantic, and Modern.* Garden City, N.Y.: Anchor Books, 1961.

Brecht, Bertolt. *Brecht on Theatre.* Tr. by John Willett. New York: Hill and Wang, 1965.

Brockett, Oscar G., and Robert R. Findlay. *Century of Innovation.* Englewood Cliffs, N.J.: Prentice-Hall, Inc., 1973.

Brustein, Robert. *Theatre of Revolt, An Approach to Modern Drama.* Boston: Atlantic Monthly Press, 1964.

Cornell, Kenneth. *The Symbolist Movement.* New Haven, Conn.: Yale University Press, 1951.

Corrigan, Robert W. (ed.). *The Modern Theatre.* New York: The Macmillan Company, 1964.

Esslin, Martin. *Brecht, the Man and His Work.* New York: Doubleday, 1960.

———. *The Theatre of the Absurd.* Garden City, N.Y.: Anchor Books, 1961.

Gray, Ronald. *Brecht.* New York: Grove Press, 1961.

Grossvogel, David. *Brecht, Ionesco, Beckett, Genet: Four Playwrights and a Postscript.* Ithaca: Cornell University Press, 1962.

Ionesco, Eugène. *Notes and Counter Notes: Writings on the Theatre.* Tr. by Donald Watson. New York: Grove Press, 1964.

Volbach, Walther. *Adolphe Appia, Prophet of the Modern Theatre.* Middletown, Conn.: Wesleyan University Press, 1968.

Willet, John. *Expressionism.* New York: McGraw-Hill Book Co., Inc., 1970.

———. *The Theatre of Bertolt Brecht.* New York: New Directions, 1959.

## EXERCISES

As preparation for acting in symbolistic, expressionistic, epic theatre, and absurdist plays, work on the following exercises:

1. Move as a puppet with strings attached to your head, elbows, wrists, and knees. As an observer calls out which string is being pulled, move the affected part of your body.
2. Move as a robot. Meet other mechanical people, bow, and talk to them in a nonrealistic voice.
3. Look at an expressionistic painting of a person by Vincent van Gogh or Paul Gauguin, and then create an improvisation involving this person.
4. Follow Brecht's suggestions as listed in this chapter for an actor's detachment or alienation from a role. Read aloud a scene from a Brecht play changing the dialogue from first to third person and from present to past tense; read aloud all stage directions. Later, say the lines as written, but try to keep a detached feeling.
5. To further practice Brecht's ideas on detachment, report to other actors about an incident that you observed recently but were not involved in, such as a fire, an automobile accident, or a fight. Report what happened unemotionally and demonstrate what occurred to the participants.
6. Some plays call for "transformations," which are fast changes of characterization. Practice walking across a stage as one of the first characters listed below; offstage quickly assume a second characterization before walking back across the stage.

137

| First Character | Second Character |
|---|---|
| Beggar | Business executive |
| Military person on leave | Blind person |
| Thief with stolen money | Religious leader |
| Shopper carrying heavy bags | Child with a ball |
| Crippled person | King or queen |

7. Some plays call for "transformations" to take place onstage. As a group exercise, move and speak as the following, changing to the next after about two minutes:
   a. Children playing games.
   b. Teenagers dancing.
   c. Middle-aged people working in a factory.
   d. Elderly people in a home for the aged.
8. Two actors should work together to improvise short scenes to demonstrate the following styles. In all four improvisations, two characters should meet in a park by accident and talk about their lives.
   a. Symbolism.
   b. Expressionism.
   c. Epic theatre.
   d. Theatre of the absurd.
9. Other situations for two or more actors to use for improvisations to demonstrate the above four styles are:
   a. Shopping in a supermarket.
   b. Getting dressed in a dormitory.
   c. Playing "trick or treat" on Halloween.
   d. Playing a video game.
   e. Being interviewed for a job.

---

## SCENE FOR ONE MAN, ONE WOMAN
### FROM ACT II, SCENE 1 OF *PELLÉAS AND MÉLISANDE* (1893)

*By Maurice Maeterlinck*

Translated by Richard Hovey

CHARACTERS: Mélisande, wife of Golaud
Pelléas, half-brother of Golaud
SETTING: A fountain in the park.
TIME: Shortly before noon.
SITUATION: Prince Golaud, an older man, discovered Mélisande in a forest and married her; but when Mélisande met Golaud's young, handsome half-brother, Pelléas, they became attracted to each other.

COMMENTS: Mélisande and Pelléas are good-looking young lovers. Notice the symbols in the following excerpt: the spring that opens the eyes of the blind and Mélisande's losing her wedding ring in the water. Note, too, the fairy-tale, mysterious atmosphere in which fate controls the action.

**Pelléas:** You do not know where I have brought you?—I often come to sit here, toward noon, when it is too hot in the gardens. It is stifling today, even in the shade of the trees.

**Mélisande:** Oh, how clear the water is! . . .

**Pelléas:** It is as cool as winter. It is an old abandoned spring. It seems to have been a miraculous spring—it opened the eyes of the blind—they still call it "Blind Man's Spring."

**Mélisande:** It no longer opens the eyes of the blind?

**Pelléas:** Since the King has been nearly blind himself, no one comes any more. . . .

**Mélisande:** How alone one is here! . . . . There is no sound.

**Pelléas:** There is always a wonderful silence here. . . . One could hear the water sleep. . . . Will you sit down on the edge of the marble basin? There is one linden where the sun never comes . . . .

**Mélisande:** I am going to lie down on the marble.—I should like to see the bottom of the water . . . .

**Pelléas:** No one has ever seen it. It is as deep, perhaps, as the sea. It is not known whence it comes. Perhaps it comes from the bottom of the earth . . . .

**Mélisande:** If there were anything shining at the bottom, perhaps one could see it . . . .

**Pelléas:** Do not lean over so . . . .

**Mélisande:** I would like to touch the water . . . .

**Pelléas:** Have a care of slipping. . . . I will hold your hand . . . .

**Mélisande:** No, no, I would plunge both hands in it. . . . You would say my hands were sick today . . . .

**Pelléas:** Oh! oh! take care! take care!
Mélisande! . . . . Mélisande! . . . Oh! your hair! . . .

**Mélisande:** *[starting upright].* I cannot . . . I cannot reach it . . . .

**Pelléas:** Your hair dipped in the water . . . .

**Mélisande:** Yes, it is longer than my arms . . . . It is longer than I . . . .
*[A silence]*

**Pelléas:** It was at the brink of a spring, too, that he found you?

**Mélisande:** Yes . . . .

**Pelléas:** What did he say to you?

**Mélisande:** Nothing;—I no longer remember . . . .

**Pelléas:** Was he quite near you?

**Mélisande:** Yes; he would have kissed me.

**Pelléas:** And you would not?

**Mélisande:** No.

**Pelléas:** Why would you not?

**Mélisande:** Oh! oh! I saw something pass at the bottom of the water . . . .

Pelléas: Take care! take care!—You will fall! What are you playing with?

Mélisande: With the ring he gave me.

Pelléas: Take care; you will lose it . . . .

Mélisande: No, no; I am sure of my hands . . . .

Pelléas: Do not play so, over so deep a water . . . .

Mélisande: My hands do not tremble.

Pelléas: How it shines in the sunlight! Do not throw it so high in the air . . . .

Mélisande: Oh! . . .

Pelléas: It has fallen?

Mélisande: It has fallen into the water!

Pelléas: Where is it? where is it? . . .

Mélisande: I do not see it sink! . . .

Pelléas: I think I see it shine . . . .

Mélisande: My ring?

Pelléas: Yes, yes; down yonder . . . .

Mélisande: Oh! oh! It is so far away from us! . . . no, no, that is not it . . . that is not it . . . It is lost . . . lost . . . . There is nothing any more but a great circle on the water . . . . What shall we do? What shall we do now? . . .

Pelléas: You need not be so troubled for a ring. It is nothing . . . . We shall find it again, perhaps. Or else we shall find another . . . .

Mélisande: No, no; we shall never find it again; we shall never find any others either . . . . And yet I thought I had it in my hands . . . . I had already shut my hands, and it is fallen in spite of all . . . . I threw it too high, toward the sun . . . .

Pelléas: Come, come, we will come back another day; . . . come, it is time. They will come to meet us. It was striking noon at the moment the ring fell.

Mélisande: What shall we say to Golaud if he asks where it is?

Pelléas: The truth, the truth, the truth . . . . [Exeunt]

---

SCENE FOR ONE MAN, ONE WOMAN
FROM SCENE 2 OF *THE ADDING MACHINE*
(1923)

*By Elmer Rice*

CHARACTERS: Mr. Zero
Daisy Diana Dorothea Devore

SETTING: In the middle of an office in a department store are two tall desks, back to back. At one desk on a high stool is Mr. Zero. Facing him at the other desk on a high stool is Miss Devore. A lamp throws light upon both desks.

TIME: Near quitting time; 1923.

SITUATION: Both wear green eye shades and paper sleeve protectors as Daisy reads figures from a pile of slips and Mr. Zero enters them upon a large sheet of paper with a pen. As they work, both are thinking of other things. Unhappily married, he is remembering a girl he used to watch who lived nearby; and when he says the line, "Gee, I wish I'd gone over there that night," he is referring to this girl. Daisy is thinking about suicide. Both attend closely to their work. Throughout, each intones figures during the other's speeches.

COMMENTS: Daisy is a plain, middle-aged, single woman. Mr. Zero is thin, sallow, undersized, partially bald, and middle-aged. You may want to consider wearing masks while speaking to each other and removing them while saying the thoughts.


**Daisy:** Six dollars. Three fifteen. Two twenty-five. Sixty-five cents. A dollar twenty. You talk to me as if I was dirt.

**Zero:** I wonder if I could kill the wife without anybody findin' out. In bed some night. With a pillow.

**Daisy:** I used to think you was stuck on me.

**Zero:** I'd get found out, though. They always have ways.

**Daisy:** We used to be so nice and friendly together when I first came here. You used to talk to me then.

**Zero:** Maybe she'll die soon. I noticed she was coughin' this mornin'.

**Daisy:** You used to tell me all kinds o' things. You were goin' to show them all. Just the same, you're still sittin' here.

**Zero:** Then I could do what I damn please. Oh, boy!

**Daisy:** Maybe it ain't all your fault neither. Maybe if you'd had the right kind o' wife—somebody with a lot of common-sense, somebody refined—me!

**Zero:** At that, I guess I'd get tired of bummin' around. A feller wants some place to hang his hat.

**Daisy:** I wish she would die.

**Zero:** And when you start goin' with women you're liable to get into trouble. And lose your job maybe.

**Daisy:** Maybe you'd marry me.

**Zero:** Gee, I wish I'd gone over there that night.

**Daisy:** Then I could quit workin'.

**Zero:** Lots o' women would be glad to get me.

**Daisy:** You could look a long time before you'd find a sensible, refined girl like me.

**Zero:** Yes, sir, they could look a long time before they'd find a steady meal-ticket like me.

**Daisy:** I guess I'd be too old to have any kids. They say it ain't safe after thirty-five.

**Zero:** Maybe I'd marry you. You might be all right, at that.

**Daisy:** I wonder—if you don't want kids—whether—if there's any way————

**Zero** [Looking up]: Hey! Hey! Can't you slow up? What do you think I am—a machine?

**Daisy** [Looking up]: Say, what do you want, anyhow? First it's too slow an' then it's too fast. I guess you don't know what you want.

**Zero:** Well, never mind about that. Just you slow up.

**Daisy:** I'm gettin' sick o' this. I'm goin' to ask to be transferred.

**Zero:** Go ahead. You can't make me mad.

**Daisy:** Aw, keep quiet. *[She reads]:* Two forty-five. A dollar twenty. A dollar fifty. Ninety cents. Sixty-three cents.

**Zero:** Marry you! I guess not! You'd be as bad as the one I got.

**Daisy:** You wouldn't care if I did ask. I got a good mind to ask.

**Zero:** I was a fool to get married.

**Daisy:** Then I'd never see you at all.

**Zero:** What chance has a guy got with a woman tied around his neck?

**Daisy:** That time at the store picnic—the year your wife couldn't come—you were nice to me then.

**Zero:** Twenty-five years holdin' down the same job!

**Daisy:** We were together all day—just sittin' around under the trees.

**Zero:** I wonder if the boss remembers about it bein' twenty-five years.

**Daisy:** And comin' home that night—you sat next to me in the big delivery wagon.

**Zero:** I got a hunch there's a big raise comin' to me.

**Daisy:** I wonder what it feels like to be really kissed. Men—dirty pigs! They want the bold ones.

**Zero:** If he don't come across I'm goin' right up to the front office and tell him where he gets off.

**Daisy:** I wish I was dead.

**Zero:** "Boss," I'll say, "I want to have a talk with you." "Sure," he'll say, "sit down. Have a Corona Corona." "No," I'll say, "I don't smoke." "How's that?" he'll say. "Well, boss," I'll say, "it's this way. Every time I feel like smokin' I just take a nickel and put it in the old sock. A penny saved is a penny earned, that's the way I look at it." "Damn sensible," he'll say. "You got a wise head on you, Zero."

**Daisy:** I can't stand the smell of gas. It makes me sick. You coulda kissed me if you wanted to.

**Zero:** "Boss," I'll say, "I ain't quite satisfied. I been on the job twenty-five years now and if I'm gonna stay I gotta see a future ahead of me." "Zero," he'll say, "I'm glad you came in. I've had my eye on you, Zero. Nothin' gets by me." "Oh, I know that, boss," I'll say. That'll hand him a good laugh, that will. "You're a valuable man, Zero," he'll say, "and I want you right up here with me in the front office. You're done addin' figgers. Monday mornin' you move up here."

**Daisy:** Them kisses in the movies—them long ones—right on the mouth———

**Zero:** I'll keep a-goin' right on up after that. I'll show some of them birds where they get off.

**Daisy:** That one the other night—"The Devil's Alibi"—he put his arms around her—and her head fell back and her eyes closed—like she was in a daze.

**Zero:** Just give me about two years and I'll show them birds where they get off.

**Daisy:** I guess that's what it's like—a kinda daze—when I see them like that, I just seem to forget everything.

**Zero:** Then me for a place in Jersey. And maybe a little Buick. No tin Lizzie for mine. Wait till I get started—I'll show 'em.

**Daisy:** I can see it now when I kinda half-close my eyes. The way her head fell back. And his mouth pressed right up against hers. Oh, Gawd! it must be grand! *[There is a sudden shrill blast from a steam whistle.]*

**Daisy and Zero:** *[Together]* The whistle!

*[With great agility they get off their stools, remove their eye shades and sleeve protectors and put them on the desks. Then each produces from behind the desk a hat—Zero, a dusty derby, Daisy, a frowsy straw . . . Daisy puts on her hat and turns toward Zero as though she were about to speak to him. But he is busy cleaning his pen and pays no attention to her. She sighs and goes toward the door at the left.]*

**Zero:** *[Looking up]:* G'night, Miss Devore. *[But she does not hear him and exits. Zero takes up his hat and goes left.]*

---

### SCENE FOR ONE MAN, ONE WOMAN
### FROM SCENE 3 OF *THE GOOD WOMAN*
### *OF SETZUAN*
### (1940)

*By Bertolt Brecht*

Translated by Eric Bentley

CHARACTERS: Shen Te, a shopkeeper
                   Yang Sun, an unemployed pilot

SETTING: The municipal park in Setzuan, China.

TIME: Evening.

SITUATION: Shen Te, a former prostitute, was rewarded by three gods for being a virtuous person. With this money, she has bought a tobacco shop; but because her generous nature has made her help the less fortunate, she has had to impersonate an imaginary evil cousin, Mr. Shui Ta, to keep her business solvent. Before this excerpt begins, Yang Sun has thrown a rope around a branch of a willow tree.

COMMENTS: Yang Sun is a young man who is dressed in rags. He is thirsty, hungry, and penniless. Shen Te is a good, soft-hearted girl who treats all honorably.

**Yang Sun:** Well, what are you staring at?

**Shen Te:** That rope. What is it for?

**Yang Sun:** Think! Think! I haven't a penny. Even if I had, I wouldn't spend it on you. I'd buy a drink of water.
*[The rain starts.]*

**Shen Te:** *[still looking at the rope]* What is the rope for? You mustn't!

**Yang Sun:** What's it to you? Clear out!

**Shen Te:** *[irrelevantly]* It's raining.

**Yang Sun:** Well, don't try to come under this tree.

**Shen Te:** Oh, no. *[She stays in the rain.]*

**Yang Sun:** Now go away. *[pause]* For one thing, I don't like your looks, you're bowlegged.

**Shen Te:** *[indignantly]* That's not true!

**Yang Sun:** Well, don't show 'em to me. Look, it's raining. You better come under this tree.

*[Slowly, she takes shelter under the tree.]*

**Shen Te:** Why did you want to do it?

**Yang Sun:** You really want to know? *[pause]* To get rid of you! *[pause]* You know what a flyer is?

**Shen Te:** Oh, yes, I've met a lot of pilots. At the tearoom.

**Yang Sun:** You call *them* flyers? Think they know what a machine is? Just 'cause they have leather helmets? They gave the airfield director a bribe, that's the way *those* fellows got up in the air! Try one of them out sometime. "Go up to two thousand feet," tell them, "then let it fall, then pick it up again with a flick of the wrist at the last moment." Know what he'll say to that? "It's not in my contract." Then again, there's the landing problem. It's like landing on your own backside. It's no different, planes are human. Those fools don't understand. *[pause]* And I'm the biggest fool for reading the book on flying in the Peking school and skipping the page where it says: "We've got enough flyers and we don't need you." I'm a mail pilot with no mail. You understand that?

**Shen Te:** *[shyly]* Yes, I do.

**Yang Sun:** No, you don't. You'd never understand that.

**Shen Te:** When we were little we had a crane with a broken wing. He made friends with us and was very good-natured about our jokes. He would strut along behind us and call out to stop us going too fast for him. But every spring and autumn when the cranes flew over the villages in great swarms, he got quite restless. *[pause]* I understand that. *[She bursts out crying.]*

**Yang Sun:** Don't!

**Shen Te:** *[quieting down]* No.

**Yang Sun:** It's bad for the complexion.

**Shen Te:** *[sniffing]* I've stopped.

*[She dries her tears on her big sleeve. Leaning against the tree, but not looking at her, he reaches for her face.]*

**Yang Sun:** You can't even wipe your own face. *[He is wiping it for her with his handkerchief. Pause.]*

**Shen Te:** *[still sobbing]* I don't know *anything*!

**Yang Sun:** You interrupted me! What for?

**Shen Te:** It's such a rainy day. You only wanted to do . . . *that* because it's such a rainy day. *[to the audience:]*

In our country
The evenings should never be somber
High bridges over rivers

The gray hour between night and morning
And the long, long winter:
Such things are dangerous
For, with all the misery,
A very little is enough
And men throw away an unbearable life.
*[Pause.]*

**Yang Sun:** Talk about yourself for a change.

**Shen Te:** What about me? I have a shop.

**Yang Sun:** *[incredulous]* You have a shop, have you? Never thought of walking the streets?

**Shen Te:** I did walk the streets. Now I have a shop.

**Yang Sun:** *[ironically]* A gift of the gods, I suppose!

**Shen Te:** How did you know?

**Yang Sun:** *[even more ironical]* One fine evening the gods turned up saying: here's some money!

**Shen Te:** *[quickly]* One fine morning.

**Yang Sun:** *[fed up]* This isn't much of an entertainment.
*[Pause.]*

**Shen Te:** I can play the zither a little *[pause]* And I can mimic men. *[pause]* I got the shop, so the first thing I did was to give my zither away. So I can be as stupid as a fish now, I said to myself, and it won't matter.
I'm rich now, I said
I walk alone, I sleep alone
For a whole year, I said
I'll have nothing to do with a man.

**Yang Sun:** And now you're marrying one! The one at the tearoom by the pond?
*[Shen Te is silent.]*

**Yang Sun:** What do you know about love?

**Shen Te:** Everything.

**Yang Sun:** Nothing. *[pause]* Or d'you just mean you enjoyed it?

**Shen Te:** No.

**Yang Sun:** *[again without turning to look at her, he strokes her cheek with his hand]* You like that?

**Shen Te:** Yes.

**Yang Sun:** *[breaking off]* You're easily satisfied, I must say. *[pause]* What a town!

**Shen Te:** You have no friends?

**Yang Sun:** *[defensively]* Yes, I have! *[change of tone]* But they don't want to hear I'm still unemployed. "What?" they ask. "Is there still water in the sea?" You have friends?

**Shen Te:** *[hesitating]* Just a . . . cousin.

**Yang Sun:** Watch him carefully.

**Shen Te:** He only came once. Then he went away. He won't be back. *[Yang Sun is looking away.]* But to be without hope, they say, is to be without goodness!
*[Pause.]*

**Yang Sun:** Go on talking. A voice is a voice.

**Shen Te:** Once, when I was a little girl, I fell, with a load of brushwood. An old man picked me up. He gave me a penny too. Isn't it funny how people who don't have very much like to give some of it away? They must like to show what they can do, and how could they show it better than by being kind? Being wicked is just like being clumsy. When we sing a song, or build a machine, or plant some rice, we're being kind. You're kind.

**Yang Sun:** You make it sound easy.

**Shen Te:** Oh, no. *[little pause]* Oh! A drop of rain!

**Yang Sun:** Where'd you feel it?

**Shen Te:** Right between the eyes.

**Yang Sun:** Near the right eye? Or the left?

**Shen Te:** Near the left eye.

**Yang Sun:** Oh, good. *[he is getting sleepy]* So you're through with men, eh?

**Shen Te:** *[with a smile]* But I'm not bowlegged.

**Yang Sun:** Perhaps not.

**Shen Te:** Definitely not. *[Pause.]*

**Yang Sun:** *[leaning wearily against the willow]* I haven't had a drop to drink all day, I haven't eaten anything for *two* days. I couldn't love you if I tried. *[Pause]*

**Shen Te:** I like it in the rain.

---

## SCENE FOR TWO MEN
## FROM ACT II OF *WAITING FOR GODOT*
### (1953)

### By Samuel Beckett

CHARACTERS: Estragon (Gogo)
Vladimir (Didi)

SETTING: A country road by a tree that has four or five leaves.

TIME: Evening.

SITUATION: Two tramps, Estragon and Vladimir, are watching wearily for the arrival of Godot. Act I depicts the first day of waiting; and Act II, the second. Pozzo and Lucky, who are imitated in the following scene, are a master and his slave.

COMMENTS: The puzzling dialogue and actions in *Waiting for Godot* have inspired many critics to interpret them, and this play is generally considered to be one of the finest written in this century.

**Estragon:** I'm going.
*Silence.*

**Vladimir:** Will you not play?

**Estragon:** Play at what?

**Vladimir:** We could play at Pozzo and Lucky.

**Estragon:** Never heard of it.

**Vladimir:** I'll do Lucky, you do Pozzo. (*He imitates Lucky sagging under the weight of his baggage. Estragon looks at him with stupefaction.*) Go on.

**Estragon:** What am I to do?

**Vladimir:** Curse me!

**Estragon:** (*after reflection*) Naughty!

**Vladimir:** Stronger!

**Estragon:** Gonococcus! Spirochete!

*Vladimir sways back and forth, doubled in two.*

**Vladimir:** Tell me to think.

**Estragon:** What?

**Vladimir:** Say, Think, pig!

**Estragon:** Think, pig!

*Silence.*

**Vladimir:** I can't!

**Estragon:** That's enough of that.

**Vladimir:** Tell me to dance.

**Estragon:** I'm going.

**Vladimir:** Dance, hog! (*He writhes. Exit Estragon left, precipitately.*) I can't! (*He looks up, misses Estragon.*) Gogo! (*He moves wildly about the stage. Enter Estragon left, panting. He hastens towards Vladimir, falls into his arms.*) There you are again at last!

**Estragon:** I'm accursed!

**Vladimir:** Where were you? I thought you were gone for ever.

**Estragon:** They're coming!

**Vladimir:** Who?

**Estragon:** I don't know.

**Vladimir:** How many?

**Estragon:** I don't know.

**Vladimir:** (*triumphantly*) It's Godot! At last! Gogo! It's Godot! We're saved! Let's go and meet him! (*He drags Estragon towards the wings. Estragon resists, pulls himself free, exit right.*) Gogo! Come back! (*Vladimir runs to extreme left, scans the horizon. Enter Estragon right, he hastens towards Vladimir, falls into his arms.*) There you are again again!

**Estragon:** I'm in hell!

**Vladimir:** Where were you?

**Estragon:** They're coming there too!

**Vladimir:** We're surrounded! (*Estragon makes a rush towards back.*) Imbecile! There's no way out there. (*He takes Estragon by the arm and drags him towards front. Gesture towards front.*) There! Not a soul in sight! Off you go! Quick! (*He pushes Estragon towards auditorium. Estragon recoils in horror.*) You won't? (*He contemplates auditorium.*) Well I can understand that. Wait till I see. (*He reflects.*) Your only hope left is to disappear.

**Estragon:** Where?

**Vladimir:** Behind the tree. (*Estragon hesitates.*) Quick! Behind the tree. (*Estragon goes and crouches behind the tree, realizes he is not hidden, comes out from behind the tree.*) Decidedly this tree will not have been the slightest use to us.

**Estragon:** (*calmer*) I lost my head. Forgive me. It won't happen again. Tell me what to do.

**Vladimir:** There's nothing to do.

**Estragon:** You go and stand there. *(He draws Vladimir to extreme right and places him with his back to the stage.)* There, don't move, and watch out. *(Vladimir scans horizon, screening his eyes with his hand. Estragon runs and takes up same position extreme left. They turn their heads and look at each other.)* Back to back like in the good old days *(They continue to look at each other for a moment, then resume their watch. Long silence.)* Do you see anything coming?

**Vladimir:** *(turning his head)* What?

**Estragon:** *(louder)* Do you see anything coming?

**Vladimir:** No.

**Estragon:** Nor I.

*They resume their watch. Silence.*

# Chapter Eleven

# Contemporary Styles

The most interesting characteristic of the contemporary theatre is its diversity of styles. While Broadway commercial theatres offer mainly musicals, modified realistic plays, revivals of past favorites, and English importations, many styles (some old and some experimental) are being offered off-Broadway, off-off-Broadway, in universities and regional theatres in this country, and in theatre centers around the world.

## PLAYS

Undoubtedly, the most successful experimenter in the United States to date was Eugene O'Neill (1888–1953), probably America's greatest playwright. He created in realistic, expressionistic, romantic, and symbolistic styles and was adept at both short and long plays. In addition to his expressionistic plays, which are listed in Chapter 10, the following are some of the his most important dramas in other styles: the realistic *Beyond the Horizon* (1920), *Anna Christie* (1921), and *Desire under the Elms* (1924); the symbolistic *The Great God Brown* (1926); *Strange Interlude* (1928), which had unrealistic asides; *Mourning Becomes Electra* (1931), in which he took the Electra-Orestes theme from classical tragedy and transferred it to America in 1865; the charming realistic comedy *Ah! Wilderness* (1933); and three realistic memory plays, *The Iceman Cometh*

(1939), *A Moon for the Misbegotten* (1943), and *Long Day's Journey into Night* (first produced in 1956).

Another major American writer who showed the influence of realism, symbolism, and expressionism was Tennessee Williams (1911–1983), whose masterpieces *The Glass Menagerie* and *A Streetcar Named Desire* were produced in 1945 and 1947. Unfortunately, while he wrote many good plays, he did not reach the level of his first two successes with *Summer and Smoke* (1948), *The Rose Tattoo* (1951), *Camino Real* (1953), *Cat on a Hot Tin Roof* (1955), *Sweet Bird of Youth* (1959), *The Night of the Iguana* (1961), and *The Milk Train Doesn't Stop Here Anymore* (1962).

Arthur Miller (1915–    ) rose to prominence as a major American playwright with *All My Sons* in 1947. His great *Death of a Salesman*, produced in 1949, is considered to be one of the finest tragedies of the twentieth century. After this came *The Crucible* in 1953, *A View from the Bridge* in 1955, *After the Fall* and *Incident at Vichy* in 1964, and *The Price* in 1968.

The biggest commercial success of the contemporary Broadway theatre, however, is Neil Simon (1927–    ) with such long-running realistic comedies as *Barefoot in the Park* (1963), *The Odd Couple* (1965), *Plaza Suite* (1968), *Last of the Red Hot Lovers* (1969), *The Gingerbread Lady* (1970), *The Prisoner of Second Avenue* (1971), *The Sunshine Boys* (1972), *The Good Doctor* (1974), *God's Favorite* (1974), *California Suite* (1976), *Chapter Two* (1977), *I Ought to Be in Pictures* (1980), and *Brighton Beach Memoirs* (1983).

Edward Albee (1928–    ) and some other famous American writers have already been mentioned in earlier chapters. Others who should be listed are Sidney Howard (1891–1939), Robert Emmett Sherwood (1896–1955), Moss Hart (1904–1961), Lillian Hellman (1905–1984), Clifford Odets (1906–1963), William Saroyan (1908–1981), William Inge (1913–1973), Robert Anderson (1917–    ), Jean-Claude van Itallie (1935–    ), Paul Zindel (1936–    ), Lanford Wilson (1938–    ), Arthur Kopit (1938–    ), David Rabe (1940–    ), Sam Shepard (1943–    ), Marsha Norman (1947–    ), David Mamet (1947–    ), and Beth Henley (1952–    ).

In England, Noel Coward (1899–1973) achieved great success with his charming, urbane comedies, musicals, and sometimes serious plays, such as *Private Lives* (1930); *Tonight at Eight-Thirty* (1936), which consists of nine one-act plays; *Blithe Spirit* (1941); and *Present Laughter* (1943).

Other important English playwrights are Robert Bolt (1924–    ), John Osborne (1929–    ), Joe Orton (1933–1969), David Storey (1933–    ), and Alan Ayckbourn (1939–    ); but the top writers in England at the present appear to be Harold Pinter (1930–    ) and Tom Stoppard (1937–    ), whose principal plays are listed in Chapter 10, and Peter Shaffer (1926– ), who has had success with *Five Finger Exercise* (1958), *The Royal Hunt of the Sun* (1964), *Black Comedy* (1965), *Equus* (1974), and *Amadeus* (1979).

The great French absurdists have already been listed in Chapter 10, but other French dramatists who must be mentioned are a neoclassical writer, Jean Giraudoux (1882–1944), who wrote *Amphitryon 38* (1929), *Judith* (1932), *Tiger at the Gates* (1935), *Electre* (1937), *Ondine* (1939), *Sodom and Gomorrha* (1943), and *The Madwoman of Chaillot* (1945); and a man who has combined many styles but is mainly a realist, Jean Anouilh (1910– ), whose plays include *Thieves Carnival* (1932), *Antigone* (1942), *Ring Round the Moon* (1947), *The Lark* (1952), *The Waltz of the Toreadors* (1952), *Beckett* (1958), *Dear Antoine* (1970), and *Do Not Awaken Madame* (1971).

In Spain, the finest dramatist of this century was Federico García Lorca (1898–1936), who wrote in expressionistic, symbolistic, and realistic styles. His best-known plays are *Blood Wedding* (1933), *Yerma* (1934), and *The House of Bernarda Alba* (1936).

In Russia, since the early days of the Soviet regime, the principal style of playwriting has been socialist realism, a basically realistic style that preaches the socialist doctrine. Few of these plays have been published in English, and those that are available have failed to gain critical approval in Western countries; however, Bertolt Brecht's epic theatre plays, which are considered the best examples of socialist realism, are widely produced around the world. (See Chapter 10.)

In West Germany, documentary drama or the theatre of fact, which was influenced by Brecht's epic theatre, became popular in the 1960s with plays by Peter Weiss (1916– ), whose best-known work in this country is *The Persecution and Assassination of Jean-Paul Marat as Performed by the Inmates of the Asylum of Charenton under the Direction of the Marquis de Sade* (known usually as *Marat/Sade*, 1964); Heinar Kipphardt (1922– ); and Rolf Hochhuth (1931– ). In Austria, Peter Handke (1942– ) has attracted attention.

In the United States in the 1960s, some avant-garde companies reduced the importance of the spoken text in their productions. Antonin Artaud (1895–1948) of France had said "no more masterpieces," and he was their inspiration as they substituted works created by the group that aimed at reviving the magic of a communal ritual. A new importance was given to the physical, nonverbal aspects of acting; close interaction with the audience; getting back to the basics of life; and dazzling sensory experiences.

In the more conservative climate of the late 1970s and 1980s, there was a swing back to reestablishing the importance of the literary text while not ignoring the lessons that were learned earlier about nonverbal values.

**Theatres.** Following World War I and again after World War II, many theatres were built in Europe and America. Some were restorations of theatres destroyed in war; others were new buildings that incorporated the latest ideas on theatre architecture. Most were built with proscenium-arch stages, but some have a thrust stage (in which the audience surrounds the actors on three sides, leaving the fourth side in back of the performers for stage decor); an arena stage (which has spectators on all four sides); or a multiform stage, which may be changed to two or three of these types.

**Experimental Groups.** During the 1950s, the Stanislavski System/Method dominated America's acting with the Actors Studio in New York, led by Lee Strasberg, as the top acting school in the country. But gradually in the 1960s, as mentioned above, under the stimulation of Antonin Artaud, certain groups began to form to find new ways to reach each other and the audience; and this experimentation, which left realism for frank theatricality, had an effect on the training of actors throughout the United States. Some actors who had formerly done nothing more strenuous onstage than carry a cocktail and a cigarette found that they were being asked to do unusual physical activity, such as swinging on trapezes or playing leapfrog. The result was that acting schools quickly changed their curricula to give new importance to stage movement, mime, dancing, fencing, circus techniques, and improvisation.

Called the theatre of cruelty by Artaud, his theory stated that the theatre should compel people to see themselves as they are. To do this, Artaud believed that the written play should be used only as a departure, that stage and auditorium should be replaced by a single area in which actors and audience mingle, and that the attention of the spectators should be held by exposing them to color, light, and sounds that vibrate and inundate.

Some experimental companies said that for theatre all they needed was "empty space" or "found space," which could change for each performance; and Richard Schechner, who in 1968 formed the Performance Group in New York, used the words *environmental theatre* for a free-form space that is shared by actors and spectators who intermingle and interact.

**Costumes.** There was a new interest, too, in the use of masks, puppets, and actors inside of huge dolls or grotesque heads. However, some avant-garde theatres did not want costumes that would make the actor appear different from the spectators. Some companies used costumes of "found" materials or everyday clothes or sometimes no clothes at all.

**Makeup.** Some experimental groups did not use any makeup because it was not "honest" or because they thought that the well-trained actor could obtain the desired appearance through physical movement rather than makeup. On the other hand, some groups used mask-like makeups instead of masks.

**Scenery.** In scene designing, the multimedia approach, which combines films, slides, closed-circuit television, stereophonic sound, music, light, and special effects with live performers, became increasingly popular in the 1960s. Because of rising production costs, there has been a trend toward more economical sets. Increasingly, designers are depending on light, sound, fragmentary sets, furniture, and props instead of large, detailed realistic settings. Nonessential items are often eliminated so that actors may have an open or free space in which to work.

**Designers.** To mention only a few of the most famous designers in the United States in the twentieth century, the following should be listed: Joseph Urban, Robert Edmond Jones, Mordecai Gorelik, Lee Simonson, Jo Mielziner, Donald Oenslager, and Norman Bel Geddes. Josef Svoboda of Czechoslovakia is a popular designer in both Europe and the United States.

**Directors.** The top director in the world in the first part of the twentieth century was Max Reinhardt (1873–1943) from Austria. Noted for taking an eclectic approach to direction, he worked in many different countries, preparing plays from all periods in a great variety of styles. Other important directors of this century in France have been Jacques Copeau, Jean-Louis Barrault, Louis Jouvet, and Jean Vilar; in Italy, Franco Zeffirelli; in Sweden, Ingmar Bergman; in West Germany, Peter Stein; in England, John Gielgud, Tyrone Guthrie, Laurence Olivier, and Peter Brook; in the United States, Harold Clurman, George Abbott, Elia Kazan, Joshua Logan, Robert Lewis, José Quintero, Alan Schneider, Joseph Papp, Harold Prince, Mike Nichols, and others.

**Actors.** Some of the greatest American stage actors in this century have been Lionel, Ethel, and John Barrymore, Alfred Lunt, Lynn Fontanne, Katharine Cornell, Helen Hayes, Laurette Taylor, Tallulah Bankhead, Ruth Gordon, Julie Harris, Jason Robards, Geraldine Page, George C. Scott, Colleen Dewhurst, Henry Fonda, Maureen Stapleton, Hume Cronyn, Jessica Tandy, Uta Hagen, and Frank Langella. England has produced Laurence Olivier, John Gielgud, Noel Coward, Gertrude Lawrence, Beatrice Lillie, Ralph Richardson, Judith Anderson, Maurice Evans, Alec Guinness, Michael Redgrave, Edith Evans, Vivien Leigh, Richard Burton, Cyril Ritchard, Rex Harrison, Claire Bloom, Joan Plowright, and Julie Andrews.

Many of the experimental groups that were formed in the United States in the 1960s and 1970s were no longer in existence by the 1980s for several reasons: economic and political changes caused a curtailment of supportive funds for the arts; a more conservative attitude toward theatre caused many to look back with disfavor upon the excesses in some of the earlier companies; and inflation pushed the costs of producing plays to an all-time high, necessitating high ticket prices that kept those of poor and moderate incomes from attending.

High production costs also forced Broadway producers to be reluctant to take chances on new playwrights, so writers such as Marsha Norman, D.L. Coburn, Sam Shepard, Beth Henley, and Michael Cristofer had the premieres of Pulitzer Prize–winning plays in resident professional theatres of the United States. These regional theatres, such as the American Repertory Theatre in Cambridge, Massachusetts, the Alley Theatre in Houston, the Mark Taper Forum in Los Angeles, the Actors Theatre of Louisville, and the Guthrie Theatre in Minneapolis, are fostering American playwrights by giving professional tryouts to both unknown and famous writers. They are also giving actors valuable experience in playing various styles of the past and present.

Acting in this country has never been better. Actors are being trained not only in Method acting but in technical acting and in a combination of the two. Training in stage movement, voice and dialects, and improvising is being emphasized. Actors are learning that they must adjust their acting to the style of the play and be versatile enough to play Oedipus or Cyrano, to act Mrs. Malaprop or Mary Tyrone.

In this country more students are studying theatre in high schools, universities, and specialized schools than ever before. More people are patronizing and working in amateur and professional theatres than before. Experimentation—motivated sometimes by exciting productions from abroad—is going on, especially in our noncommercial resident theatres, universities, and small traveling troupes. If we can continue to provide enjoyable or thrilling or valuable learning experiences for our audiences, our theatres should prosper.

## SUGGESTED READING

Artaud, Antonin. *The Theatre and Its Double.* Tr. by Mary C. Richards. New York: Grove Press, 1958.

Brockett, Oscar G., and Robert R. Findlay. *Century of Innovation.* Englewood Cliffs, N.J.: Prentice-Hall, Inc., 1973.

Brook, Peter. *The Empty Space.* New York: Avon, 1969.

Hainaux, René (ed.). *Stage Design Throughout the World, 1960–1970.* New York: Theatre Arts Books, 1972.

————. *Stage Design Throughout the World, 1970–1975.* New York: Theatre Arts Books, 1976.

Hethmon, Robert H. *Strasberg at the Actors Studio.* New York: Viking Press, 1965.

Saint-Denis, Michel. *Theatre: The Rediscovery of Style.* New York: Theatre Arts Books, 1960.

Schechner, Richard. *Environmental Theatre.* New York: Hawthorn Books, Inc., 1973.

## EXERCISES

Acting in the contemporary theatre requires great versatility. To increase your skills, do the following:

1. Improvise a scene in which a politician is trying to convince a group to vote for him or her in the following ways. The group responds similarly:
   a. Use only screams and loud sounds.
   b. Use nonvocal sounds (clapping your hands; hitting your face, other parts of your body, or props; stamping your feet or kicking props).
   c. Use dance movements with no sounds.
   d. Use realistic dialogue and movements.
2. Using the same four ways from Exercise 1, two actors may improvise on these situations:
   a. Selling a painting.
   b. Begging a member of the opposite sex to marry you.
   c. Scolding a child.
   d. Arguing with a parent.
3. As a movement exercise, use slow motion with no physical contact as you box with another actor. As one throws a blow, the other should react as though struck although no contact is actually made. Continue until one slowly falls to the floor.
4. As an exercise in using different tempos of moving and speaking, a group may improvise a picnic. Start with realistic dialogue and movements. After several minutes, the instructor may say "Slow," at which time the actors should move in slow motion and elongate their words. After several more minutes, the instructor may say "Fast," and the actors should move and talk very rapidly.
5. Directors sometimes use "role reversal" to help an actor understand another character's viewpoint. After you have rehearsed a scene several times, try reversing roles to see if this brings you a deeper insight into the meaning of the play.

6. Another device used by directors is to have actors improvise an incident that is talked about in the play but not shown onstage. For example, the actress playing Cathleen in *Long Day's Journey into Night* (see the excerpt from this play in this chapter) may find it valuable to improvise her meeting with the man in the drug store, which she describes in this scene.

7. Improvisations may also be used to prepare actors for entering a scene with the right attitude, mood, and thoughts. Look at the excerpt from *Chapter Two* and improvise what either Jennie or George has been doing for five minutes before this scene begins.

8. Playing opposite values is another rehearsal technique used to explore conflicting emotions in a role. If a part calls for anger, as in the excerpt from *The Crucible* in this chapter, try playing it with kindness in rehearsal; when fear is indicated, try boldness, and so forth.

---

### SCENE FOR TWO WOMEN
### FROM ACT III OF *LONG DAY'S JOURNEY INTO NIGHT*
### (WRITTEN EARLIER, FIRST PRODUCED IN 1956)

*By Eugene O'Neill*

CHARACTERS: Mary Cavan Tyrone
               Cathleen, second girl

SETTING: The living room of James and Mary Tyrone's summer house. At the right are a screen door to the porch and windows that look over the front lawn to the harbor. On a table are a reading lamp and a tray with a bottle of whiskey, glasses, and pitcher of ice water.

TIME: About 6:30 P.M. on a day in August 1912.

SITUATION: Mary, who has become addicted to drugs, has had a prescription filled during the day and has taken some to relieve her pain. She talks to Cathleen, her servant, with familiarity as if she were an old intimate friend. Cathleen has been drinking and is holding an empty whiskey glass in her hand as she stands near the table.

COMMENTS: Mary is fifty-four. She is a little plump but still has a graceful figure. She uses no makeup; her high forehead is framed by thick, white hair, which is slightly disheveled. Rheumatism has knotted the joints of her fingers so that now they have an ugly crippled look. Her nervousness causes her to move her hands constantly. Cathleen is a buxom Irish peasant girl in her early twenties who is amiable, clumsy, and ignorant.

**Cathleen:** *Worriedly.* What time is it, Ma'am? I ought to go back in the kitchen. The damp is in Bridget's rheumatism and she's like a raging divil. She'll bite my head off.
*She puts her glass on the table and makes a movement toward the back parlor.*
**Mary:** *With a flash of apprehension.* No, don't go, Cathleen. I don't want to be alone, yet.

**Cathleen:** You won't be for long. The Master and the boys will be home soon.

**Mary:** I doubt if they'll come back for dinner. They have too good an excuse to remain in the barrooms where they feel at home.

*Cathleen stares at her, stupidly puzzled. Mary goes on smilingly.*

Don't worry about Bridget. I'll tell her I kept you with me, and you can take a big drink of whiskey to her when you go. She won't mind then.

**Cathleen:** *Grins—at her ease again.* No, Ma'am. That's the one thing can make her cheerful. She loves her drop.

**Mary:** Have another drink yourself, if you wish, Cathleen.

**Cathleen:** I don't know if I'd better, Ma'am. I can feel what I've had already. *Reaching for the bottle.* Well, maybe one more won't harm. *She pours a drink.* Here's your good health, Ma'am. *She drinks without bothering about a chaser.*

**Mary:** *Dreamily.* I really did have good health once, Cathleen. But that was long ago.

**Cathleen:** *Worried again.* The Master's sure to notice what's gone from the bottle. He has the eye of a hawk for that.

**Mary:** *Amusedly.* Oh, we'll play Jamie's trick on him. Just measure a few drinks of water and pour them in.

**Cathleen:** *Does this—with a silly giggle.* God save me, it'll be half water. He'll know by the taste.

**Mary:** *Indifferently.* No, by the time he comes home he'll be too drunk to tell the difference. He has such a good excuse, he believes, to drown his sorrows.

**Cathleen:** *Philosophically.* Well, it's a good man's failing. I wouldn't give a trauneen for a teetotaler. They've no high spirits. *Then, stupidly puzzled.* Good excuse? You mean Master Edmund, Ma'am? I can tell the Master is worried about him.

**Mary:** *Stiffens defensively—but in a strange way the reaction has a mechanical quality, as if it did not penetrate to real emotion.* Don't be silly, Cathleen. Why should he be? A touch of grippe is nothing. And Mr. Tyrone never is worried about anything, except money and property and the fear he'll end his days in poverty. I mean, deeply worried. Because he cannot really understand anything else. *She gives a little laugh of detached, affectionate amusement.* My husband is a very peculiar man, Cathleen.

**Cathleen:** *Vaguely resentful.* Well, he's a fine, handsome, kind gentleman just the same, Ma'am. Never mind his weakness.

**Mary:** Oh, I don't mind. I've loved him dearly for thirty-six years. That proves I know he's lovable at heart and can't help being what he is, doesn't it?

**Cathleen:** *Hazily reassured.* That's right, Ma'am. Love him dearly, for any fool can see he worships the ground you walk on. *Fighting the effect of her last drink and trying to be soberly conversational.* Speaking of acting, Ma'am, how is it you never went on the stage?

**Mary:** *Resentfully.* I? What put that absurd notion in your head? I was brought up in a respectable home and educated in the best convent in the Middle West. Before I met Mr. Tyrone I hardly knew there was such a thing as a theater. I was a very pious girl. I even dreamed of becoming a nun. I've never had the slightest desire to be an actress.

**Cathleen:** *Bluntly.* Well, I can't imagine you a holy nun, Ma'am. Sure, you never darken the door of a church, God forgive you.

**Mary:** *Ignores this.* I've never felt at home in the theater. Even though Mr. Tyrone has made me go with him on all his tours, I've had little to do with the people in his company, or with anyone on the stage. Not that I have anything against them. They have always been kind to me, and I to them. But I've never felt at home with them. Their life is not my life. It has always stood between me and— *She gets up—abruptly.* But let's not talk of old things that couldn't be helped. *She goes to the porch door and stares out.* How thick the fog is. I can't see the road. All the people in the world could pass by and I would never know. I wish it was always that way. It's getting dark already. It will soon be night, thank goodness. *She turns back—vaguely.* It was kind of you to keep me company this afternoon, Cathleen. I would have been lonely driving uptown alone.

**Cathleen:** Sure, wouldn't I rather ride in a fine automobile than stay here and listen to Bridget's lies about her relations? It was like a vacation, Ma'am. *She pauses—then stupidly.* There was only one thing I didn't like.

**Mary:** *Vaguely.* What was that, Cathleen?

**Cathleen:** The way the man in the drugstore acted when I took in the prescription for you. *Indignantly.* The impidence of him!

**Mary:** *With stubborn blankness.* What are you talking about? What drugstore? What prescription? *Then hastily, as Cathleen stares in stupid amazement.* Oh, of course, I'd forgotten. The medicine for the rheumatism in my hands. What did the man say? *Then with indifference.* Not that it matters, as long as he filled the prescription.

**Cathleen:** It mattered to me, then! I'm not used to being treated like a thief. He gave me a long look and says insultingly, "Where did you get hold of this?" and I says, "It's none of your damned business, but if you must know, it's for the lady I work for, Mrs. Tyrone, who's sitting out in the automobile." That shut him up quick. He gave a look out at you and said, "Oh," and went to get the medicine.

**Mary:** *Vaguely.* Yes, he knows me.

*She sits in the armchair at right rear of table. She adds in a calm, detached voice.*

I have to take it because there is no other that can stop the pain—all the pain—I mean, in my hands.

*She raises her hands and regards them with melancholy sympathy. There is no tremor in them now.* Poor hands! You'd never believe it, but they were once one of my good points, along with my hair and eyes, and I had a fine figure, too.

*Her tone has become more and more far-off and dreamy.* They were a musician's hands. I used to love the piano. I worked so hard at my music in the Convent—if you can call it work when you do something you love. Mother Elizabeth and my music teacher both said I had more talent than any student they remembered. My father paid for special lessons. He spoiled me. He would do anything I asked. He would have sent me to Europe to study after I graduated from the Convent. I might have gone—if I hadn't fallen in love with Mr. Tyrone. Or I might have become a nun. I had two dreams. To be a nun, that was the more beautiful one. To become a concert pianist, that was the other.

*She pauses, regarding her hands fixedly. Cathleen blinks her eyes to fight off drowsiness and a tipsy feeling.* I haven't touched a piano in so many years. I couldn't play with

158

such crippled fingers, even if I wanted to. For a time after my marriage I tried to keep up my music. But it was hopeless. One-night stands, cheap hotels, dirty trains, leaving children, never having a home— *She stares at her hands with fascinated disgust.* See, Cathleen, how ugly they are! So maimed and crippled! You would think they'd been through some horrible accident!
*She gives a strange little laugh.* So they have, come to think of it.
*She suddenly thrusts her hands behind her back.* I won't look at them. They're worse than the foghorn for reminding me— *Then with defiant self-assurance.* But even they can't touch me now.
*She brings her hands from behind her back and deliberately stares at them—calmly.* They're far away. I see them, but the pain has gone.

**Cathleen:** *Stupidly puzzled.* You've taken some of the medicine? It made you act funny, Ma'am. If I didn't know better, I'd think you'd a drop taken.

**Mary:** *Dreamily.* It kills the pain. You go back until at last you are beyond its reach. Only the past when you were happy is real.

---

### SCENE FOR ONE MAN, ONE WOMAN
### FROM SCENE VII OF *THE GLASS MENAGERIE*
#### (1945)

*By Tennessee Williams*

CHARACTERS: Laura Wingfield
                Jim O'Connor, the gentleman caller

SETTING: The Wingfield apartment in St. Louis. This is a memory play, so the setting need not be realistic but should be rather poetic. Downstage is the living room, which has a sofa, some chairs, a what-not with many transparent glass animals, and on the floor two sofa pillows and a candelabrum on a newspaper. A dining–room table and chairs are upstage. Because the electric lights have gone out, this scene is played by candlelight.

TIME: After dinner on a Friday evening in the 1930s.

SITUATION: At his mother's request, Tom Wingfield has invited a young man from the warehouse where he works to come to dinner to meet his sister, Laura. Laura has admired Jim since they went to high school because he was a popular student in many activities. Laura was as shy in high school as she is now, but Jim finally remembered that he used to call her Blue Roses when they had a singing class together. He has just explained to her that he is taking a night course in radio engineering.

COMMENTS: A childhood illness left Laura crippled; but according to the playwright, this defect need not be more than suggested on the stage. Laura is like a piece of her own glass collection, exquisitely fragile. Jim is a nice, energetic young man. Both Laura and Jim are twenty-three. The slides projected on a screen, which are indicated in this excerpt, were not used in the original New York and most subsequent productions.

**Jim:** Now how about you? Isn't there something you take more interest in than anything else?

**Laura:** Well, I do—as I said—have my—glass collection— [*A peal of girlish laughter from the kitchen.*]

**Jim:** I'm not right sure I know what you're talking about. What kind of glass is it?

**Laura:** Little articles of it, they're ornaments mostly! Most of them are little animals made out of glass, the tiniest little animals in the world. Mother calls them a glass menagerie! Here's an example of one, if you'd like to see it! This is one of the oldest. It's nearly thirteen.

[*Music: "The Glass Menagerie."*]

[*He stretches out his hand.*]

Oh, be careful—if you breathe, it breaks!

**Jim:** I'd better not take it. I'm pretty clumsy with things.

**Laura:** Go on, I trust you with him! [*Places it in his palm.*] There now—you're holding him gently! Hold him over the light, he loves the light! You see how the light shines through him?

**Jim:** It sure does shine!

**Laura:** I shouldn't be partial, but he is my favorite one.

**Jim:** What kind of a thing is this one supposed to be?

**Laura:** Haven't you noticed the single horn on his forehead?

**Jim:** A unicorn, huh?

**Laura:** Mmm-hmmm!

**Jim:** Unicorns, aren't they extinct in the modern world?

**Laura:** I know!

**Jim:** Poor little fellow, he must feel sort of lonesome.

**Laura:** [*Smiling*]. Well, if he does he doesn't complain about it. He stays on a shelf with some horses that don't have horns and all of them seem to get along nicely together.

**Jim:** How do you know?

**Laura:** [*Lightly*]. I haven't heard any arguments among them!

**Jim:** [*Grinning*]. No arguments, huh? Well, that's a pretty good sign! Where shall I set him!

**Laura:** Put him on the table. They all like a change of scenery once in a while!

**Jim:** [*Stretching*]. Well, well, well, well—Look how big my shadow is when I stretch!

**Laura:** Oh, oh, yes—it stretches across the ceiling!

**Jim:** [*Crossing to door*]. I think it's stopped raining. [*Opens fire-escape door.*] Where does the music come from?

**Laura:** From the Paradise Dance Hall across the alley.

**Jim:** How about cutting the rug a little, Miss Wingfield?

**Laura:** Oh, I—

**Jim:** Or is your program filled up? Let me have a look at it. [*Grasps imaginary card.*] Why, every dance is taken! I'll just have to scratch some out. [*Waltz music: "La Golondrina."*] Ahh, a waltz! [*He executes some sweeping turns by himself then holds his arms toward Laura.*]

**Laura:** [*Breathlessly*] I—can't dance!

**Jim:** There you go, that inferiority stuff!

160

**Laura:** I've never danced in my life!

**Jim:** Come on, try!

**Laura:** Oh, but I'd step on you!

**Jim:** I'm not made out of glass.

**Laura:** How—how—how do we start?

**Jim:** Just leave it to me. You hold your arms out a little.

**Laura:** Like this?

**Jim:** A little bit higher. Right. Now don't tighten up, that's the main thing about it—relax.

**Laura:** *[Laughing breathlessly]* It's hard not to.

**Jim:** Okay.

**Laura:** I'm afraid you can't budge me.

**Jim:** What do you bet I can't? *[He swings her into motion.]*

**Laura:** Goodness, yes, you can!

**Jim:** Let yourself go, now, Laura, just let yourself go.

**Laura:** I'm—

**Jim:** Come on!

**Laura:** Trying!

**Jim:** Not so stiff—Easy does it!

**Laura:** I know but I'm—

**Jim:** Loosen th' backbone! There now, that's a lot better.

**Laura:** Am I?

**Jim:** Lots, lots better! *[He moves her about the room in a clumsy waltz.]*

**Laura:** Oh, my!

**Jim:** Ha-ha!

**Laura:** Oh, my goodness!

**Jim:** Ha-ha-ha! *[They suddenly bump into the table. Jim stops.]* What did we hit on?

**Laura:** Table.

**Jim:** Did something fall off it? I think—

**Laura:** Yes.

**Jim:** I hope that it wasn't the little glass horse with the horn!

**Laura:** Yes.

**Jim:** Aw, aw, aw. Is it broken?

**Laura:** Now it is just like all the other horses.

**Jim:** It's lost its—

**Laura:** Horn! It doesn't matter. Maybe it's a blessing in disguise.

**Jim:** You'll never forgive me. I bet that that was your favorite piece of glass.

**Laura:** I don't have favorites much. It's no tragedy, Freckles. Glass breaks so easily. No matter how careful you are. The traffic jars the shelves and things fall off them.

**Jim:** Still I'm awfully sorry that I was the cause.

**Laura:** *[Smiling]* I'll just imagine he had an operation. The horn was removed to make him feel less—freakish! *[They both laugh.]* Now he will feel more at home with the other horses, the ones that don't have horns . . .

**Jim:** Ha-ha, that's very funny! *[Suddenly serious.]* I'm glad to see that you have a sense of humor.

You know—you're—well—very different! Surprisingly different from any-

161

one else I know! [*His voice becomes soft and hesitant with a genuine feeling*].
Do you mind me telling you that? [*Laura is abashed beyond speech.*] I mean it in a nice way . . . [*Laura nods shyly, looking away.*] You make me feel sort of—I don't know how to put it! I'm usually pretty good at expressing things, but— This is something that I don't know how to say! [*Laura touches her throat and clears it—turns the broken unicorn in her hands. Even softer*]. Has anyone ever told you that you were pretty?
[*Pause: Music.*]
[*Laura looks up slowly, with wonder, and shakes her head.*]
Well, you are! In a very different way from anyone else. And all the nicer because of the difference too. [*His voice becomes low and husky. Laura turns away, nearly faint with the novelty of her emotions.*]. I wish that you were my sister. I'd teach you to have some confidence in yourself. The different people are not like other people, but being different is nothing to be ashamed of. Because other people are not such wonderful people. They're one hundred times one thousand. You're one times one! They walk all over the earth. You just stay here. They're common as—weeds, but—you—well, you're—*Blue Roses!*
[*Image on screen: Blue Roses.*]
[*Music changes.*]

Laura: But blue is wrong for—roses . . .

Jim: It's right for you!—You're—pretty!

Laura: In what respect am I pretty?

Jim: In all respects—believe me! Your eyes—your hair—are pretty! Your hands are pretty! [*He catches hold of her hand.*] You think I'm making this up because I'm invited to dinner and have to be nice. Oh, I could do that! I could put on an act for you, Laura, and say lots of things without being very sincere. But this time I am. I'm talking to you sincerely. I happened to notice you had this inferiority complex that keeps you from feeling comfortable with people. Somebody needs to build your confidence up and make you proud instead of shy and turning away and—blushing—Somebody—ought to—ought to—*kiss* you, Laura! [*His hand slips slowly up her arm to her shoulder.*]
[*Music swells tumultuously.*]
[*He suddenly turns her about and kisses her on the lips. When he releases her, Laura sinks on the sofa with a bright, dazed look.*]

---

### SCENE FOR ONE MAN, TWO WOMEN
### FROM ACT II OF *THE CRUCIBLE*
### (1953)

*By Arthur Miller*

CHARACTERS: John Proctor
Elizabeth Proctor, his wife
Mary Warren, their servant

SETTING: The common room of Proctor's house on a farm near Salem, Massachusetts.

TIME: Evening; spring, 1692, at the start of the witchcraft trials.

SITUATION: Seven months earlier, John was unfaithful to Elizabeth with their former servant, Abigail Williams, who with some other young girls is accusing women of witchcraft. Elizabeth, who knows of his infidelity, has urged John to go to Salem to tell the court that Abigail is a fraud. In a scene immediately before the following excerpt, the strained relations between the two have been evident.

COMMENTS: John is a powerfully built, independent farmer who is in his middle thirties. Elizabeth is a dutiful wife and mother. Mary is a naive, frightened, young girl of eighteen.

*(He starts for the door as Mary Warren enters. As soon as he sees her, he goes directly to her and grabs her by her cloak, furious.)* How do you go to Salem when I forbid it? Do you mock me? *(Shaking her.)* I'll whip you if you dare leave this house again! *(Strangely, she doesn't resist him, but hangs limply by his grip.)*

**Mary Warren:** I am sick, I am sick, Mr. Proctor. Pray, pray, hurt me not. *(Her strangeness throws him off, and her evident pallor and weakness. He frees her.)* My insides are all shuddery; I am in the proceedings all day, sir.

**Proctor:** *(with draining anger—his curiousity is draining it)* And what of these proceedings here? When will you proceed to keep this house, as you are paid nine pound a year to do—and my wife not wholly well? *(As though to compensate, Mary Warren goes to Elizabeth with a small rag doll.)*

**Mary Warren:** I made a gift for you today, Goody Proctor. I had to sit long hours in a chair, and passed the time with sewing.

**Elizabeth:** *(perplexed, looking at the doll)* Why, thank you, it's a fair poppet.

**Mary Warren:** *(with a trembling, decayed voice)* We must all love each other now, Goody Proctor.

**Elizabeth:** *(amazed at her strangeness)* Aye, indeed we must.

**Mary Warren:** *(glancing at the room)* I'll get up early in the morning and clean the house. I must sleep now. *(She turns and starts off.)*

**Proctor:** Mary. *(she halts.)* Is it true? There be fourteen women arrested?

**Mary Warren:** No, sir. There be thirty-nine now— *(She suddenly breaks off and sobs and sits down, exhausted.)*

**Elizabeth:** Why, she's weepin'! What ails you, child?

**Mary Warren:** Goody Osburn—will hang!
*(There is a shocked pause, while she sobs.)*

**Proctor:** Hang! *(He calls into her face.)* Hang, y'say?

**Mary Warren:** *(through her weeping)* Aye.

**Proctor:** The Deputy Governor will permit it?

**Mary Warren:** He sentenced her. He must. *(To ameliorate it)* But not Sarah Good. For Sarah Good confessed, y'see.

**Proctor:** Confessed! To what?

**Mary Warren:** That she *(in horror at the memory)* —she sometimes made a compact with Lucifer, and wrote her name in his black book—with her blood— and bound herself to torment Christians till God's thrown down—and we all must worship Hell forevermore. *(Pause.)*

**Proctor:** But—surely you know what a jabberer she is. Did you tell them that?

**Mary Warren:** Mr. Proctor, in open court she near to choked us all to death.

Proctor: How, choked you?

Mary Warren: She sent her spirit out.

Elizabeth: Oh, Mary, Mary, surely you—

Mary Warren: *(with an indignant edge)* She tried to kill me many times, Goody Proctor!

Elizabeth: Why, I never heard you mention that before.

Mary Warren: I never knew it before. I never knew anything before. When she come into the court I say to myself, I must not accuse this woman, for she sleep in ditches, and so very old and poor. But then—then she sit thère, denying and denying, and I feel a misty coldness climbin' up my back, and the skin on my skull begin to creep, and I feel a clamp around my neck and I cannot breathe air; and then *(entranced)* —I hear a voice, a screamin' voice, and it were my voice—and all at once I remembered everything she done to me!

Proctor: Why? What did she do to you?

Mary Warren: *(like one awakened to a marvelous secret insight)* So many time, Mr. Proctor, she come to this very door, beggin' bread and a cup of cider—and mark this: whenever I turned her away empty, she *mumbled*.

Elizabeth: Mumbled! She may mumble if she's hungry.

Mary Warren: But *what* does she mumble? You must remember, Goody Proctor. Last month—a Monday, I think—she walked away, and I thought my guts would burst for two days after. Do you remember it?

Elizabeth: Why—I do, I think, but—

Mary Warren: And so I told that to Judge Hathorne, and he asks her so. "Goody Osburn," says he, "what curse do you mumble that this girl must fall sick after turning you away?" And then she replies *(mimicking an old crone)* — "Why, your excellence, no curse at all. I only say my commandments; I hope I may say my commandments," says she!

Elizabeth: And that's an upright answer.

Mary Warren: Aye, but then Judge Hathorne say, "Recite for us your commandments!" *(leaning avidly toward them)*— and of all the ten she could not say a single one. She never knew no commandments, and they had her in a flat lie!

Proctor: And so condemned her?

Mary Warren: *(now a little strained, seeing his stubborn doubt)* Why, they must when she condemned herself.

Proctor: But the proof, the proof!

Mary Warren: *(with greater impatience with him)* I told you the proof. It's hard proof, hard as rock, the judges said.

Proctor: *(pauses an instant, then)* You will not go to court again, Mary Warren.

Mary Warren: I must tell you, sir, I will be gone every day now. I am amazed you do not see what weighty work we do.

Proctor: What work you do! It's strange work for a Christian girl to hang old women!

Mary Warren: But, Mr. Proctor, they will not hang them if they confess. Sarah Good will only sit in jail some time— *recalling)* and here's a wonder for you; think on this. Goody Good is pregnant!

**Elizabeth:** Pregnant! Are they mad? The woman's near to sixty!

**Mary Warren:** They had Doctor Griggs examine her, and she's full to the brim. And smokin' a pipe all these years, and no husband either! But she's safe, thank God, for they'll not hurt the innocent child. But be that not a marvel? You must see it, sir, it's God's work we do. So I'll be gone every day for some time. I'm—I am an official of the court, they say, and I— *(She has been edging toward offstage.)*

**Proctor:** I'll official you! *(He strides to the mantel, takes down the whip hanging there.)*

**Mary Warren:** *(terrified, but coming erect, striving for her authority)* I'll not stand whipping any more!

**Elizabeth:** *(hurriedly, as Proctor approaches)* Mary, promise now you'll stay at home—

**Mary Warren:** *(backing from him, but keeping her erect posture, striving, striving for her way)* The Devil's loose in Salem, Mr. Proctor; we must discover where he's hiding!

**Proctor:** I'll whip the Devil out of you! *(With whip raised he reaches out for her, and she streaks away and yells.)*

**Mary Warren:** *(pointing at Elizabeth)* I saved her life today! *(Silence. His whip comes down.)*

**Elizabeth:** *(softly)* I am accused?

**Mary Warren:** *(quaking)* Somewhat mentioned. But I said I never see no sign you ever sent your spirit out to hurt no one, and seeing I do live so closely with you, they dismissed it.

**Elizabeth:** Who accused me?

**Mary Warren:** I am bound by law, I cannot tell it. *(To Proctor)* I only hope you'll not be so sarcastical no more. Four judges and the King's deputy sat to dinner with us but an hour ago. I—I would have you speak civilly to me, from this out.

**Proctor:** *(in horror, muttering in disgust at her)* Go to bed.

**Mary Warren:** *(with a stamp of her foot)* I'll not be ordered to bed no more, Mr. Proctor! I am eighteen and a woman, however single!

**Proctor:** Do you wish to sit up? Then sit up.

**Mary Warren:** I wish to go to bed!

**Proctor:** *(in anger)* Good night, then!

**Mary Warren:** Good night. *(Dissatisfied, uncertain of herself, she goes out. Wide-eyed, both, Proctor and Elizabeth stand staring.)*

**Elizabeth:** *(quietly)* Oh, the noose, the noose is up!

**Proctor:** There'll be no noose.

**Elizabeth:** She wants me dead. I knew all week it would come to this!

**Proctor:** *(without conviction)* They dismissed it. You heard her say—

**Elizabeth:** And what of tomorrow? She will cry me out until they take me!

**Proctor:** Sit you down.

**Elizabeth:** She wants me dead, John, you know it!

**Proctor:** I say sit down! *(She sits, trembling. He speaks quietly, trying to keep his wits.)* Now we must be wise, Elizabeth.

**Elizabeth:** *(with sarcasm, and a sense of being lost)* Oh, indeed, indeed!

## SCENE FOR ONE MAN, ONE WOMAN
## FROM ACT I, SCENE 6 OF *CHAPTER TWO*
### (1977)

*By Neil Simon*

CHARACTERS: Jennie Malone
George Schneider

SETTING: The living room of Jennie's apartment in New York City; it is modern, bright, attractive, and cheerful.

TIME: About 9:30 P.M.

SITUATION: Jennie, a divorcée, and George, a widower, have never met, although his brother, Leo, and her friend, Faye, have been trying to get them together. Attempting to call an elderly Mrs. Jurgens to do some research for him, George used the wrong number left by Leo and talked to Jennie instead. They got along well on the telephone, so they have agreed to a quick five-minute look at each other in her apartment. Jennie has just opened the door.

COMMENTS: George, a writer, is forty-two. Jennie, an attractive actress, is thirty-two.

*(George stands there, arm extended, leaning against the doorframe. They look at each other . . . Finally he smiles and nods his head)*

**George:** Yeah! Okayyyyyy!

**Jennie:** Is that a review?

**George:** No. Just a response . . . Hello.

**Jennie:** *(Smiles)* Hello.
*(They are both suddenly very embarrassed and don't quite know what to say or how to handle this situation)*

**George:** *(Good-naturedly)* This was a dumb idea, wasn't it?

**Jennie:** Extremely.

**George:** *(Nods in agreement)* I think I've put undue pressure on these next five minutes.

**Jennie:** You could cut it with a knife.

**George:** I think if I came in, it would lessen the tension.

**Jennie:** Oh, I'm sorry. Please, yes.
*(He steps in. She closes the door behind her)*

**George:** *(Looks around the room and nods)* Aha!

**Jennie:** Does that mean you comprehend my apartment?

**George:** No. It means I like it. "Aha" can be used in many situations, this being one of them.

**Jennie:** Can I get you anything to drink?

**George:** No, thanks. I don't drink.

**Jennie:** Oh, neither do I.
*(There is an awkward pause)*

**George:** Although I'd love a glass of white wine.

**Jennie:** So would I. *(She goes to the kitchen)* Please, sit down.

**George:** Thank you. *(But he doesn't. He wanders around the room looking at things. She brings in an opened bottle of white wine in an ice bucket set on a tray with two glasses. He spots a framed photograph of a football player in action)* Is it all right if I pry?

**Jennie:** Sure.

**George:** You can scrutinize later. *(He examines the picture)* Oh, are you a football fan?

**Jennie:** That's my ex-husband. He was a wide receiver for the New York Giants.

**George:** No kidding! What's his name?

**Jennie:** Gus Hendricks.

**George:** *(Looks at picture again)* Gus Hendricks? . . . Funny, I can't remember him. How wide a receiver was he?

**Jennie:** He was cut the beginning of his second year. Bad hands, I think they call it. Couldn't hold on to the football.

**George:** Well, some coaches are very demanding. What does he do now?

**Jennie:** Well, he was in mutual funds, he was in the saloon business, he was in broadcasting, he was in sports promotion—

**George:** Very ambitious.

**Jennie:** He did all those in three months. He has some problems to work out.
*(She pours the two glasses of wine)*

**George:** Who doesn't?

**Jennie:** True enough.
*(She hands him a glass)*

**George:** Thank you.

**Jennie:** Here's to working out problems.
*(They both drink. He looks at her)*

**George:** Leo was right. You're very attractive.

**Jennie:** Thank you.

**George:** I'm curious. You don't have to answer this . . . How was I described?

**Jennie:** "Not gorgeous, but an intelligent face."

**George:** *(Smiles)* That's true. I have. You can ask my face anything. *(Jennie sits. George is still standing)* No matter how old or experienced you are, the process never seems to get any easier, does it?

**Jennie:** What process?

**George:** Mating.

**Jennie:** *Mating?* My God, is *that* what we're doing?

**George:** *(Sits next to her on the sofa)* Haven't you noticed? First thing I did as I passed you, I inhaled. Got a little whiff of your fragrance. In our particular species, the sense of smell is as determining factor in sexual attraction.

**Jennie:** This is just a guess. Do you write for *Field and Stream?*

**George:** *(Laughs)* Please, give me a break, will you? I haven't done this in fourteen years. If you're patient, I get interesting with a little kindness.

**Jennie:** You're not uninteresting now.

**George:** I'll tell you the truth. You're not the first girl Leo's introduced me to. There were three others . . . All ranked with such disasters as the *Hindenburg* and Pearl Harbor.

**Jennie:** *Now* I see. That's when the Five-Minute Plan was born.

**George:** Necessity is for the Mother of Calamity.

**Jennie:** Tell me about them.

**George:** Oh, they defy description.

**Jennie:** Please. Defy it.

**George:** All right. Let's see. First there was Bambi. Her name tells you everything.

**Jennie:** I got the picture.

**George:** Then there was Vilma. A dynamite girl.

**Jennie:** Really?

**George:** Spent three years in a Turkish prison for carrying dynamite . . . Need I go on?

**Jennie:** No, I think I've had enough.

**George:** Since then I've decided to take everything Leo says with a grain of panic . . . And now I feel rather foolish because I was flippant with you on the phone, and now I find myself with an attractive, intelligent and what appears to be a very nice girl.

**Jennie:** You won't get a fight from me on that.

**George:** With an appealing sense of adventure.

**Jennie:** You think so?

**George:** It's your five minutes, too.

**Jennie:** I was wondering why I said yes. I think it's because I really enjoyed talking to you on the phone. You're very bright, and I found I had to keep on my toes to keep up with you.

**George:** Oh. And is that unusual?

**Jennie:** I haven't been off my heels in years . . . What kind of books do you write?

**George:** Ah, we're moving into heavy territory. What kind of books do I write? For a living, I write spy novels. For posterity, I write good novels. I make a good living, but my posterity had a bad year.

**Jennie:** Name some books.

**George:** From column A or column B?

**Jennie:** Both.

**George:** Well, the spy novels I write under the name of Kenneth Blakely Hyphen Hill.

**Jennie:** Hyphen Hill?

**George:** You don't say the hyphen. You just put it in.

**Jennie:** Oh, God, yes. Of course. I've seen it. Drugstores, airports . . .

**George:** Unfortunately, not libraries.

**Jennie:** Who picked the name?

**George:** My wife. You see, my publisher said spy novels sell better when they sound like they were written in England. We spent our honeymoon in London, and we stayed at the Blakely Hotel, and it was on a hill and the hall porter's name was Kenneth . . . If we had money in those days, my name might have been Kenneth Savoy Grill.

**Jennie:** And from column B?

**George:** I only had two published. They were a modest failure. That means "Bring us more but not too soon."

**Jennie:** I'd like to read them someday.

**George:** I'll send you a couple of cartons of them. (*They both sip their wine. He looks around, then back at her*). I'm forty-two years old.

**Jennie:** Today?

**George:** No. In general.

**Jennie:** Oh. Is that statement of some historic importance?

**George:** No. I just wanted you to know, because you look to be about twenty-four and right now I feel like a rather inept seventeen, and I didn't want you to think I was too young for you.

**Jennie:** I'm thirty-two.

(*They look at each other. It's the first time their gaze really holds*)

**George:** Well. That was very nice wasn't it? I mean, looking at each other like that.

**Jennie:** I wasn't scrutinizing.

**George:** That's okay, I wasn't prying.

---

# Appendix

❧

## BRIEF DESCRIPTIONS
## OF MAJOR PLAYWRITING STYLES

The following is a list of the major playwriting styles covered in this book:

1. Classical—This term pertains to the plays of ancient Greece and Rome, which adhered to a rigid form with traditional standards of simplicity, unity, and proportion. (See Chapters 2 and 3.)
2. Neoclassical—This label is used for plays of the Renaissance to modern times that are written in imitation of the ancient Greek and Roman drama. (See Chapters 4, 6, and 7.)
3. Romantic—This name is applied to plays that subordinate form to content and that emphasize freedom of expression, imagination, emotion, and individualism, as opposed to the restrictions of classicism. (See Chapters 5 and 8.)
4. Realistic—Plays that purport to show life as it is are given this name. The difference between a realistic and a naturalistic dramatist is that the former has a greater desire to follow standard play construction and is more selective of the details to be included in the play than the latter. (See Chapters 9 and 11.)
5. Naturalistic—Plays in which the author presents "a slice of life" with accuracy and frankness, without regard for form, are called naturalistic. (See Chapter 9.)

6. Symbolistic—When the playwright uses symbols and symbolic language to express ideas and emotions, the play may be labeled symbolistic. (See Chapter 10.)

7. Expressionistic—This term is applied to plays that present a distorted view of life as seen by one character or by the playwright, who is trying to effect social changes. (See Chapter 10.)

8. Epic theatre—This name refers to the didactic plays of Brecht and others that present an episodic, analytical view of a subject of social significance. (See Chapter 10.)

9. Theatre of the absurd—This label is applied to irrational, illogical plays that often feature extreme exaggerations, surrealism, and symbolism to make a point about our chaotic world or the meaninglessness of life. (See Chapter 10.)

## BRIEF DESCRIPTIONS
## OF MAJOR ACTING STYLES

The following is a list of the major acting styles:

1. Classical or heroic—This presentational style, which may be used for classical and neoclassical tragedies, strives for a dignified, restrained, larger-than-life effect. Movements are usually majestic and rhythmic, and voices display great vocal variety and dramatic intensity.

2. Romantic—Characterized by emotional intensity and an abundance of action, this presentational style demands graceful movements and flexible voices with excellent diction. Also, actors in romantic plays often have to fence, dance, sing, or play musical instruments.

3. Realistic—This representational style requires the actor to present a truthful view of life. Since realistic acting is so prevalent today, it is often used not only for realistic and naturalistic plays but also for other types.

4. High comedy—Comedies of character, wit, and manners demand a high comedy or drawing-room comedy style of acting. Sophisticated, worldly, appealing to the intellect, the lines of this presentational style have subtle nuances of meaning that must be communicated by astute pointing of lines and excellent timing. A flexible voice and an expressive face and body are mandatory for playing high comedy.

5. Low comedy—Farce, burlesque, and some satiric and situation comedies may require a low comedy style of acting. This can involve slapstick, horseplay, pratfalls, clowning, and lots of exaggerated action in a fast-paced show. Vitality is a prime requisite for this presentional style.

6. Epic—Used for epic theatre plays, this presentational style, which was advocated by Bertolt Brecht, requires the actor to remain detached from the part—to display the character and demonstrate the events—so that the actor's performance may involve a comment on the character.

7. Nonrealistic—This is a catch-all label for the presentational acting demanded by some plays that may require actors to move and talk in nonhuman ways like, for example, automatons, puppets, or animals.

## BRIEF DESCRIPTIONS OF
## CURRENT MAJOR
## PRODUCTION STYLES

The following is a list of the major production styles used in contemporary theatre:

1. Formalistic—Levels, steps, ramps, screens, and columns form a neutral type of stage that does not suggest any one locale until it is established by the dialogue. Permanent architectural settings and unit sets are included in this category.

2. Romantic—This name is used for a nineteenth-century form of the wing-drop-border set. This version featured large, painted backdrops with the wings pushed farther to the sides than in the Renaissance.

3. Realistic—The designer using this representational style selects scenic details that will give the illusion of an actual place.

4. Naturalistic—The naturalistic designer attempts to put all of the details of a locale on the stage, using little or no selectivity.

5. Selective realistic—As the name implies, this style is more selective than realism—just the minimum number of essential details of a place is used with greater emphasis on theatricality.

6. Impressionistic—The designer of an impressionistic set heightens the mood of the scenes in a nonrealistic but atmospheric way. As with expressionism, the audience may see the world as a major character does.

7. Symbolistic—The designer of this type of setting uses symbols to suggest meanings to the audience; for example, one window may symbolize a large church.

8. Constructivistic—This style uses ramps, ladders, platforms, steps, and beams to suggest the skeletal construction of a building.

9. Expressionistic—This is a distorted, frankly theatrical style representing a place as seen through the eyes of one of the characters or the playwright.

10. Theatrical—With this style, the audience knows that it is in a theatre watching a play as no attempt is made at illusion. Lights may be visible, stagehands may change the scenery in front of the audience, some properties may be imagined, and so forth.

11. Epic theatre—This is another theatrical style that involves the use of signs, projections, turntables, treadmills, escalators, elevators, and other technical devices to teach the message of the playwright.

12. Multimedia—Slide, movie, or television projections on multiple screens, stereophonic sound, unusual lighting, and special effects may combine with live acting, dancing, and music for another theatrical style.

# CHARACTER ANALYSIS FORM

PLAY: Title:
     Author:
     Brief resumé of plot:


     Theme:

     Dramatic form (tragedy, comedy, farce, drama, etc.):
     Style of play (classical, romantic, realistic, etc.):
     Locale and time of play:


CHARACTER: Physical appearance
                 Age:
                 Weight and height:
                 Posture:
                 Movements and stage business:

                 Clothing:
                 Hair:

     Vocal characteristics:

     Intellectual characteristics and education:

     Emotional characteristics:

     Social and economic status:

     Personality:

     Super-objective (major goal) for entire play:

SCENE: Emotional state of your character in this scene:


     Attitude and relationship of your character to other people in scene:


     Main objective of your character in this scene:

# Index

Schneider, Alan, 153
*School for Scandal, The* (Sheridan), 85, 89–90
*School for Wives, The* (Molière), 71, 90
  scene, 74–77
Scott, George C., 153
Scribe, Eugène, 110
Selective realism, 1, 73, 134, 153, 172
Seneca, 26, 28–29, 32, 35, 41–42, 81
Sense memory, 4, 115, 117
Shaffer, Peter, 151
Shakespeare, William, 3, 8, 10, 39, 42–52,
  55, 57, 60, 63, 99–100
Shaw, George Bernard, 111, 121
Shepard, Sam, 150, 154
Sheridan, Richard Brinsley, 85–86, 89, 95
Sherwood, Robert Emmett, 150
Siddons, Sarah, 101
Simile, 45–46, 51
Simon, Neil, 150, 166
Simonson, Lee, 153
Snuff, 87–89
Soliloquies, 2, 37, 44, 47–48, 51
Sophocles, 9–12, 15, 20
Stanislavski, Constantin, 3–4, 113–15,
  117–18, 135, 152, 154
Stapleton, Maureen, 153
Stein, Peter, 153
Stoppard, Tom, 132, 150
Storey, David, 150
Strasberg, Lee, 152
Strindberg, August, 112
*Sturm and Drang* movement, 99
Styles:
  acting, 1–3, 5, 171–72
  definition, 1–2
  playwriting, 1–3, 170–71
  presentational, 2–3, 12–13, 27–28, 36–37,
    44–48, 72–73, 86–87, 129–36
  production, 1–3, 172
  representational, 2–3, 111–16, 149–51
Subtext, 114, 118
Superobjective, 114
Svoboda, Josef, 153
Symbolism, 1–2, 14, 129–30, 132–33,
  134–35, 138, 149–50, 171–172
  plays, 129–130, 149–50
  productions now, 134–35
  productions then, 132–33
Synge, John Millington, 111

Talma, François Joseph, 101
*Taming of the Shrew, The* (Shakespeare), 43
  scene, 55–57
Tandy, Jessica, 153
*Tartuffe* (Molière), 71, 74
  scene, 77–80

Taylor, Laurette, 153
Teatro Farnese, 35–36
Teatro Olimpico, 35
Technical acting, 114–15, 154
Tempo-rhythm, 115
Terence, 24–28, 35–36, 41–42
Terry, Ellen, 112
Théâtre Libre, 113
Theatre of cruelty, 28, 151–52
Theatre of fact, 151
Theatre of the absurd. (*See* Absurd)
Theatrical production styles, 1–3, 172
Thespis, 9
*Three Sisters, The* (Chekhov), 111
  scene, 123–25
Toller, Ernst, 130
*Tragical History of Doctor Faustus, The*
  (Marlowe), 42
  scene, 52–54
Transformations, 136–38
Turgenev, Ivan, 110
*Twin Captains, The* (Scala):
  scene, 39–40

Urban, Joseph, 153

Vanbrugh, John, 85–93
van Itallie, Jean-Claude, 136, 150
Vilar, Jean, 153
Vitruvius, 26
*Volpone* (Jonson), 43
  scene, 65–69

*Waiting for Godot* (Beckett), 131
  scene, 146–48
Warm-up exercises, 4, 8
Weill, Kurt, 131
Weiss, Peter, 131, 151
Weist, Edward C, 29
Well-made play, 110
Wilbur, Richard, 74, 77
*Wild Duck, The* (Ibsen), 111, 129, 134
Wilder, Thornton, 131
Williams, Tennessee, 150, 159
Wilson, Lanford, 150
Worth, Irene, 28
*Would-Be Gentleman, The* (Molière), 71, 74
Wycherley, William, 85, 90

Yeats, William Butler, 111, 130

Zeffirelli, Franco, 153
Zindel, Paul, 150
Zola, Émile, 111